Divine Representations

SUNY series in Western Esoteric Traditions

David Appelbaum, editor

Divine Representations

The Rise of the Mystical Novel in Twentieth-Century England

CARLA A. ARNELL

SUNY
PRESS

Cover credit: Hilma af Klint, *Group IX UW No. 25, The Dove, No. 1* (1915). Public domain.

Published by State University of New York Press, Albany

Printed in the United States of America

EU GPSR Authorised Representative:
Logos Europe, 9 rue Nicolas Poussin, 17000, La Rochelle, France
contact@logoseurope.eu

For information, contact State University of New York Press, Albany, NY
www.sunypress.edu

Library of Congress Cataloging-in-Publication Data

Name: Arnell, Carla A., author.
Title: Divine representations : the rise of the mystical novel in twentieth-century England / Carla A. Arnell.
Description: Albany : State University of New York Press, [2026]. | Series: SUNY series in western esoteric traditions | Includes bibliographical references and index.
Identifiers: LCCN 2025023438 | ISBN 9798855805321 (hardcover : alk. paper) | ISBN 9798855806960 (epub) | ISBN 9798855805345 (PDF)
Subjects: LCSH: English fiction—20th century—History and criticism. | Mysticism in literature. | Experience (Religion) in literature. | Transcendence (Philosophy) in literature. | Literature and society—England—History—20th century. | Mysticism—England—History—20th century. | LCGFT: Literary criticism.
Classification: LCC PR888.M93 A76 2025 | DDC 823/.91409—dc23/eng/20250709
LC record available at https://lccn.loc.gov/2025023438

For my mother

in memoriam

Contents

Acknowledgments

With a grateful heart, I wish to acknowledge the people who have contributed to this project over the course of many years. I am indebted to the work of my student research assistants, many of whom worked with me at different stages of this project as Richter Scholars or Fielding Fellows: Cara Goldstone, Samuel Bickersteth, Denzel Marufu, Caroline Warrick-Schkolnik, Natalie Briggs, Kendra Foberts, Isabel MacKenzie, Nina Codell, Aleksandar Markovic, Kalina Sawyer, E. Caitlin Brown, Lauren Bell, Paul Henne, and Stephen "Buzz" Beeaker. Thanks especially to Finn Bunta for his significant research assistance during my work on the Arts and Crafts movement. Thanks to Jack Farrell for his research assistance and many fruitful, energizing conversations about A. E. Waite and Charles Williams. And, above all, thanks to Elena Vaux, whose stellar and outstanding research assistance and editing have touched all areas of this book. These wonderful students, and so many more whom I do not have space to name, have been a daily inspiration through their intellectual adventuresomeness and deep questions.

Thanks to the Richter Scholar Program at Lake Forest College and Randy and Melvin Berlin, whose generous gift to the English department made some of this research support possible. Thanks to James Peltz, the acquisitions editor at SUNY Press, for championing my project and to the SUNY Press editorial staff, especially Julia Cosacchi, for their help.

Portions of chapter 3 were previously published as "Work for the Soul: Medievalism, the Arts and Crafts Movement, and the Development of a Practical Spirituality in Evelyn Underhill's Novel *The Gray World*" in *Studies in Medievalism* (Summer 2019), pp. 53–76. © Boydell and Brewer; reproduced with permission of the Licensor through PLSClear.

Thanks also to Lake Forest College reference librarians past and present, especially Cory Stevens, Nancy Bohm, and Kim Hazlett, for their patient help with specific research questions and to Michael Karsten for his diligent work on interlibrary loans.

Thanks to those who have read portions of this book and offered suggestions or encouragement. Lois Barr offered helpful suggestions about a version of my Underhill chapter. Dan LeMahieu spurred me along with his kind inquiries about my book and his useful comments about twentieth-century British middlebrow culture. Henry Carrigan offered helpful counsel at an early stage as well as faithful friendship. Ann Boaden, who has been a kind, wise, and lifelong mentor, knows George MacDonald better than anyone I have met and offered welcome comments on my MacDonald and Waite chapter. Elizabeth Clemmitt has been a supportive and gentle conversationalist in sharing ideas about the Christian mystical tradition. Gary Saul Morson taught me so much about the novel as a genre and continues to teach and inspire. Richard Kieckhefer's course on Christian mysticism long ago, his patient responses to theological questions, and his keen insights about particular chapters have been a great benefit. Barbara Newman has provided unflagging encouragement, generous mentorship, and brilliant insights about things modern and things medieval as well as astute observations about sections of this manuscript. This book would not be a book without her perennial inquiries about its progress. To her I offer thanks beyond measure.

Special thanks to the late Elizabeth Dipple, an early and kind mentor in the field of twentieth-century British literature, and to my former colleague and "other mother," Judy Dozier, a gifted spiritual mentor, wise guide, and devoted friend.

Thanks to my husband, Paul Lucas, and my children, John, Elisabeth, and Susanne, for their patience with all the time spent on this book. Thanks also to my father, Richard Arnell, for his generous support, enthusiasm, and willingness to read my work.

Finally, loving thanks Karin Youngberg, an extraordinary teacher, whose college course on "Mystics and Visionaries" first introduced me to Evelyn Underhill and Charles Williams. For that and so much more, I am greatly in her debt.

This book is dedicated to Paula Y. Arnell, my remarkable mother, whose last words to me were "I think you should write more."

Introduction

The Mystical Revival in Turn-of-the-Century England

On the eve of World War I, during the last months of peace, the British writer Evelyn Underhill prepared an introduction to *Practical Mysticism* (1914), a book originally subtitled "a little book for normal people." In that introduction, despite initial reservations about publishing her book with war impending, she affirmed the modern relevance of mysticism—a seemingly arcane topic that she had spent over a decade researching and writing about for ordinary readers. Conscious that the emerging world-historical crisis might quash the previous decade's signs of a "spiritual renaissance" and serve as cause for dismissing mysticism as irrelevant or inconsequential, she asserted that the value of mysticism "is increased rather than lessened when confronted by the overwhelming disharmonies and sufferings of the present time" (13). Here and elsewhere, Underhill would argue that mysticism is spiritually and ethically salutary for modern times, providing wisdom and healing for lost souls in a broken world.

Underhill's perseverance in popularizing a modern discourse about mysticism, even at a time of world-historical crisis, illustrates her powerful, tenacious role in what came to be known as the twentieth-century mystical revival. According to Philip Reynolds, "During its heyday, which coincided with the Edwardian era, the phrase 'mystical revival' was used by the leading lights of the movement, such as William Inge, Rufus Jones, and Evelyn Underhill. They were referring primarily to the steady publication of widely-read books on the topic . . . , but they saw themselves as reviving an ancient tradition that had somehow fallen silent: a tradition to be found chiefly in the Middle Ages and in the Spanish Counter-Reformation" (Reynolds 17). The historian Jane Shaw concurs in observing, "The early twentieth century saw a surprising but very definite revival of interest in religious experience generally, and mysticism in particular, after decades, even centuries, of disparagement of the subject in the British context" ("Varieties" 226). This revival was attested to by the Edwardian priest and novelist R. H. Benson at the opening of his 1907 Westminster lecture on mysticism; therein, he asserted, "Of all phases in religious thought that at the present day are attracting attention, none is more prominent than that of Mysticism. It is a subject that is engrossing widely differing minds of every variety of creed, Christian and non-Christian" (5). Although Underhill sought to present mysticism in a new key, tuned to the modern ear, her work nonetheless revived ideas sounded many centuries before, for the Christian tradition's first efflorescence of mysticism was rooted in the high Middle Ages, where it was given voice to by writers as diverse as Julian of Norwich, Hadewijch, Hildegard of Bingen, and Meister Eckhart. In England, however, interest in mysticism as a form of the Christian religion experienced a second major flowering at the start of the twentieth century, thanks to the work of pioneering scholars and writers such as Underhill, Inge, A. E. Waite, Friedrich von Hügel, and Carolyn Spurgeon. In different ways, each of these writers dedicated themselves to studying past mystical experience and, in some cases, recording their own personal mystical experiences. Moreover, some of the writers who were part of this early twentieth-century mystical revival were novelists as well as students of mysticism. In that imaginative role, they bequeathed to us a small but significant oeuvre of literary experiments, fascinating for their attempts to capture mystical experience in novelistic form, thereby making that experience accessible to ordinary readers, not just a gnostic few.

Decades after this mystical revival, the British novelist and philosopher Iris Murdoch identified the "mystical novel" as one of two types of novel that became popular in the twentieth century (*Existentialists* 223). Explaining her distinction between the "mystical novel" and the "existentialist novel," she argued that "[t]he existentialist novel shows us freedom and virtue as the assertion of will. The mystical novel shows us freedom and virtue as understanding, or obedience to the Good" (Murdoch, *Existentialists* 223). She continued, "What is characteristic of this [mystical] novel is that it keeps in being, by one means or another, the conception of God. . . . I call these novels mystical . . . because they are attempts to express a religious consciousness without the traditional trappings of religion" (Murdoch, *Existentialists* 225). Although Murdoch's philosophical discussion of the mystical novel specifically referred to a group of mid-century authors, not to Edwardian writers, her discussion nonetheless drew attention to an important twentieth-century literary development. Yet, for many years after the publication of her 1970 essay, Murdoch's claims about a "mystical novel" languished, relatively unnoticed by scholars of twentieth-century literature, focused as they primarily were on social and political literary topics. Since the 2000s, though, an increasing number of scholars have turned to the topic of mysticism and literature through journal articles focused on particular twentieth-century novelists who evinced an interest in mysticism or, in rare cases, through book-length studies such as David Garrett Izzo's *Influence of Mysticism on 20th Century British and American Literature* (2009) or James Clemens's *Mysticism and the Mid-Century Novel* (2012).

Clemens takes his cue directly from Murdoch's essay, selecting for his study some of the mid-century novelists she identified as authors of "mystical novels": William Golding, Patrick White, and Saul Bellow (to which he, rightly, adds Murdoch herself). Clemens distinguishes these novels from their Modernist predecessors by their inauguration of "a new form of realism; one that refused to ignore the philosophical ideas that had led to the novel's apparent impoverishment—the opacity of language, and the loss of stable external sources of meaning—and sought new techniques and structures to overcome them" (3). In making this claim about the novels he has chosen for his study, he quickly dismisses instances of mystical fiction in the preceding decades of the twentieth century, writing:

> Admittedly, there are many exceptions to this rather simplistic picture [of Modernism], as many modernist works have mystical overtones that gesture towards a reality beyond subjective experience. An interest in such metaphysical speculation in the form of occultism and theosophy was apparent from early in the era, and was a subject of great interest for poets and writers such as William Butler Yeats and D. H. Lawrence; however, this early strain of mysticism was less concerned with the development of an objective, moral vision than with the intricacies of arcane cosmologies and a solipsistic "perfecting of the I." (4)

While Clemens's claim may be true of certain early twentieth-century novelists who pursued occult knowledge and practices or of the high Modernists he names, his claim does not accurately reflect some of the novelists most responsible for reintroducing mystical experience to a twentieth-century audience. The Edwardian era, far from being a minor blip in the history of mysticism and modern literature, is in fact the seedbed of twentieth-century scholarship about mysticism and the novelistic fiction that seeks to represent that form of spiritual experience. Because the story of these early twentieth-century mystical novelists has thus far been untold as an integrated story, my study seeks to fill that significant gap in our literary history.[1]

In a loose sense, to be sure, mystical fiction did not arise ex nihilo in the Edwardian era. During the Victorian era, there had been decades of experimentation with what readers and writers *called* mystical fiction, some of which was dubbed so because it included stories of ghosts, seances, hypnotists, alchemical processes, and the like. As Knight and Mason point out, the sacramental theology increasingly popular in the Victorian era ushered in "an openness to eclecticism, heterodoxy, and mysticism" (192). Some Victorians, such as Anna Kingsford, sought to forge links between such practices and their own idiosyncratic Christian vision. Others, such as Marie Corelli, sought to merge Christian moralism with newfangled spiritual-scientific language that linked concepts like electricity to the energy of the Divine. But the group of Edwardian writers who helped to define the Edwardian mystical revival sought to separate mysticism from other magical or occult spiritual traditions, looking instead to Christian mystical texts and legends from the medieval past for the foundation of their mystical vision.

It might at first seem paradoxical that such a renaissance of mysticism would arise at the start of the twentieth century, after a century of growing scientific positivism, historical biblical criticism, and subsequent questioning of orthodox religious faith. And indeed, many scholarly narratives about early twentieth-century literature have drawn a distorted picture of this age's literary culture as suddenly and solely an age of secularism, perhaps because of scholarly emphasis on Europe's most avant-garde writers: Forster, Woolf, Joyce, and Beckett, to name just the British exemplars. For instance, Richard Ellmann argued that Edwardian literature is "thoroughly secular" (191), suggesting that "[t]he Edwardians were looking for ways to express their conviction that we can be religious about life itself. . . . The capitalized word for the Edwardians is not God but Life" (196). Similarly, in a 2005 chapter on "Edwardian Literature," John Batchelor claims that it is "broadly true to say that the Edwardian imagination was secular" (127). History, however, does not move in predictable patterns, and its story is not one of linear "progress" away from religious or spiritual inclinations. As Naomi Carle, Samual Shaw, and Sarah Shaw remark in a more recent corrective of the conventional narrative about Edwardian literary history:

> It would be wrong to suggest that Edwardian society had become emphatically secularized. A range of recent historical, political, feminist, and religious scholarship has revealed the Edwardian period to be one in which religion continued to play an influential role in both public and private life. Although by the turn of the century attendance at Anglican churches was diminishing, there continued to be a robust participation amongst nonconformist denominations. The first two decades of the twentieth century also witnessed a surge of interest in the history and psychology of mysticism, with comprehensive publications such as Williams James's *The Varieties of Religious Experience* (1902), Rufus M. Jones's *Studies in Mystical Religion* (1909), and the prolific Evelyn Underhill's *Mysticism* (1911) and *The Mystic Way* (1913). (5)

Likewise, the historian Alex Owen's study of British occultism and the culture of the Modern makes abundantly clear that the growing secularism of the early twentieth century was counterpointed by a vigorous interest in spiritualism, the occult, and other esoteric religious interests and practices, including mystical experience, all of which took root in the Victorian era and burgeoned in the Edwardian one. Those spiritual interests were reflected by the literary culture as well as in other places.

Recently, Susan Johnston Graf has offered a helpful literary history of four writers who were central to that early twentieth-century occult movement. The writers in her study include W. B. Yeats, Arthur Machen, Algernon Blackwood, and Dion Fortune. As Graf points out, they achieved popularity (both then and now) for their literary explorations of occult and esoteric spiritual traditions. Stimulated by their involvement in the Order of the Golden Dawn, these writers sought to "change consciousness and to control the imagination by active participation in psychic events" (Graf 8). Her study, therefore, seeks to illuminate the "linkages between the imaginative literature these writers produced and the occult beliefs and practices they engaged in" (5). However, insofar as these writers sought to explore the power of the will to change or shape reality, their understanding of spiritual development exemplifies Clemens's characterization of earlier twentieth-century novelists and, therefore, differs radically from that of another group of writers active at the same time.[2] Several of these other writers also had roots in the same Order of the Golden Dawn, but they came to make a key distinction between mysticism on the one hand and magic on the other, ultimately devoting their life, fiction, and other writings to clarifying that distinction, explaining the nature of true mysticism, as they understood it, and popularizing the "mystical path." Despite their major contributions to the history of mysticism and literature, however, no study has yet thoroughly examined the relationship among these writers and the diverse ways in which they sought to adapt the middlebrow English novel to an exploration of mystical experience. As Chad Stutz notes at the end of his monograph on R. H. Benson, one of the writers in this study, it remains to be explored how Benson's tales "relate to other tales of a similar kind written during the Edwardian period" (170).

At the center of this group of mystical novelists are A. E. Waite and Evelyn Underhill, both important to the early twentieth-century revival of mysticism for different reasons, with Waite's novels first published at the end of the 1800s and Underhill's in the first decade of the twentieth-century. R. H. Benson was connected to Underhill as a spiritual advisor, and his novels joined hers in distinguishing mysticism from magic in the century's first decade. Arthur Machen was a friend of both Waite's and Underhill's, and his late fiction provides a significant contribution to the genre of mystical fiction and lays the groundwork for Charles Williams's novelistic use of Arthurian mythology to explore mystical and metaphysical ideas in the mystical novels he published in the 1930s and 1940s. Beyond a shared interest in mysticism and fiction writing, all of these Edwardian writers sought to integrate their religious backgrounds with their sometimes heterodox study of mystical experience, bringing their deep knowledge of medieval religious and literary traditions to bear on their modern spiritual explorations. Some of this fiction has been explored by Glen Cavaliero, Alison Milbank, and Zoë Lehmann Imfeld, among others, as examples of neo-Gothic, horror, or, generally supernatural fiction. I argue, however, that the "mystical novel" is a both a more precise and a more capacious category for considering the kind of fiction that these writers developed during the Edwardian era, focused as they were on exploring mystical experience in relation to the Christian tradition. Through their work, they created different variations on what Murdoch has called the "mystical novel," a genre whose features are distinctly different from those Graf lays out in her study of novelists like Dion Fortune and Algernon Blackwood. In fact, the ethical vision of these four writers is closer to that outlined by Iris Murdoch in her definition of the mystical novel than it is to the ethical worldview of occult writers like Yeats or Fortune. In the chapters to follow, I shall focus on one novel from each of these four writers as a case study in the development of the mystical novel, using the publication history of the novels to be explored as my organizational pattern: Waite's novel *The Golden Stairs* was first published in 1893, Benson's *The Light Invisible* first in 1903, Underhill's *The Gray World* first in 1904, and Machen's revised and completed version of *A Fragment of Life* was first published in 1906 (an early version appeared in 1904 in serial form in *Horlick's Magazine*, and the 1906 edition was republished as a stand-alone edition in 1928).

Among the writers in this study, A. E. Waite may have the most enduring fame, with first editions of his books now commanding exorbitant sums. He is considered a father of occult studies, despite his attempts to Christianize ceremonial magic and direct his thinking, writing, and ritual practices away from the occult magic practiced by spiritual adversaries like Aleister Crowley. Waite was a prolific scholar, whose studies of the Jewish kabbalah, the Grail legend, and the tarot system still merit vigorous discussion. By contrast, his imaginative literature is relatively unknown, and yet it represents one of the earliest instances of mystical exploration in the English novel through *The Golden Stairs*, which was first published in 1893 and then republished as *The Quest of the Golden Stairs* in 1927. Both hearken back to the Victorian fantasy fiction of George MacDonald and the medieval knightly romances popular during that era. My chapter on Waite explores the impact of his mystical studies on his work as an imaginative writer and fiction editor and the legacy he bequeathed to other fiction writers who were part of the mystical revival. Although he was an imaginative writer whose conservative aesthetic tastes were more Victorian than modern, his ideas about mysticism and his edited fictions (including Underhill's first short stories) provided a bridge to modern novelistic explorations of mysticism.

By contrast to A. E. Waite with his penchant for fantasy fiction in the style of medieval romance, the Roman Catholic priest and novelist R. H. Benson represents the first forays into portraying mystical experience in the context of traditional literary realism. Among the novelists in this study, Benson may be the least well-known today, but he was exceedingly famous in his own time, popular both for his sermons and his novels, some of which exemplify his efforts at exploring mystical experience. His 1903 novel *The Light Invisible*, a priest's stories about the mystical experiences that shaped his spiritual development, is particularly significant for this study. As Benson's biographer Janet Grayson observed, that book opened new doors of mystical insight for ordinary readers: "To many readers a mystical side of religion was revealed for the first time, full of insight and transcendence" (xv). That Benson was interested in mysticism was evinced even more explicitly in a 1907 Westminster lecture on "mysticism," subsequently published as a book by the same title. My chapter will explore Benson's early experiment with mystical fiction in the novel *The Light Invisible* as an example of how the novel of literary realism could be used to explore a sacramental mysticism rooted in Benson's deep faith in the presence of Christ in ordinary life.

Benson was an early spiritual and literary influence on Evelyn Underhill, the third writer in this study, though she came to distance herself from his fiction as it became more doctrinaire. Underhill is in many ways at the heart of the English mystical revival both as a scholar and as a novelist. Despite being overshadowed by the American academic William James and his famous theoretical study of mysticism in *The Varieties of Religious Experience* (1902), Underhill was responsible for recuperating a vast number of medieval mystical texts, which she read, translated (or co-translated), and edited, thanks to access she gained to the British Museum through her friend J. A. Herbert, keeper of manuscripts at the British Museum. As a result of that research, she wrote a comprehensive study of mysticism, called simply *Mysticism*, which was published in 1911 and has never since been out of print. Underhill's scholarly study of mysticism aimed to identify the commonalities among mystics from diverse places and times (though mostly from the Middle Ages) and attempted to delineate the typical stages of the mystical path. For this publication and others, Bernard McGinn has called her contributions to the study of mysticism "unprecedented in English scholarship" (22). During the decade leading up to the publication of *Mysticism*, however, Underhill was at work on three novels, all of which attempted to portray mystical experience within the context of the ordinary lives of twentieth-century English characters. My chapter will explore how she integrates elements from the medieval mystical tradition within a narrative tradition of literary realism to figure forth mystical experience in *The Gray World* (1904), the first and, arguably, most accomplished of her three mystical novels. *The Gray World* explores how the mundane world of "arts and crafts" can be a vehicle of mystical experience and, notwithstanding its strong Neoplatonic features, it adumbrates her growing turn towards a Christian sacramental mysticism.

Connected to Underhill and Waite is their friend Arthur Machen; Machen admired Underhill's contributions to modern spirituality, but also found some of her mystical fiction lacking and confronted similar artistic challenges in his own work adapting the representation of mystical experience to the novel of literary realism. Though Machen began his career as a writer of fiction we might now call horror literature, and though Susan Graf and many other critics have categorized Machen as an occult writer, Machen was a protean literary figure, whose writings and intellectual perspective changed significantly over time, making him difficult to categorize within a single literary group or mode. Unquestionably, however, he himself attested to having had mystical experiences (often called "ecstasies" earlier in his career), and, as Geoffrey Reiter has shown, over time, he shifted his fictional focus from exploring the horror of a godless world to illustrating how ordinary life is infused by a divine presence ("*Man Is Made a Mystery*" 127). Toward this end, Machen plundered the riches of Arthurian mythology for writing two mystical novels, *A Fragment of Life* (1904) and *The Secret Glory* (1922). My chapter will explore the first and most successful of those two novels, *A Fragment of Life*, and how his use of the Grail myth adds a mystical dimension to the traditional novel of literary realism.

All of these writers, therefore, were students of the mystical tradition (whether Christian, Jewish, Eastern, or some combination thereof), but unlike Yeats, Forster, and other spiritual seekers from this period, they did not reject Christianity as an outmoded belief system. Thanks to the spiritual direction of Benson and Baron von Hügel, Underhill increasingly grew to accept the Christian faith into which she had been christened as a child. Benson spent his adult years first as an Anglican priest, then as a Roman Catholic one. Machen was a regular attendee at Anglo-Catholic mass and wrote passionately about the Celtic Christianity inherited from his Welsh rector father. And though Waite's beliefs befuddled even his close friend Arthur Machen (*Selected Letters* 100), and he was once dubbed "a Sacramentalist rather than a Catholic" (Shirley 11), his biographer Gilbert concludes that "Waite *was* a Christian, but he was certainly not orthodox" (*Magician* 164).

Consequently, the fictions of Waite, Underhill, Machen, and Benson reflect an attempt to reconcile mystical insight and Christian belief in ways that set them apart from other spiritual-seeking peers of that era.

Moreover, they each share Underhill's general definition of mysticism as "the art of union with Reality," making them all realists in the sense of professing faith in a transcendent divine reality within and beyond ordinary, sensible reality. In my study, I will explore the roots of each writer's interest in mysticism, the nature of each one's contribution to mystical reflection, and the different ways in which they make the English novel new by adapting its traditional form to the representation of mystical experience. In that regard, the title of my book deliberately echoes Ian Watt's seminal history *The Rise of the English Novel*, a study of the roots of literary realism in the eighteenth-century English novel.

In his study of the English novel's origins, Ian Watt popularized the idea that the English novel is, at root, a secular genre. Though subsequent literary historians have nuanced or even challenged that view, Watt's account remains a kind of touchstone of literary history, to which all subsequent accounts of the English novel's origins allude and respond. If the English novel arose in the eighteenth century (as Ian Watt argues), one of the features that distinguished that new genre from older genres—the epic or the romance—is the absence of the Divine from the narrative action and religion from the narrative topics. That is not to say the societies portrayed in eighteenth- and nineteenth-century English novels lack any religious character, but the Divine does not make its presence known in *Robinson Crusoe* or *Pamela* or *Pride and Prejudice* or *Bleak House* in the way that it had in the dominant genres of previous eras. Even the Gothic novel, with which the modern mystical novel has some affinity, may use religious trappings for literary background or characterization (for instance, as in Matthew Lewis's infamous novel *The Monk*), but such novels often avoid any purposeful theological or metaphysical exploration.[3] The English novel's typical purview is, as Blakey Vermeule describes it, "middle-class subject matter and focus on courtship and marriage" (147). And where religious characters are present in such fictions, those characters typically serve as actors within a social or moral drama (Austen, Trollope, Dickens) rather than agents of religious experience. Indeed, novels that dabbled in religious experience seemed anathema to one of the most distinguished of English novelists, George Eliot. As Eliot once observed about the religious novel: "Religious novels are more hateful to me than merely worldly ones: they are a sort of centaur or mermaid, and, like other monsters that we do not know how to class, should be destroyed for the public good as soon as born" (40). Given the seeming dominance of Eliot's view within the world of nineteenth-century novelistic realism,

Cavaliero notes, "The majority of English novels are naturalistic, faithful to observed reality and imagined within the confines of tangible experience" (*Poet* 54); he cites Emily Brontë's *Wuthering Heights* as the only novel, even within the Gothic tradition of supernaturalism, that "stands out as a truly comprehensive vision of both spiritual and physical reality" (*Poet* 54).

In the twentieth century, however, the English novelists in this study adapted the novel to the more ambitious metaphysical topics that once seemed the province of only Continental and Russian novelists like Dostoevsky. Even more daringly than their Russian predecessors, they turned the mirror of mimesis not only to the social or psychological world, but also to the world of religious experience. In that regard, these mystical novelists represent a new adventure in novelistic realism, thickening the plot of the English novel's history by navigating the new imaginative territory created by a confluence of two traditions: the novel's traditional literary realism and the philosophical realism they share as students of mysticism. In different ways, each of the four novelists I will be discussing takes seriously a vertical axis of reality to counterpoint the novel's traditional horizontal axis of social reality. By anchoring that divine axis within the familiar coordinates of the ordinary, everyday world, they sought to make mysticism accessible to middle-class readers. In the priest R. H. Benson's view, Christianity had already, through the historical Incarnation, begun to make the mysteries that pagan peoples imperfectly tried to pursue accessible to the many rather than the few. In his lecture on mysticism, he asserted, "For the first time . . . in history these things became the property of the vulgar as well as the hidden treasure of the mystics, for the very reason that now these mysteries had come forward for enactment upon the historical stage" (*Mysticism* 15). For him, as well as for others of his era, the genre of the novel, with its rootedness in everyday life and its common readership, became a fitting vehicle for embodying Christian mystical experience and further "drawing up" the "veil" within the stage of popular fiction (15).

It is my argument, then, that these four writers—Waite, Benson, Underhill, and Machen—drew upon their knowledge of mysticism to pioneer for English fiction a strange but remarkably intriguing "centaur novel," creating thereby a new tradition of English metaphysical fiction, or, as Murdoch put it, a "mystical novel," to be further explored in later decades by novelists such as Graham Greene, William Golding, Muriel Spark, and Murdoch herself. While this chapter of English literary history is an important one to tell simply because it is a missing chapter, it also raises provocative questions beyond literary history. The novels of Waite and his Edwardian peers invite fascinating questions about the virtues and defects of the novel as a vehicle for metaphysical exploration, the accessibility of mystical experience for the middlebrow[4] reader, and the ethical and spiritual effects of mystical depictions when experienced vicariously through a fictional narrative. Thus, my book ultimately addresses from a literary perspective the question Evelyn Underhill herself once posed: In what ways is mystical experience "practical" for the ordinary person?

Chapter 1

A. E. Waite, George MacDonald, and the Golden Stair from Victorian Fantasy to Edwardian Mystical Fiction

> Remember that true pathways lead beyond themselves.
>
> —A. E. Waite, *Shadows of Life and Thought*, 19

A. E. Waite's spiritual life began in a rainstorm, and with that small but momentous occasion so, one might say, was an important seed of the Edwardian era's Christian mystical literary revival first watered. Prior to that time, the Victorian era had seen decades of writing devoted to séance participation, astral exploration, tarot reading, mesmerism, magic, and other forms of heterodox activity often referred to as "mystical," given that word's persistent philological fluidity. As the historian Alex Owen explains, the term "was used across the ideological board to identify a range of spiritual alternatives to religious orthodoxy that sprang up in the 1880s and 1890s and gained momentum and prominence as the old century gave way to the new," resulting in what came to be called a "mystical revival" (20). Waite's impact on this revival was so great that even his archenemy, the magician Aleister Crowley, conceded, "Waite certainly did start a revival of interest in Alchemy, Magic, Mysticism, and all the rest" (qtd. in Gilbert, *Magician* 11).

Over time, however, Waite sought to rectify his age's understanding of mysticism and align it with his Christian faith in ways that influenced and intersected with the writings of several other prolific Edwardian writers, such as Evelyn Underhill, Arthur Machen, and R. H. Benson. By the time he wrote *Lamps of Western Mysticism* in 1923, he had concluded that "we must separate in our minds certain things from Mysticism which are liable to be identified therewith" (4), establishing what the scholar Aren Roukema calls a "cordon sanitaire" between occultism and Christianity (68). For Waite, the subject of mysticism was "essentially religious, and the sum of real religion"; indeed, he went so far as to assert that "all Mysticism worthy of the title had in the West for many centuries its home and abiding place within the Sanctuaries of the Church" (*Lamps* 5).[1] Waite thus "became," as Joscelyn Godwin observes, "a more exclusively Christian mystic as he grew older, leaving behind a whole library of works that, for better or worse, define the Western esoteric tradition for the general readership to this day" (346). This essay will explore how A. E. Waite fostered a literary movement anchored in his distinctive Christian understanding of mysticism, a movement that had profound consequences for the spiritual lives of many Edwardians, for subsequent decades of spiritual writers, and even for the relationship between mysticism and religion in our own day and time.

In his autobiography *Shadows of Life and Thought*, Arthur Edward Waite (1857 to 1942) recounts the decisive but seemingly chance moment when he and his mother

> were walking out, once on an afternoon, when it pleased God to send us rain in summer, and we were driven into the refuge of a Church. That gates may open strangely, on strange unknown realms, is on record full often in the high romance of mind. They open on the Land of Psyche and also on the Land of Nous. Moreover, rain in summer may itself be even as a figurative golden gate. It was eminently such in this case, for that towards which it led me was world without end in God. (19)

Thenceforth, his mother embarked upon a path toward Roman Catholicism, and he took up lodging in that Church's sheltering space—sometimes as a skeptic, sometimes a disaffected son, sometimes an apologist, but a permanent lodger nonetheless. For, ever after, he kept one foot of his spiritual compass within the Church even as the other foot would trace a wide circuit within the hidden realms of occult studies.

Despite this fundamental rootedness in the Roman Catholic Church, A. E. Waite is now known largely, if inaccurately, as an occultist.[2] His works are published in occult venues, as with one recent reissue of his essays, titled *The A. E. Waite Reader: A Selection of Occult Essays* and marketed within the publisher's Esoteric Classics series.[3] Early editions of his amateur scholarship on the kabbalah, alchemy, ritual societies, and the like, command high prices among modern readers interested in occult studies. He is also regarded as the father of one of the most famous tools of occult practice, still in use today: the Rider-Waite tarot deck. Gilbert, by contrast, calls him a "major, even if unrecognised, mystic" ("One" 3). The difficulty in classifying Waite's spiritual orientation was expressed well by Arthur Machen, who wrote in a 1925 letter,

> I have known my very dear friend A. E. Waite for 38 years; and I have not the faintest notion as to his real beliefs. . . . He was brought up strictly in the Roman Faith, and has always had the warmest enthusiasm for the Roman Church—"as a great system of symbolism," as he once explained to me. I have often told him that his case is exactly like that of the late President Thiers, who once said: "Je ne suis pas Chrétien: mais je suis toujours Catholique Romain." It is a strange case. (*Selected Letters* 100)

Yet, even with so many contributions to the study of occultism, mysticism, and religion, Roukema notes that Waite has received scant "research dedicated to his life and work" (49). Rethinking Waite within the context of mysticism is important for understanding his life and work, his privileging of mysticism over occultism, and the trend within the work of his Edwardian peers to separate mysticism from occultism. And typically missing from the conventional portrait of Waite as an occultist is the degree to which he sought to stay anchored in a Catholic Christian world view even as he wandered the fields of gramary in search of fruitful spiritual seeds.[4]

Not only is Waite today known more as an occultist than as a religious or mystical figure, so, too, is he known more for his amateur scholarship than for his literary endeavors. But literature was central to Waite's life and imagination from the very start. He wrote and published as a poet and novelist, despite Robert Browning's warning in 1876 to "[d]o *anything* rather than attempt to live by literature" (qtd. in Gilbert, *Magician* 76). And he both participated in and fostered an Edwardian-era Christian movement dedicated to the literary exploration of mystical experience for the common reader. This is the story of Waite's work as a literary artist and his influential contributions to a unique literary movement. It is, in short, the story of the rise of a particular kind of mystical novel in Edwardian England, characterized by a convergence of medieval and modern sensibilities and expressive of a distinctive sacramental theology.

In the years preceding Waite's scholarly and literary work in England, there had been sundry Victorian writers who authored what might be called Christian occult fiction or who considered themselves Christian mystics but whose mysticism was explored in nonfiction rather than fiction. In the former category, Marie Corelli (1855 to 1924) was a prolific and enormously popular fiction writer whose novels, such as *The Sorrows of Satan*, explored all manner of heterodox Christian ideas, leading reviewers in her own day and modern scholars to refer to her work as "mystical" (Knight 379), but Waite wrote little about her fiction over the course of his career (*Bibliography* 162–81) and when he did, he implied that her fiction's popularity was no test of its greatness ("Dealings" 406).

In the latter category, Waite's literary work was also preceded by that of writers like Anna Kingsford (1846 to 1888), a physician, onetime president of the Theosophical Society, passionate anti-vivisectionist, Roman Catholic, and self-described Christian mystic. Kingsford laid out her own heterodox Christian ideas in a work called *The Perfect Way, or the Finding of Christ* (1882), an attempt to synthesize Christianity with various theosophical ideas and her own dream visions. Like Corelli, Kingsford did write Christian fiction, and some of it, like "Caedmon: The Story of a Saxon Poet," hearkened back to the Middle Ages (with the "Caedmon" tale imagining how Caedmon came to write his famous creation hymn), but such fictions did not focus on the exploration or representation of mystical experience. Further, though Waite was much influenced by Kingsford's close collaborator Edward Maitland, whom he referred to as a fellow mystic (Waite, *Light* 115), it was Maitland's nonfiction work that inspired him, not Maitland's utopian science fiction novel *By and By: An Historical Romance of the Future*, and Waite ultimately dismissed Kingsford herself as "more zealous in the crusade against vivisection than as an evangelist in mysticism" (*Light* 116).[5]

By Waite's own account, his literary life was first set aflame by his enchantment with penny dreadfuls and a book of *Arabian Tales*, the latter, ironically, given to him by a friend "deputed by the Dominicans to oversee the spiritual welfare of Mrs. Waite and her children" (Gilbert, *Magician* 26). While such literature was later castigated by Mrs. Waite and that very same friend as " 'dangerous rubbish' " (Gilbert, *Magician* 26), only in hindsight does it become clear that these stories indirectly inspired the spiritual fiction Waite himself came to write and sought to foster in fellow writers, thereby fulfilling his family friend's deputation after all. Through the *Arabian Tales*, his life was lit up with stories of "hidden cities, sorcerers, and enchanted princesses" that exposed him to the potential for literature to transcend the ordinary world of getting and spending and transport the reader to other realms (Gilbert, *Magician* 26).

The earliest stages of Waite's own writing career were marked by his own twenty-something attempts at the penny dreadful (Gilbert, *Magician* 27), a genre he loved so much that he dedicated a full study to it and even collected a rare edition when the occasion arose (Gilbert, *Magician* 29–30). While he considered poetry to be the highway of literature and relegated such fiction to the "By-Ways of Periodical Literature" (the title of a Waite article), Gilbert rightly notes that Waite's subsequent scholarly interest in the genre betrays a prescient understanding of the value of "popular literature" (*Magician* 28). Although Waite himself eventually had reservations about how his enthusiasm for penny dreadfuls would tarnish his image as a writer of serious spiritual matters, over the course of his career Waite's experimentation in fiction for a popular audience and his advocacy for other writers of popular fiction helped to usher in a literary movement that sought to synthesize the heights of mystical experience and the accessibility of popular fiction. Yet, Waite was not the first to experiment with such a synthesis, nor were penny dreadfuls and the *Arabian Tales* his only literary influences. As Patrick Pazdziora has noted, the fiction of the Victorian novelist George MacDonald had a profound influence on Waite's thinking and writing and paved the way for the kind of "mystical fiction" Waite tried—and often failed—to write well (285).

In 1867, George MacDonald, the Scottish pastor, popular storyteller, and pioneer of fantasy fiction (known especially for classics such as *The Light Princess* and *The Princess and the Goblin*), penned a new collection of fantasy stories, *Dealings with the Fairies*, a collection that contained his now-famous novella *The Golden Key*. MacDonald's short fantasy fiction reflects one of the first English fictional narratives of mystical experience in prose form.[6] His novel is written using the fairy-tale genre popularized during the Victorian era through writers like Christina Rossetti, William

Morris, Andrew Lang, and others. Although MacDonald's *Dealings with the Fairies* was dedicated to his children (Hein 187), the stories therein have been enjoyed since the Victorian era by adults as well as children for the profound way in which they convey a world "[w]here," as the epigraph puts it, "more is meant than meets the eye" (qtd. in Hein 187). MacDonald's story relates how a child named Mossy finds a golden key at the foot of a rainbow, leading him and Tangle, the girl with whom his story becomes interwoven, through a series of adventures that climax in a mystical experience: Tangle "had a marvellous sense that she was in the secret of the earth and all its ways. Everything she had seen, or learned from books; all that her grandmother had said or sung to her . . . all was plain: she understood it all, and saw that everything meant the same thing, though she could not have put it into words again" (59). Through the course of their adventures with a wise old grandmother; with fishes and strange trees; with water, air, and fire, the two young people grow into deeper understanding that the ordinary world is as strange as it is familiar because, as Hopkins famously put it, "charged with the grandeur of God" (128). Their own process of growth and sanctification is reflected through a deepened knowledge of the transcendent within the ordinary.

Many dimensions of MacDonald's religious vision and aesthetic attracted and inspired Waite: MacDonald's use of fairy lore as a way of encoding individual spiritual experience, his prizing of purgatorial suffering, his sacramentalism, his doctrine of universal salvation, and, most importantly, his emphasis on mystical experience as profound interior insight about the nature of reality, which even the most ordinary folk can aspire to and grow into. In Waite's autobiography, he suggests that reading MacDonald's *Phantastes* "marked an epoch" in his life "perhaps because it gave me . . . a second sense in literature" (*Shadows of Life and Thought* [*SLT*] 66–67). Explicit references to MacDonald appear elsewhere in Waite's writing, for, according to J. Patrick Pazdziora, "Waite quotes [MacDonald's novel *Phantastes*] no fewer than three times in his mystical treatise, *Azoth; or the Star in the East: A New Light of Mysticism* (1893)," a work from relatively early in Waite's career (293). The words that so interested him are the "fairy-gifted poet beholds THE SAME THING EVERYWHERE" (qtd. in Pazdziora 292). This passage, noted repeatedly in Waite's comments, suggests that MacDonald's stress on the poet's imaginative experience of universal truth spoke to Waite's universalizing inclinations and his faith in the poet's ability to apprehend universal truth through individual experience.

Pazdziora remarks that it is "intriguing" to discover such admiration on Waite's part, "by an author who, as a practicing occultist, appropriates MacDonald into a religious understanding seemingly at odds with 'the fictionalization of Christianity'" (292). This discovery should occasion surprise, however, only if one sees Waite primarily as an occultist. Nonetheless, Pazdziora is right to acknowledge MacDonald's unique impact on Waite: "Waite seems to be advancing MacDonald as an authority on poetry and mysticism . . . [H]e positions MacDonald's image of 'the fairy-gifted poet' as portraying a specific way of perceiving the world through the transfigured soul of the mystic, thereby transfiguring and ennobling the material world itself" (295). In Pazdziora's view, Waite finds in MacDonald's work a spiritual worldview that the former appropriates and extends in his own fiction and distinctive vision, and he describes this shared sensibility as a "willingness to look beyond the immediate surface of things, the realm of the material and materialism, to allow for a broader, more imaginative . . . embrace of the world" (299).

It is this "second sense" that Waite adopts and adapts from MacDonald. Toward that end, Waite uses fairy lore as a way to explore how the world is shot through with glimmers of transcendent glory and always, everywhere, suffused with spiritual significance. Thus, he builds upon MacDonald's use of the prose fairy novel for spiritual ends. Although Waite's most explicit references to MacDonald appear in his quotations from *Phantastes*, Waite's 1893 fiction, *The Golden Stairs*, clearly illustrates how he draws upon MacDonald's *The Golden Key* in developing a form of novel that tells the soul's story and, ultimately, tries to portray the varieties of mystical experience in popular form.[7]

The Golden Stair from MacDonald to Waite

After the fashion of many of MacDonald's fantasy fictions, all of Waite's attempts at narrative fiction embed his stories in the world of faerie. The poetic mode of this supernatural literature was one Waite traced through the whole history of English poetry by collecting and publishing a medley of English fairy poetry, *Elfin Music: An Anthology of English Fairy Poetry*. Writing in 1888, he introduced this collection by opining that his literary era was an opportune one due to "the initial signs of a revival of that romantic or supernatural element," which he considered the potential "salvation of modern poetry" (*Elfin Music* ix). Through an etymological history, Waite traces the word *faerie* to words meaning to "enchant" and suggests that the word came to be employed "not only for illusion, but for the land which was *par excellence* the home of all gramary, illusion, and *envoutement*" (*Elfin Music* x). That such *faerie* poetry was furthermore connected to the spiritual or mystical is evinced by his comments about the third section of the anthology, which he describes as poetry "devoted to those wonderful and mystical travels or spiritual pilgrimages into Fairyland, which have been occasionally undertaken by favoured and adventurous mortals" (*Elfin Music* xxxiv). From Waite's vantage, poetry could be considered "truly great only when it contained profound mystical insights" (Gilbert, "One" 8).[8]

Waite's own adventures in writing started with several attempts at poetry, and according to Gilbert's comprehensive bibliography, Waite's "Lyric of the Fairyland and other Poems" (1879) was one of his first publications, with the *Anthology of English Fairy Poetry* published not long thereafter in 1888 (Gilbert, *Magician* 199). When Waite turned to fiction writing, his first sustained novel was the 1889 *Prince Starbeam: A Tale of Fairyland*. That was followed by *The Golden Stairs: Tales from the Wonder-World* in 1893, *Belle and the Dragon: An Elfin Comedy* in 1894, and *The Quest of the Golden Stairs*, a 1927 revised and remixed version of his earlier fairy stories. The course of Waite's long and prolific writing career reflects a gradual shift from authorship of poetry and fiction to translation of occult texts; essays and scholarship on the occult and mystical; liturgies and manuals related to the ritual Orders with which he was involved; and editorial work. Given how much the latter work has loomed large in his reputation, he is now most well-known for *The Hidden Church of the Holy Graal* (1909), *The Pictorial Key to the Tarot* (1911), *The Secret Tradition in Freemasonry* (1911), *The Secret Doctrine in Israel* (1913), and *The Holy Kabbalah* (1929). This shift in trajectory as a writer is consistent with his eventual desire to be identified solely in accord with his *Who's Who* self-description: as "the exponent in poetical and prose writings of sacramental religion and the higher mysticism" (qtd. in Gilbert, *Magician* 29). Yet, a close reading of his forays into fiction illuminates how much his fiction was shaped to suit that very same end.

Waite's *The Golden Stairs: Tales from the Wonder-World* appeared in 1893 in a first edition with back-page advertisements illustrating the literary milieu in which he had found favor: *Gypsy Sorcery* by Charles Godfrey Leland; *The Wonder-Light and Other Tales* by Mrs. J. Campbell Ver-Planck, Folk Lore and Legends featuring tales of German, Oriental,

Scottish, Scandinavian, North American Indian, and Russian provenance; *Indian Fairy Tales* edited by Joseph Jacobs; *Sacred Mysteries Among the Maya and Quiches* by A. Le Plongeon (about freemasonry before the Temple of Solomon); and *The Mystic Quest: A Tale of Two Incarnations* by William Kingsland. These books and Waite's novel were all published by the Theosophical Publishing Society, whose library still today houses some of the few first editions (or even copies) of Waite's *Prince Starbeam.*

Waite's *Golden Stairs* interlinks the stories of several different princes, each of whom has a quest related to the world of fairy land. The stories imitate the fairy-tale genre collected by Andrew Lang and popularized by MacDonald in novel form. Unlike Lang and akin to MacDonald, Waite uses fairy as a way of telling the "soul's story," and the princely figures who populate his tales are both ordinary young men and "soul heroes," a key phrase that appears in the chapter called "The Seven Sapphires."[9] There, a prince named Metron is prophesied to have "a great destiny," a future interpreted throughout the boy's palace to mean that he would become a "splendid and powerful ruler who would subdue the whole world" (47).[10] Counter to that conventional interpretation of his future, an anonymous old woman teaches Prince Metron "to value the nobility of life above the accidents of rank and wealth, a pure heart more than the pride of princes, and the welfare of humanity above his private interests. She told him *tales of soul heroes* [emphasis mine], and of the bright crowns which they attain in that far country which is the Home of the Spirit" (47–48). Through such a prophecy, Waite emphasizes spiritual questing and sanctification as the great, truly heroic calling of life, more important than material or worldly success.[11]

The phrase "soul hero" is an apt descriptor for the type of hero Waite's own stories feature, and it represents a distinctive shift from the types of heroes previously common to the English novel as a genre—from Robinson Crusoe and Clarissa to Catherine Morland and Pip. That is, Waite's heroes are drawn to what he elsewhere calls "the Unknown World," the metaphysical realm that beckons and hovers "ever at our doors" ("Dealings" 405). Significantly, Waite's *Golden Stairs* relates the story not of one prince or even two central characters like Mossy and Tangle, but of several princes. In that respect, *The Golden Stairs* may seem as much a collection of tales as a novel. Waite acknowledges this structure explicitly in the final story, "An Elfin Legacy," using a well-known mystical image, the mystic rose, to convey how readers should regard the stories. Reflecting on the separate stories, he suggests that they are "tales of many meanings, *even as one rose is composed of many petals* [emphasis mine]" (101). Thus, the very structure of Waite's novel mirrors his conception of mystical experience as a unitary path with diverse expressions. As each story features a different princely protagonist, neither story intersects by plot with that of any of the others, though there are common motifs and symbols and a unifying metafictional interpretation that yoke the stories together. On the one hand, the aristocratic pedigree of his princely heroes bespeaks the spiritual elitism for which Waite's thinking was sometimes criticized.[12] On the other, though, Waite's rejection of a single main character or narrative and his inclusion of so many different princes displays his conviction that there are more people inclined to step upon the mystic path than one might expect, and different paths to the one end of joy and mystical union.

The opening chapter of *The Golden Stairs*, also called "The Golden Stairs," most directly recalls MacDonald's work and brings together many motifs already present in MacDonald's fantasy fictions, but particularly MacDonald's *Golden Key*, for that work directly bequeaths to Waite the idea of a "golden stair." When Mossy first views the rainbow at the foot of which he finds the "golden key," he perceives the rainbow "as large as the column of a church" and "he could faintly see beautiful forms slowly ascending as if by *the steps of a winding stair* [emphasis mine]" (5–6). This stair image recurs in the final moments of MacDonald's novel, when Tangle and Mossy's spiritual ascent is marked by climbing the rainbow: "Stairs beside stairs wound up together, and beautiful beings of all ages climbed along with them" (78). Waite adapts this idea of the spiritual stairway and plays upon it in varied ways in his several stories.

In Waite's chapter called "The Golden Stairs," the protagonist, Hildebrand, is the inheritor of a "grey, half-ruinous building, with a wide and wild garden round it" (9). The House's Master (capitalized, significantly) sets sail to restore the house's fortunes and, upon return, establish a "Golden Age" (12); in language that implies his divine nobility, he is later described as a "fairy prince and a prince of spells" (11), with dominion over land, air, and sea, and even the "great Kraken" (11), a Norse mythological analogue to the biblical Behemoth and Leviathan. These associations suggest that the Master of the House is to be read as God, Christ, or Arthur (who, as the once and future king, has traditionally had Christlike associations and bears the hope of redeeming the broken Round Table). The story's structure parallels that of the redemptive story of Adam and Christ, beginning in ruin and wilderness and ending with the Master's completion of his redemptive quest, the restoration of the fortunes of the "house" of the world. If the Master of the House is read as Christ, then Hildebrand is akin to, simultaneously, the Christian setting off from the Church, Galahad embarking on a quest for the Grail, and the soul leaving its earthly abode to seek its true home.

Like Mr. Vane in MacDonald's last novel *Lilith*, Hildebrand finds himself the inheritor of an ancestral house, its library, and the books therein. In the library, Hildebrand discovers a "great book of knightly romances, containing the Quest of the Golden Stairs" (10). Illustrative of Waite's synthesizing imagination, Hildebrand experiences a kind of merger of the book's story and his father's quest, for, "the Quest of the Golden Stairs and the quest of his father, blending in his mind, became one wonderful story" (11). His vision merges and unifies, reflecting MacDonald's idea in *Phantastes* that the poet is able to see the same thing everywhere. No sooner does he experience that merger than the story he is reading becomes his as well, and he lives into what he has read. He sets out on a journey into Nature with a "clean heart and a 'seeing sense' " (16), a phrase that echoes MacDonald's Romantic concept of the poet's gift for all-embracing perception. As a further extension of Waite's attempts to correlate multiple levels of reality, Waite's metafictional play with the "Quest of the Golden Stairs" title implies that we ourselves are reading the story that Hildebrand reads and lives into—and, as the final section of the novel asserts, we are called to pursue the same quest.

The Role of Suffering in Spiritual Progress

For both Waite and MacDonald, successful progress along a spiritual quest depends upon sacrificial suffering. In MacDonald's *Golden Key*, one of the strangest creatures Tangle encounters in her adventure are the fish who willingly jump into pots of boiling water (13–14), some to be eaten and others to be transformed into Ariel-like spiritual beings (Aëranths), evolving from an earthly existence to a spiritual one. Tangle is at first horrified by this self-immolation until she better understands that self-sacrifice is a fundamental principle of the cosmic economy. The Grandmother assures Tangle, "In Fairyland . . . the ambition of the animals is to be eaten by the people; for that is their highest end in that condition. But they are not therefore destroyed. Out of that pot comes something more than the dead fish, you will see" (25). Indeed, when the Lady removes the lid, "[a] lovely little creature in human shape, with large white wings, rose out of it" (26). Having learned from the fish how self-sacrifice paves the way for spiritual progress, she herself experiences this when she throws herself into an abyss where the stairs she has been following give way (58), only to find that her demise downward leads to a "cool mossy cave," the place of her mystical enlightenment and her spiritual path upward (59).

Waite draws upon this idea of purgative and transformational suffering in the story of Prince Asphodel, but whereas MacDonald uses a wise grandmother to educate the children about the role of suffering, Waite uses a more explicitly Christian figure. Instructed by an Angel about the mysterious discarnate beings in a "pool of souls," Prince Asphodel learns that they, like he, are "seeking a higher life" (*The Golden Stairs* 32). The Angel explains, "They pass thee here in pain, because pain is inseparable from progression . . . by suffering they earn their title to existence" (32). Waite returns to this idea again in a direct address to the reader within the final story, "An Elfin Legacy." Like the fish who swim into the boiling water to become nourishment for others, "so," Waite writes, "must you renounce yourself for the good of others" (106). This suffering is necessary, he says, "[i]f you would climb the Golden Stairs, if you would attain the Crown of Life, the Seven Sapphires, and a Throne in Paradise" (106). In fact, in Hildebrand's story, Waite obliquely invokes an alchemical allusion for such suffering in suggesting that Hildebrand's heart needs to be tried to see if it is "true gold" before he is worthy to ascend the Golden Stairs (20); the microcosm must mirror the macrocosm.[13]

The Representation of Mystical Experience

In MacDonald's *Golden Key*, Tangle's story builds toward an experience of ultimate knowledge and mystical union, and so "The Golden Stairs" chapter in Waite's book climaxes in a mystical experience for Hildebrand. The "seeing sense" so important to Hildebrand's soul quest fosters his mystical vision, which hews closely to the mystical vision Tangle and Mossy experience. Just as Mossy has been tutored only by his great-aunt's oral stories prior to his adventure, Prince Hildebrand's mystic quest begins in a place of stories—a library where he devotes himself to scholarly study. Yet, like Vane in MacDonald's *Lilith*, Hildebrand learns nothing about the true nature of reality till he directly experiences it. For, the mystic, as William Philip Downes notes in his 1920 essay "Mysticism," "Knowledge of God must be . . . personal, direct, intuitive" (623). So, Waite's narrator relates, “Hildebrand began . . . his search for the Golden Stairs among the books and the vellum manuscripts. At the end of the year he had filled his head with wonders, but of his quest he had learned nothing” (15). Despite Hildebrand’s initial inclination to find the Golden Stairs through reading and study alone (analogous to Waite himself), Waite privileges direct experience over secondhand knowledge for the fulfillment of Hildebrand’s quest. As in *The Golden Key*, Hildebrand must leave “home” and venture into the world of Nature; only “after a gallant roaming, which passed like that mystical pause when ‘there was silence in heaven for the space of half-an-hour’ ” (17), is he is gifted with the sight of a rainbow.

Here the tale explicitly alludes to the rainbow in MacDonald’s *Golden Key*. Hildebrand even wonders if the rainbow is the “wonderful staircase” he seeks (17); in both narratives, the rainbow serves as an image of the bridge between earth and heaven, and it reflects one instance of the nature mysticism present in the fiction of both authors. Nature’s graceful gifts—the “sea’s voices,” the stars’ “bright meteoric circles” (13) help to foster a sense of wonder and awe that opens Hildebrand to mystical knowledge. The narrator relates, “All Nature began to interpret itself in song and music to the mind of the listening boy . . . [F]or earth, and sky, and sea had taken voice together, and his own soul was speaking to him” (25). And just as in *The Golden Key*, Mossy’s turning of the lock with his golden key is accompanied by Aeolian music (77), so, too, Hildebrand experiences “the melody of a great wind sweeping over Aeolian harp-strings. . . . Then out of the bright confusion of these hues there was developed a divine harmony of a single beautiful colour which was unlike anything he had ever seen before” (18). When the key opens the lock “the gates rolled open with the shrill sweetness of a sudden burst of flute-notes, and the world of wonder opened its red-rose vistas and wild sky-pageants in front of them” (21), a vision displayed by Hildebrand’s guiding Spirit in order that he might choose his earthbound existence or an ascent upon the Golden Stairs to the supreme Reality.

Several of the others stories in Waite’s *Golden Stairs* also depict or allude to mystical experience: the kind of experience William James, lecturing in 1902, described as “passive,” “transient,” “ineffable,” ultimately “noetic” (380–82). In Waite’s “The Renewed Youth,” a forest boy named Lolo teaches Prince Ernest the joy embedded in the natural world and the transcendent mysteries opened by music, for Lolo is distinguished by a preternatural gift for song. Waite explores the spiritual importance of music in another story, “The Bells of Fairyland,” which relates the special effects of a "circular, stringed instrument" that sounds from the woodland pavilion near a secluded village (90–91). The story's poet-father explains to his son, Amaranth, on whom the story centers,

> Doubtless this music is a key to many secrets of Nature. The instrument is the work of a person of soul-power—one who has attained a great height . . . Those few, "chosen out of all," who hear—not merely listen to—this music are lifted out of themselves, for it is the true language of the spheres, the secrets of the sun and moon. By the sympathy of comprehension they are raised to communion with the heavenly intelligences whose divine thoughts radiate from burning centres in life-giving and illuminating beams. (93)

In the course of the story, the boy-hero Amaranth becomes a martyr in order to restore the instrument to its high place, losing his life but creating a "Mystic Bridge" or "Bridge of Harmony" for his fellow villagers, who had lost their connection to the transcendent world (98–99).

Like this musical instrument in "The Bells of Fairyland," which provides a mystical stair from the ordinary world to the fairy one, from the earthly to the spiritual realm, so Lolo's own musical instrument, his voice, expresses his interior insight and creates a similar bridge between him, Prince Ernest, and all of reality. The story ends with a union between the two men and a mystical vision of the greater reality of which they are a part. Lolo articulates this vision when he cries, " 'The whole earth is before us; there is no end to it, and it is all ours. This is true reality' . . . They stood for a moment side by side . . . [T]hey were joined to the universal spirit of the blithe world, and they could want for nothing" (45–46). Just as Tangle and Mossy mature toward a mystical union with all other beings in the radiance of a rainbow, so, too, Ernest and Lolo experience this blissful union.

Sacramental Theology

The insights to which Waite's stories lead reflect a sacramental understanding of reality analogous to the one shaping MacDonald's vision. As Ann Boaden puts it, "A bone-deep heritage of Celtic lore taught him [MacDonald] that the forces of nature—from wide skies and whirling storms, to the gentle and majestic moon, to the tiny primroses starring earth—bore sacramental significance" (9). This sacramental sense of life, inherited both from MacDonald's theology and from Waite's own Catholicism, is attested to in many places throughout Waite's large oeuvre. Notably, in a poem titled "The Extreme Sense," Waite laments how "Man treads a path with signs and lights ablaze/Yet scarce conceives of sacrament or sign," often led astray by "[f]alse sacraments," missing what "Nature's mystic life . . . unfolds" (*Book of Mystery and Vision* 23). In his 1923 scholarly study of mysticism, he emphasizes how rooted the great Western mystics have been in the Church's sacraments as "the outward sign of an inward grace" (*Lamps of Western Mysticism* 8–9). The stories within *The Golden Stairs* reflect sacramentalism in both a specific and a general sense.

In "The Golden Stair" chapter, we see him explicitly alluding to the sacramentalism of Christian ritual. For, when Hildebrand reaches the foot of the rainbow, Waite substitutes a golden chalice for MacDonald's golden key, foreshadowing the former's growing interest in the "Graal" and Christian interpretations of the Eucharistic sacrament it represents. The narrator relates, "Whoever reaches the foot of the rainbow will find a golden chalice, says one old legend, but according to another he will be rewarded by the possession of the Golden Key; the Key just fits the lock of the golden Gates, and through the Gates of Gold it is a certain thing that one passes into many marvels, indeed into a strange land where there is a strange sun and a strange bright light over everything" (17). Although Waite's "Golden Stairs" tale uses the imagery of the chalice to root Hildebrand's mystical experience in the Christian sacramental tradition, in "The Renewed Youth" chapter, the narrator describes art and Nature as forms of sacrament, capable of renewing and even revivifying life. The forest boy Lolo sings an ineffable song expressing "the praise of beauty, the praise of life, the praise of that divine mystery which is hidden in all we see" (39). Like Niggle's painting in Tolkien's famous story about the painter as "sub-creator," Lolo's song is both revelation of the divine mystery within God's natural creation and, as sub-creation, a "floral paradise created by song-power" (43). The sacrament of song has such great healing power that it causes a kind of reverse aging for Prince Ernest, who had become wearied, withered, and aged from long years as the reluctant ruler of his earthly kingdom.

Waite returns to the nature mysticism so strongly present in "The Renewed Youth" in his final chapter, "An Elfin Legacy," suggesting that the fairy-gifted poet is imbued with a sacramental sensibility available to the reader as well. The narrator explains,

> When you can find in old ocean something more than a tract of blue water, and more in high heaven than an expanse of cloud and azure; when you feel that in looking upon the world you are coming into contact with an unbottomed mystery which is full of grace and loveliness, a fountain of intelligence, an inexhaustible well of joy, you may be sure that you are being taught of Nature, and that it is possible for you also to hear the melody . . . (104)

Waite's novel, thus, pushes readers beyond the horizontal sphere of reality—the everyday, ordinary, social world—emphasized by writers like Defoe, Richardson, Fielding, and Austen, implying a hidden sphere of reality accessible to those who would recognize the ordinary world's sacred depths, an unknown world knowable through the homely graces of everyday life.

The Kingdom of God Lies Within

In *The Golden Key*, MacDonald's fantasy story draws attention to the primacy of the individual's role in the spiritual quest and that quest's profound interiority. When Mossy protests that he does not know what to do with the golden key, the wise and kindly Lady insists that he must go it alone: "You must look for the keyhole. *That is your work. I cannot help you.* I can only tell you that if you look for it you will find it [emphasis mine]" (31). Not only must individuals rely upon themselves to seek and find, but they must also find the quest's fulfillment within themselves. MacDonald gives the name *Mossy* to the male protagonist in his story, and, in the story's literal narrative, moss is where the golden key is to be found. The convergence of the external location of the key and the name for Mossy himself suggests that the key to divine fulfillment is as much an internal state of perception as it is an external place to be reached.[14]

Waite adopts this emphasis on interiority in several of his tales. For instance, in "The Golden Stairs," Hildebrand "knew that there was a universe within him as well as without him, and he felt the presence of the Christ in his heart" (25–26). Here, Waite shifts out of the coded language of fairy and speaks in explicitly Christian theological language to suggest that the foot of the rainbow may well be Hildebrand's own heart. Waite stresses this interiority of vision even more strongly in the final section, "An Elfin Legacy"—which is, in fact, more a meta-commentary on the whole novel than a story. Directly addressing the reader, he insists that each prince is really the reader, as, for instance, "Prince Metron is also yourself . . ." (105) or "You also are that most fair Prince Asphodel . . . and you are taking the same journey. You are in search of the Crown of Life" (103) and the "Queen of Fairies may be your own bright and starry bride . . . She also is within you, my dear one—the pure and shining soul" (107). Elsewhere he adds that "the presence of this Spirit is within you, as it is within me, an instructing, guiding light" (102). The final words of his book enjoin the reader not to look elsewhere but to look within for the spiritual salvation that the quest represents. Waite concludes with this counsel: "Once more then, do not go in search of that land; it is within you and round you" (109). With that injunction, Waite hints at what he elsewhere calls "a Church behind the Church on a more inward plane . . . that . . . is formed of those who have opened the indescent [*sic*] shell of external doctrine and have found that which abides within it" (*SLT* 170–71). Such words about "a Church behind the Church" point up the tensions that underlie his worldview, which is at once moored to the historical Church and its ecclesiastical authority and yet idiosyncratically individualistic.

Assurance of Universal Salvation

Early in Hildebrand's story, when he is still reading of rather than experiencing the Golden Stairs, he reads that the existence of the Golden Stairs is universally credited, and, moreover, all have hope of ascending them: "There was no doubt of their existence, everyone had heard of them, many had seen them; indeed there were some persons, whose opinion was worth hearing, who were quite certain that neither man nor woman would ultimately fail to mount them" (12–13). MacDonald was surely possessed of that theological certainty, and subsequent allusion to Hildegard's mother agreeing with "Wise Men and the Fairies that some day probably they would be trodden by every man and woman" may be a direct reference to MacDonald as one such wise man (14). This view of human salvation is wholly consistent with MacDonald's soteriology, an unorthodox theology that created friction and eventual alienation between him and his parishioners in the 1850s (Hein 81) and characterized his thinking "throughout the rest of his life," though it was most creatively imagined at the end of his career in his 1895 novel, *Lilith* (82).

Waite returns to this assurance of universal salvation later in *The Golden Stairs*. In one of the final chapters, "The Budget of Fairyland," Waite again invokes echoes of MacDonald's soteriology. Even as Waite turns to the high legends of Arthur for this tale of fairy, a legend that might seem larger than life and distant from ordinary people, he continues to adopt MacDonald's idea of universal salvation, reminding readers that "All are agreed . . . that there is a Fairyland, and that most persons, if they choose, may enter it" (60). In the final chapter, "An Elfin Legacy," where Waite encourages readers to see themselves in each of the princely characters, he simultaneously assures readers that if they seek the mystic stairs, they, too, will find ultimate salvation. With an optimism for all, Waite's farewell to the reader offers only tender mercies and makes no mention of fear or damnation:

> You are the dear Childe Hildebrand, and the house in which he lived in is the house that you have lived in . . . The great lessons which the Spirit taught Hildebrand are the lessons that you must learn, and then you also, at the right time, shall go up the Golden Stairs which lead to God and immortality, and to that happy state of peace and knowledge, which is the end of your life and of my life. (102)

This dimension of Waite's mystical theology evinces a paradox; he is at once the elitist who sees mysticism as the province of a spiritual nobility, chosen "princes" with access to the secret church within, but he is at the same time the purveyor of assurances that there is a mystical path and salvation for all who would step upon the golden stairs. Pazdziora highlights the degree to which Waite's work was prone to spiritual elitism. He observes that "Waite was most certainly guilty" of Chesterton's "charge of 'celestial snobbishness' " (298), adding that Chesterton saw in Waite a man who believed " 'only a few can enter into his feelings, that he writes for a select circle of the initiated' " (qtd. in 298). And, to be sure, the esoteric topics Waite explored, from Kabbalah to alchemy, as well as his "circumlocutory prose" (Martin 192) and the arcane Celtic fairy lore he drew upon for embedding his spiritual ideas, substantiate Pazdziora's claims about his gnostic tendencies.

Pazdziora's characterization of Waite, however, captures only a partial truth. In the very same review of Waite's *Book of Mystery and Vision*, Chesterton observed, half seriously, half sardonically, that we seem to have become "all mystics now" (246).[15] More recently, Christine Ferguson has identified a contrary, strongly "egalitarian impulse" (47) in Waite's thinking and writing, turning to his journalistic "Dealings in Bibliomania" as an example. In Ferguson's view, that article, different from his earlier "By-Ways of Periodic Literature," signals a democratic shift in his thinking away from his earlier, condescending view that popular fiction fell short of the sublime highway of true poetry. She suggests that his "Dealings in Bibliomania" "[d]ramatically extended his argument for pulp fiction's value by lauding its incantatory powers and aligning its collection with the quest for occult wisdom" (Ferguson 46). Ferguson argues that "the further Waite immersed himself in esoteric study, the more vocal a defender of popular fiction he became" (46), but "it was not the social world with which [such] popular fiction concerned itself, but rather the Unknown one. Portals into this numinous space were omnipresent, in railway book kiosks, cheap newsagents, and lending libraries. Popular fiction offered . . . the possibility of sheer spiritual bliss and occult citizenship" (54). Even Waite's nonfiction writing, such as his 1891 primer *The Occult Sciences*, was aimed at making esoteric topics popularly accessible in the face of similar studies that he found both expensive and "unsuited to an elementary reader" (v). Thus, in contrast to Pazdziora's emphasis on the gnostic and elitist dimensions of Waite's thinking, Ferguson thinks that "Waite's meditations on the Unknown World of the popular text challenge prevailing characterizations of the late Victorian occult revival as furtive, secretive, elitist, and hierarchical in nature, emphasizing instead British occulture's long-running dependency on popular literary forms and investment in mass-mediated as well as individuated forms of spiritual experience" (Ferguson 54–55). For Waite, however, it was ultimately not "occult citizenship" that he sought to purvey through popular fiction, but rather *mystical membership* in the one body of Christ.

Waite's paradoxical position as spiritual elitist and democrat is reflected in the different ways he helped to fire the Christian mystical revival in the first decades of the twentieth century—on the one hand, through a rectification of mysticism that included his secret order, the

Fellowship of the Rosy Cross, and, on the other hand, through his publication of popular fiction by writers whose views of mysticism aligned with his own. That he sought not only to write mystical literature but also to inaugurate a movement of it is evident in some of his critical commentaries. In Waite's introduction to his 1902 collection of poetry, *A Book of Mystery and Vision*, he describes the select "secret school" of the "awakened" who have experienced a mystic vision (ix) at the same time that he concedes that "[s]uch persons are more numerous than would perhaps be thought possible" (ix). Moreover, at the start of the new century, he observes "a quickening that has come within recent years" and the need for this "school" to "create its literature anew for the century which has now opened" (x–xi). He describes its chief "pretension . . . as a first-hand attempt to present the sacramental nature of life in a literary form" (xi). Indeed, his review of his own work from this period describes it as "voices of a sacramental world, from a poet's point of view" (*SLT* 155). While the elaborately allegorical narratives encoded by fairy lore and the baroque prose style of Waite's own fiction precluded him from realizing a mystic literature for a growing "school" of readers, he nonetheless recognized the need for a new "literary form" and directly or indirectly encouraged friends and fellow writers—Evelyn Underhill, Arthur Machen, R. H. Benson, Charles Williams, among others—to continue his experiment in literary form and the adoption of novelistic fiction as a viable genre for representing Christian mystical experience.

Waite's mundane employment as the manager of advertising for the Horlick's Malted Milk Company may have shaped his sympathy for making his ideas—including those about the nature of mysticism—accessible and relevant to the middlebrow reader. Waite began his business career with the London office of that American food company in 1899 and worked there for ten years (Gilbert, *Magician* 84). But it was the year 1904 that "marked the beginning of an experiment": He recounts, "It was decided to divert from the normal channels a part of the large annual sum then expended on advertising Horlick's Malted Milk and to establish a high-class monthly periodical under the name of Horlick's Magazine" (*SLT* 167). Taking advantage of his office as editor of that magazine, he seized the opportunity to showcase literary works that explored the vertical dimension of human existence and the human quest to experience a transcendent reality. While the periodical survived for just fifteen issues (*SLT* 167), the writers who published within it found success beyond its pages. The mystical fiction that friends or acquaintances like Machen and Underhill wrote therein (and elsewhere) mirrored Waite's conception of mysticism, but those fellow writers of mystical fiction eschewed the fairy stories so popular during the Victorian world. Instead, shifting with the winds of a new century, they spirited in a fresh approach to representing mystical experience for the modern reader, embedding mystical experiences of the Divine within stories and novels rooted in the English novel's tradition of literary realism, from R. H. Benson's *The Light Invisible* (1903) and Evelyn Underhill's *The Gray World* (1904) to Arthur Machen's *A Fragment of Life* (1906) and, decades later, Charles Williams's *Greater Trumps*.

This group of writers subscribed neither to the blurring of boundaries between mysticism and magic so characteristic of many Victorian predecessors nor to the path traced by the poet Alice Meynell, who "insisted on distinguishing religion from mysticism," as she did in her introduction to Cashmore's 1910 *Mount of Vision: Book of English Mystical Verse* (Knight and Mason 208). Instead, through weighty tomes such as *Studies in Mysticism* (1906), Waite and the company he kept sought to distinguish mysticism from the occult and thereby to integrate mysticism with Christian religious traditions dating back to the Middle Ages. And in a story that is still to be told, each of these Edwardian novelists of mystical fiction, whether nominally Anglican or Roman Catholic, cultivated a sacramental sensibility through the merger of medievalism and modernism, mysticism and literary realism.[16] It is perhaps an irony of literary history that this sacramental mysticism and the mystical fiction that arose in the Edwardian era is in part traceable, via Waite, to an unorthodox Scottish Protestant master of fantasy fiction.

To be sure, Waite's reliance on the Victorian-style fantasy inherited from MacDonald was not successful by the economic measure of copies sold or the aesthetic measure of his reviewers' judgments.[17] Nonetheless, his prolific writing about mysticism and his editorial efforts to set a new direction for the revival of Christian mystical fiction had notable effects on writers who had more popular success in the Edwardian era and even, for better or worse, on subsequent generations of seekers drawn to individual spiritual quests—whether with or without religious moorings. Through his combined work as novelist and poet, scholar, book reviewer, ritualist, and editor, Waite paved a spiritual path for other writers to pursue using a different literary mode—one still aimed at conjuring the awe and transcendence central to mystical experience, but within the framework of an ordinary, everyday world rather than a remote world of faerie.[18]

Chapter 2

The Mystical Novel and Incarnational Realism

R. H. Benson's *The Light Invisible*

> I thought I saw in you one to whom the supernatural was more than a beautiful and symbolical fairy-story, and one who held it not impossible that this unseen should sometimes manifest itself.
>
> —An anonymous letter writer to the novel's priestly tale-teller in *The Light Invisible* (88)

"If you have not read 'The Light Invisible' by Robert Benson: do so quickly—*liber vere mysticus*," Arthur Machen enthused in a letter to his fellow actor Paul England (qtd. in *Selected Letters* 221). While Robert Hugh Benson's popular spiritual fiction may not generate the same enthused response today, except among certain Catholic circles, Benson was something of a literary phenomenon in his own day. His most recent biographer, Janet Grayson, compares him to "a comet hurtling across the sky, drawing all eyes to it" during the Edwardian era, for, "[f]rom first novel to last, Benson enjoyed an immense audience, an international audience drawn from all classes including royalty and stretching across two continents" (xiii–xiv). Among this audience of interested readers, he attracted the admiration of the theologian Teilhard de Chardin and the Catholic intellectuals Jacques and Raissa Maritain (xxviii). He also surfaced in F. Scott Fitzgerald's fiction as one of the favorite writers of the character Amory in Fitzgerald's first novel, *This Side of Paradise*, published in 1920 (xxii). And, within the short span of his forty-two years of life, he was incredibly prolific, publishing twenty novels in eleven years, in addition to sermons, lectures, poetry, children's books, plays, and copious letters (Grayson xiv).

But like a comet, he "passed out of mind almost as rapidly" (Grayson xiii). And not only did his readership decline precipitously as decades passed, but so also has the scholarship about this prolific and once-popular novelist been sparse. Broad studies of the Edwardian literary world have tended to leave him aside in their focus on Forster, James, Kipling, Haggard, Stevenson, and other writers who better fit the story of modernist secularization.[1] He has made periodic appearances in studies of early twentieth-century Catholic writers, though those have given higher profile to Chesterton, Huysmans, and Meynell.[2] Glen Cavaliero's seminal study of the supernatural in English literature casts him as a writer of polemical novels and ghost stories, classifying *The Light Invisible* and *Mirror of Shalott* as "collections of ghost stories" (*Supernatural* 105). In that vein, he is sometimes referenced in connection to writers of English Gothic, horror, or decadent fiction, though even in Alison Milbank's important *God and the Gothic: Religion, Romance, and Reality in the English Literary Tradition*, he merits only two footnotes (290, 294). Typically missing from this scholarly assessment is an account of his contributions to the Edwardian mystical revival as novelist, poet, preacher, and lecturer, and the striking synergies between his novelistic explorations of mysticism and those of A. E. Waite, Evelyn Underhill, and Arthur Machen.

Benson's contributions to the Edwardian mystical literary revival demand closer attention, for they help us to understand the revival's theological emphases and aesthetic inclinations. Like his peers and in contrast to many Victorian predecessors, he was interested in distinguishing mysticism from forms of occultism with which it might be confused. Although he did not harbor the same skepticism Waite and Machen did about the practical power of occult activities such as communicating with the dead, in his novel *The Necromancers* and elsewhere, he shadowed forth the dangers of dabbling in occult activities and the importance of trusting to the orthodox rituals and teaching of the Church.

Through his fiction, he also sought to give ordinary readers a felt sense of the spiritual dimension of human life and the mystical experiences that made that dimension visible. To that end, he adapted the novel of literary realism so popular in the nineteenth century for the purpose of making seemingly esoteric spiritual experiences familiar to a broad audience of middle-class, modern readers. As Paschal Baumstein notes, "Benson used novels because he believed theology had to be simple and accessible in order to have the greatest impact. And he drew his doctrine always from the most basic theological principles: God is" (97). Further, he deeply believed that God's presence was made manifest through the things of this world—through the rising sun and the fallen thrush, through human hands held in prayer and feet burdened by pain, and, of course, through ordinary bread and wine. Following from that conviction, he created narratives rooted in precise details about ordinary life, presenting esoteric ideas in prosaic form and departing from the fairy fiction so popular among Victorian writers like George MacDonald.[3]

Despite this shift from fantasy fiction to realist novel, Benson's mystical novels share in the sacramental thinking evident in the fairy fiction of MacDonald and Waite. Comparing Benson to Charles Williams and the fiction Williams wrote in the '30s and '40s, Glen Cavaliero observes, "Both writers portray occult studies as dangerous, and Christian supernaturalism as affirmative and sane. In this they reflect the influence of fictive naturalism, which of its very nature has to posit that the material world is one in whose significance it is necessary to believe. Such a conviction is likewise the basis of Christian sacramentalism, in which body and spirit are mutually interdependent" (*Supernatural* 105–06). This sacramental mysticism reflects what Mark Knight and Emma Mason have described as the sacramental emphasis in late Victorian literature and early twentieth-century literature, an emphasis that sprang from a growing interest in Incarnational theology (199–206). As evidence of this growing interest, they cite Boyd Hilton's study of nineteenth-century Evangelicalism and his argument that the Victorian era saw a shift from a theology of Atonement, popularized during the first half of the nineteenth century, to a theology of Incarnation; they also point to Philip Davis's alternately framed account of a Victorian turn from a theology of transcendence to one of immanence (161–62). Michael Wheeler concurs that such a shift in emphasis took place, in his view partly due to the receding prominence of Evangelicalism in the second half of the nineteenth century (56). While Knight and Mason caution against drawing theological lines that are too sharp,[4] they suggest that an emphasis on Christ's immanence in material creation is especially affiliated with Catholic theology, for "Catholic theology tends to hold a higher view of the created order and is more likely to seek God's revelation in the natural world. The importance of creation in Catholic theology, and the related interest in sacramental theology, was given fresh impetus in the latter part of the nineteenth century by

Vatican I and a revival of interest in the work of Thomas Aquinas" (199). Elaborating further, they describe "the resulting theological sacramentalism" as characterized by "its understanding of a God who is really present (rather than just echoed) in the material world" (202). As we have seen, however, a turn toward sacramental theology was evident even in novelists outside of the Catholic fold. From George MacDonald's prolific literature and preaching, for instance, Timothy Larsen has adduced extensive evidence of an Incarnational theology, noting that a theology of Incarnation circulated widely in the Congregational church during the Victorian era, but "[t]his new doctrinal emphasis was, if anything, even stronger in the communion that MacDonald made his spiritual home for most of his adult life, the Church of England" (14). Indeed, Benson's own father could be said to be one of the architects of this Incarnational turn, with his designing and popularization of the Anglican Festival of Nine Lessons and Carols service in 1880, which helped to center and elevate the liturgical celebration of Christ's birth.

It is not surprising, therefore, that even Benson's first novel, *The Light Invisible*, written during his short time as an Anglican priest and just before his conversion to Roman Catholicism, manifests such a strongly sacramental theology. As Grayson observes, Benson felt that "[f]iction conveying a religious idea was tantamount to a sacramental and as such was conveying truth as nothing else could. It is the writer's business to see that the inner and invisible mystery is adequately portrayed and presented outwardly through the right visible sign" (142). However, not all literary proponents of a sacramental theology saw the convergence Benson eventually did between sacramentalism and mysticism. In fact, for some Christian writers, mysticism seemed contrary to a sacramental theology, given the strong strain of Platonism in some traditions of mysticism. Mason and Knight observe that G. K. Chesterton's sacramental theology led him to object to the interchangeable use of religion and mysticism; according to them, he believed that "whereas the Catholic religion affirmed the value of the material world by insisting on its ongoing relation to the God who created it; mysticism tended to downplay the material world by collapsing any distinction between Creator and creation and suggesting that material particularity was merely an illusion, the uncovering of which would reveal an essential unity" (209). Benson did not share that understanding of mysticism; rather, he used the realist novel, with its deep rootedness in the things of this world, as way of showcasing the potential confluence of mysticism and sacramental religion, developing a sacramental mysticism that warrants comparison to the sacramentalism in the mystical novels of Waite, Underhill, and Machen.

Yet, insofar as Benson's mystical fiction is marked by a sacramental theology, it has a distinctive character that also sets it apart from the mystical fiction of those peers. Namely, he is unabashedly Christological in his representation of mysticism. Waite's mysticism, as a contrasting example, reflects a constant search for the unity among perennial traditions of mysticism; as Gilbert observes, "For Waite the end of the mystical quest was not union but Unity; his last word could only have been 'Unitas' " (*Magician* 160). While Benson concurred with Waite and Underhill that mysticism is the "Art of Divine Union" (*Mysticism* 45), Benson's mystical fiction manifests a Christological character that is unique to the type of Incarnational realism he developed. In the chapter to follow, I shall focus on Benson's first novel, *The Light Invisible*, to argue that his deep devotion to the person of Christ led him to use the novel of realism as a vehicle for illustrating how ordinary, everyday life bears witness to the body and blood, the birth, suffering, and death of Christ. Influenced by the medieval mysticism of writers such as Julian of Norwich and Richard Rolle as well as J. Henry Shorthouse's 1881 novel *John Inglesant*, Benson's *Light Invisible* aims to make the real presence of Christ—as a mystical body—visible to the reader.

Benson the Man: Ghost Lover, Artist, Priest

Unlike A. E. Waite, Robert Hugh Benson (1871 to 1914) was a man of the cloth, ordained in 1895 as an Anglican priest; then, converted to Roman Catholicism and ordained as a Catholic priest in 1903. He hailed from a family whose ties to institutional Christianity could not have been stronger, for he was born to a legacy of Anglican leadership as the son of Edward White Benson, bishop of Truro and later archbishop of Canterbury. His father was so well-known that when the archbishop died, his funeral was attended by the future king of England, among other dignitaries (Grayson 24). Though Benson differed from his father in significant ways, he "inherited many traits from his father, boundless energy, a spiritual nature tending to the mystical, the artist's fondness for ritual, a love of liturgy and church ornament down to the last detail" (Grayson 3). According to Benson's own account, though, his father's intellectual approach to religion, evident from early lessons with his father, seemed arid, leaving him emotionally distant from religion. Lessons with his father, he said, reflected "the predominance of the mind element over the soul. I do not remember that these lessons made it easier to love God . . . I do not, with all reverence to my father's memory, even now believe that in myself they developed the spiritual side of religion" (*Confessions* 12–13). This perceived imbalance in his father's approach to religion, privileging mind over spirit, may account for his growing interest in the spiritual side of religion.

Benson grew up among a large brood of children; though he was the only child to follow his father's religious vocation, several of his siblings had either scholarly or artistic inclinations. A bit like the famous Brontë children, R. H., or "Hugh" as he was known to his familiars, grew up writing stories and enacting them. Grayson goes so far as to say that "[o]f all literary families in Edwardian England, surely this was the most gifted" (2). Arthur (A. C.) went on to become a celebrated biographer and literary critic as well as a short-story writer, and Edward (E. H.) wrote numerous ghost stories, earning fame for his *Mapp and Lucia* novels. Though his sister Maggie suffered from mental illness, resulting in periods of stay in a sanitarium, she, too, was an artist and author who achieved some distinction as an Egyptologist. This bent for artistic creation emerged early in Benson's life, for "[t]here was from childhood a strong artistic dimension, a love of opulence and an affinity for color and sensation and detail that was to permeate his life and works" (Grayson 8). Passion for the artistic dimension of life so defined Benson that his brother Arthur later observed,

> I believe that all his life he was an artist in the largest sense, in the fact that his work was the embodiment of dreams, the expression of beauty which he constantly perceived. His ideal was in one sense a larger one than the technically artistic ideal, because it embraced the conception of moral beauty even more ardently than mere external beauty. The mystical element in him was for ever reaching out in search of some Divine essence in the world. (134–35)

Yet Arthur qualified this assessment by observing that Benson was never a mystic in the stereotypical sense of a dreamer who lives cut off from the world, for "[h]e lived in the visible and tangible world . . . and he was a mystic only in the sense that he had an hourly and daily sense of the presence of God" (253).

Benson's earliest experience of narrative art seems to have come through tales of the supernatural. From a young age, he and his siblings enjoyed ghost stories, but they were not just a matter of fiction for Benson. He and his brother Edward were both reputed to believe in ghosts (Grayson xvii), a fascination that stayed with Benson into adulthood. He had been a child with a fertile imagination, even fearful of dark rooms due to the ghosts and spirits that might inhabit them (Grayson 5). Later, as a college student at Trinity College, Cambridge, he was known for dabbling in some of the heterodox spiritual movements popular in his day. After a European tour, upon returning to London, he became "vaguely interested by Theosophy" (*Confessions* 23). He also seems to have been drawn to hypnotism, at which he became "tolerably proficient" (*Confessions* 27). According to Grayson, "[h]e managed to hypnotize a couple of local rustics and dabbled in other occultist crazes like crystal-ball gazing and mind reading" (15). And having discovered that religion at Cambridge "left him flat" (Grayson 16), he even briefly toyed with Swedenborgism, though he disliked that its spiritual perspective did not credit animals with the potential for immortality (Martindale 92). Benson eventually rejected heterodox forms of religion and occult activities as dangerous, but these early spiritual vagaries found fictional form in his novels. So convincing was his portrayal of spiritualist seances in his 1909 novel *The Necromancers* that Arthur Machen wrote in a book review, "I should think that the author has mingled a good deal in the circles which hover about the foolish and forbidden and dangerous thing called 'occult science' " ("Trying" 726).

Benson's interest in writing about occultism and mysticism seems to have been shaped not only by his personal forays into supernatural activity, but also by the literature he read—popular fiction as well as medieval religious literature. The record of his time as a member of the Anglican Mirfield community reflects an abiding interest in ghost stories and "his love for the occult"; writing in a letter to India in 1902, he recounts,

> We told ghost stories . . . last night till prayer-time—and I nearly had a fit with fright when I found myself alone in my room—with ghostly curtains round my bed . . . I expected them to be parted by bony fingers, and a face to look through. And there were curious thumpings in the hall at 11 P.M. that

> terrified me. My eldest brother has lately written some mystical stories which he has asked me to criticise [*The Hill of Trouble*]. They are quite fascinating. (qtd. in Martindale 157)

His penchant for mystical literature is recorded in his comments about the reading he did while working for the Eton Mission in 1895. During that time, he describes his room there as having "an immense lot of books—many of them novels (in which I am my mamma's son). *Several also dealing with drawing-room mysticism* (in which also I am my mamma's son) [emphasis mine]" (qtd. in Martindale 115). Unfortunately, he does not name specific novels representative of "drawing-room mysticism," but his reference here makes clear the impact of earlier Victorian writers of "mystical fiction" upon his imagination. We also know that during his time with the Mirfield community he returned to the novel he fell in love with during his teenage years, J. Henry Shorthouse's *John Inglesant*, and to that added Walter Pater's *Marius the Epicurean*, Huysmans, Zola, George Sand, and Maeterlinck, a favorite of Underhill's whom he found "very morbid and odd and French, but really moving" (qtd. in Martindale 155).

His views about Maeterlinck, Sand, and Huysmans are especially interesting because those writers seem to have attuned him to the sacramental potential of novelistic fiction, shaping the mystical perspective he was soon to develop in his own fiction. About Maeterlinck, he observed in 1903, "The very dullest things become significant, with him to describe them" (qtd. in Martindale 155–56). Further, he considered Maeterlinck along with the wildly popular George Sand and Huysmans as gifted in the art of "transfiguring" ordinary things and connecting them to the mystery of the cosmos: "[George Sand], too, he finds, transfigures the commonplace; but not like Maeterlinck, by making you feel that there are huge, mysterious Powers behind, but by making the very things and characters *themselves* interesting, quite apart from their 'significance' and 'symbolism.' Huysmans, too, and to a lesser extent Zola, seemed to him to achieve this transfiguring effect, though Huysmans did it the more easily, as he 'puts the whole thing into a mystical frame' " (156). At Mirfield, he was also exposed to an even older tradition of mysticism through his reading of medieval religious literature. According to Grayson, it was during his time at Mirfield that he immersed himself in and became passionate about Julian of Norwich's *Revelations of Divine Love* (35). Thus, Benson's own first experiment with novelistic fiction seems to have arisen out of the confluence of his interest in the supernatural, his love of ghost stories, his reading of popular novels that made the everyday seem strange and wonderful, and his study of medieval religious literature. The result was a novel, *The Light Invisible*, that is neither a ghost story nor a conventional novel of literary realism. It is a strange hybrid creature: a mystical novel aimed at transfiguring ordinary life in the image of Christ's mystical body. In the ensuing sections, I shall first explore the origins and structure of Benson's novel, then its debt to medieval religious literature, and finally, though a close reading of the novel, an examination of his Incarnational realism and the way in which the protagonist's narrative and the individual stories he tells represent different facets of Benson's Christological mysticism.

First Glimmers of *The Light Invisible*

The Light Invisible was the first of Benson's novels to see print, begun in the summer and autumn of 1902 when he was still an Anglican priest and first published in 1903. Prior to writing this novel, Benson had written some fiction in a fairy tale vein during his time working with children at the Eton Mission. There he used Andrew Lang's Green Fairy Book as a way of engaging the young people with whom he worked, and he coached children in enacting "a Christmas pantomime, which he had himself written, on the *Rose and the Ring*" (Martindale 118). But when he came to write literature for adults, he found particular inspiration in J. Henry Shorthouse's historical novel *John Inglesant*, which he adored so much as to have it almost memorized. According to George Shuster, Shorthouse "was a mystic Quaker who revived in fiction the idea of sacramentalism. His novels are gorgeous pageants glowing with a deep quest for spiritual realities and the instincts of medievalism" (211). Among the many things that drew Benson to that book was its "interweaving of the preternatural, and indeed of the elfish and bizarre, with the realistic" (Martindale 71), but in the view of Benson himself, what most attracted him was the way it made vividly visible "the adorable Person of Christ, which, remembering the lessons of 'John Ingelsant,' I endeavoured to make the centre of my teaching" (*Confessions* 67). In addition to the Christian sacramentalism that loomed large in his mind during the early days of his writing career, so, too, did his era's growing mania for mysticism. He later recalled, "Before, during, and after the writing of this book [*The Light*

Invisible] I was more and more becoming interested in mystical lines of thought. I put away from me the contemplation of cold-cut dogma and endeavoured to clothe it with the warm realities of spiritual experience; and in the book itself I attempted to embody dogma rather than to express it explicitly" (*Confessions* 80). Benson's use of the word *embody* here is particularly significant because it speaks to the theology of Incarnation that he sought to make visible through the concrete details of character and scene rather than through abstract ideas. Thus, a Christ-centered sacramentalism, along with a growing interest in the experiential dimension of mysticism, framed his writing of *Light Invisible*.

Beyond Shorthouse's influence and Benson's own penchant for mysticism, he was prompted to write *The Light Invisible* by a book of ghost stories his brother Arthur had given him: a manuscript copy of *The Hill of Trouble*, a collection of "mystical" tales eventually published in 1903 (Martindale 176). Benson explained its appeal in remarking, "The last one . . . 'The Closed Window,' terrified me for hours. What I like so much is your device . . . of making the supernatural world open out directly from the natural. I do believe that is the secret of effective supernatural stories" (qtd. in Martindale 176). With that account of his brother's fictional strategy, Benson succinctly outlines the premises for his own artistry in *The Light Invisible*, a novel set within a natural, ordinary world, described with spare, but precise and exacting detail, yet a world that, story after story, opens out upon an invisible supernatural reality. In *The Light Invisible*, this strategy is aimed not at conjuring conventional Gothic terrors, but at evoking what Rudolf Otto has called the presence of "the numinous" (11). Yet, the numinous has a specifically Christian inflection in Benson's fiction, for he uses vignettes of everyday life to make visible the mystical body of Christ.

These vignettes are framed by the story of an anonymous narrator who visits an unnamed priest on repeated occasions during the final stages of the priest's life, with the priest's spiritual evolution creating an integrated narrative that gives the novel coherence and makes it more than a mere collection of short stories told by the priest to the narrator. Because so many of the priest's stories focus on mystical experience, the priest pauses at the start of the novel to explain the faculty that renders mystical experience possible. Mystical experience depends not upon faith, but upon "spiritual perception," he says, and spiritual perception is "common to us all in our measure. It is the faculty by which we verify for ourselves what we have received on authority and hold by faith. Spiritual life consists partly in exercising this faculty" (*The Light Invisible* 18). Offering the narrator a kind of epistemological lesson, he tries to explain what it means to *know* through spiritual experience. Toward that end, he makes an analogy between spiritual perception and artistic perception, suggesting that just as the artist can see beauty where others cannot, so the mystic can perceive spiritual realities to which others are blind. It is a kind of gift or grace, for "it is no sort of credit to you or to me, any more than is the colour of our eyes" (18).[5] Like Waite, he seems to believe all are capable of such perception, but not all may be gifted with spiritual vision. That this spiritual perception connects to what Benson understood mysticism to be is clear from Benson's 1907 Westminster Lecture, "Mysticism." Therein, he suggests that the mystic's faculty offers a spiritual vantage on the world no less valuable than the geologist's, the farmer's, and the poet's (8–9). The Mystic, he argues, is "the artist of the spiritual life," and just "[a]s the poet sees things invisible to the farmer and the geologist, as he is kindled by a sight of colour and form, unperceived by the others, yet objectively real, so the Mystic, looking upon the same facts, whether natural or revealed . . . is aware of certain elements, and even of revelations and significances invisible to these" (19–20). For someone gifted with this mystical vision, the hidden becomes visible. As the priest explains to the narrator in the first chapter, this perception sometimes sharpens to such a degree "that the spiritual world appears to me as visible as what we call the natural world" (19).

The priest's attempts to share his mystical visions of the spiritual world with the narrator become the content of the stories he relates during his many meetings with the narrator at the priest's country house. Despite the spare and simple style of the novel's stories, the novel possesses a complex narrative structure, for the novel operates on multiple levels: At one level, the novel traces the priest's spiritual coming of age, from the retold stories of the priest's childhood, adolescence, and earlier life to the direct representation of his final stages of spiritual development; at another level, the novel interlaces and juxtaposes embedded stories of myriad other characters, whose experiences the priest relates to the narrator because of their connection to the priest's spiritual evolution. And beyond that, there are minor characters, such as the priest's servant, Parker, whose experiences are also woven into this tapestry of tales.

Benson's Medievalism: An Invisible Light from the Dark Ages

A further layering of structural significance within the novel comes from the epigraphs that introduce each chapter. While the priest's life story and the stories he tells appear to take place solely in a modern world, each chapter is prefaced by a unique epigraph. Some epigraphs come from more recent provenance, drawn from William Blake, Maeterlinck, or Benson's brother Arthur, but the epigraphic debt to the medieval world deepens as the chapters progress, with quotations drawn from Dante, the Persian Omar Khayyam, Julian of Norwich, the medieval Abbey of the Holy Ghost, and St. Leander of Seville. Even the Victorian writer Julia Cartwright's *Pilgrim's Way*, source of one epigraph, is a book about the medieval pilgrimage to Canterbury. Many of the epigraphs, therefore, are like invisible ghosts from the medieval past, illustrating Benson's awareness that mysticism is neither wholly modern nor solely individualistic because of the past thinkers who share the modern spiritual perceptions his stories trace.

But Benson's interest in medieval religious ideas was not limited to the epigraphs he chose for the novel. According to Grayson, medievalism was one of Benson's passions, along with carving and gardening (147–48). He even spoke to the Mediaevalist Club on one of his visits to Chicago (Grayson 156). This broader interest in medievalism sheds further light on the kind of sacramental mysticism informing *Light Invisible* and suggests another tie to his Edwardian peers—Waite and Machen, whose fascination with the Middle Ages led them to delve deeply into Arthurian lore about the Holy Grail, and Underhill, whose love of medieval art and research into medieval mysticism shaped her entire life as a student of mysticism. Benson's interest in medieval religious literature was so thoroughgoing that in the year after he wrote *The Light Invisible*, he collected, edited, and published *A Book of the Love of Jesus*, subtitled "A Collection of Ancient English Devotions in Prose and Verse," that drew especially upon the medieval writings of Richard Rolle, the fourteenth-century hermit of Hampole. As Martindale notes about this devotional book, "A brief account of this English mystic, whom Benson loved second only to Juliana, the ankress of Norwich, is added in an appendix to the prayers, and Rolle himself will reappear as the foundation of the exquisite *Richard Raynal*, the book which its author loved best of all his writings" (314).[6] Despite the historical nature of the appendix's apparatus, with its notes about medieval manuscript sources and brief history of Rolle's life, Benson intended this collection of verse not for antiquarian admiration, but for ordinary devotion; in that regard, it is one of many instances of Benson's efforts to make mystical theology accessible to modern readers, in this case for the practical purpose of daily devotions. For, in his preface, he notes that he does not want modern readers to be excluded from these "spiritual treasures" due only to the barrier of archaic language or the foreignness of the literary forms (*Love of Jesus* viii).

Benson's book of medieval devotional literature helps to illuminate the Christological character of his mysticism, particularly his focus on the humanity of Christ. The book is dedicated "To Jesus Christ, God and man, and to all his true lovers," and as a frontispiece, it features a magnified image of Jesus's head and torso on the cross from Velásquez's 1632 *Christ Crucified*, a strikingly human portrait of Jesus's crucifixion, displaying an almost photographic realism in its depiction of Jesus's downcast head, encircled by a crown of thorns. In the preface that accompanies this image, Benson laments the disappearance of devotion to Jesus's "Sacred Humanity" from the time of the Middle Ages and over the course of three hundred years of "non-Catholic English devotion" (*Love of Jesus* xvi). The human suffering of Jesus was once central to mystical spirituality, he argues in an additional commentary about the characteristics of this early English verse, and he laments again the loss of devotion to that image. Suggesting that focus on the suffering Jesus is foundational to true mysticism, he writes:

> In almost every mystic the details of the sufferings of our Lord form the ground from which acts of love and contrition and "ruth" spring. This devotion distinguishes sharply the true mystic from his modern imitator, who mistakes vagueness for spirituality, and idealism for intuition. It is supposed to be a mark of modern delicacy and spiritual instinct to despise and shrink from realism; to dwell upon the risen Christ, the robed and crowned King, or upon the stainless child of Bethlehem, and to avoid the vision of the bloodstained Man of Sorrows, with his torn limbs. But the true mystic reads the awfulness of sin in the awfulness of the Cross—the story of his own life written so carefully and accurately over the white body and soul of his Saviour—and he sees the infinite love of God in the infinite sufferings that He so willingly undertook; the full fragrance of the Beloved is not perceptible except when He is bruised and torn. And therefore the medieval souls of prayer loved to follow him with tears and "still mourning" and "love-longing," step by step along the Way of Sorrows; to finger gently each running wound; to plunge their whole hands

> into his side, and there to "feel Christ's heart so hot loving" them. (xxiii–xxiv)

Benson's comments here about the "true mystic" are crucial for understanding both the mystical theology and the literary character of *The Light Invisible*. For his commentary's emphasis on "realism" in the Christian mystic's devotion to Christ helps to explain the literary realism he adopts as his novel's mode. Benson's commentary also helps to nuance our understanding of the "Incarnational" theology undergirding his sacramental mysticism. While Victorians such as MacDonald may have construed that Incarnational turn as a call to emphasize Christ's birth event, even to prioritizing it over the Passion story, for Benson, Christ's suffering on the Cross is as important to a full understanding of the Incarnation as is his birth in the manger. In his view, both are necessary for adoration of the mystical body of Christ, a body both beautiful and terrible, adorable and awful.

Christ the Babe

Benson's literary interest in the birth of Christ is prominent in *The Light Invisible* as well as in his drama and poetry. An exploration of the Incarnation appears early in his career with the *Mystery Play in Honour of the Nativity of Our Lord*, a drama written during his Cambridge days and inspired by medieval drama (Martindale 321). The importance of the Incarnation also emerges in his poetry, which was collected and published posthumously in a book called *Poems*. Within that very slim volume, several poems illustrate Benson's attention to the Incarnation, especially a lengthy nativity poem called simply "A Christmas Carol" (73–77) and "Ave Verum Corpus Natum" (78), a brief poem hailing the body of Christ at both his birth and his crucifixion. In "Lines: Written Before August 1903," he addresses Christ as the Incarnate one: "Creative Lord Incarnate, let me lean/My heavy self on thee" and "Grant me to rest on Thee, Incarnate Mind/ And Word of God" (27). Another poem, "After the Retreat," celebrates the "God incarnate" by suggesting that it is not ecstasy or elevation to transcendent heights that spiritual retreats induce in their prayerful participants, but rather embodied knowledge: knowledge of God's voice, his hands, and his incarnate Love (50).

Benson's emphasis on the significance of Christ's birth extends to *The Light Invisible* through both setting and story. The most obvious evidence of his focus on the Nativity is the number of times Christmas is mentioned as the occasion either for the narrator's conversation with the priest or as the backdrop of one of the stories the priest relates: This is true for the chapters titled "Consolatrix Afflictorum" (87), "Unto Babes" (167), "The Traveller" (190), and "The Sorrows of the World" (209). Even the story within "With Dyed Garments" takes place on a frosty December afternoon (156). Thus, the liturgical seasons of Advent and Christmas frame five of the fifteen chapters. No other liturgical seasons are specifically singled out, with the novel's time frames otherwise denoted by "one afternoon," "one evening," or some other signifier of ordinary time.

Benson focuses the reader on Christ "the Babe" for several reasons, one of which is to suggest that an apprehension of the cosmic mystery depends upon having the disposition and receptivity of a baby. The chapter "Unto Babes" begins during Christmastide, with the priest offering the narrator a discursive critique of intellectualism as the path to knowledge of the Divine, a criticism reminiscent of Benson's personal reservations about his father's intellectual rather than spiritual or emotional approach to religion. The priest asserts that it is the pure of heart, not the "profound or acute of intellect," that "shall see God" (172–73). To exemplify the former, he describes his encounter with a famous critic and poet whose elegance of thought and language were dazzling, but whose spiritual sense was like that of an "ill-bred boor" (174). Give me the faith of a coal merchant, he says in a French exclamation that oddly mirrors the desire of Ivan Karamazov's devil for the faith of a two-hundred-pound, churchgoing woman. Were spiritual devotion not more important than intellectual acuity, he continues, clever people would have a "better hope of salvation than stupid people," creating an absurdity (175).[7]

This chapter's introduction frames a tale told to the priest by a friend in Cornwall, illustrating how the body of Christ becomes mystically present to an intellectually stunted, orphan boy at Christmas. The "idiot" boy's head "had the look of a mule," and he imitated some of the behaviors of a mule, "snorting and stamping and neighing when he was much excited" and "stabl[ing] himself in a corner of the wide dark kitchen, and munch[ing] grass" (177). The use of the verb *stable* here immediately connects the boy to the baby Christ, who was once stabled in a manger, but the nameless boy is treated not as the face of Christ, but as a mule-like animal (177). His seeming idiocy leads his Calvinist grandmother to regard him as damned (176), and the spectacles through which she looks at the boy, along with her fireside scrutiny of Scripture, signify the distorted intellectual lens through which she interprets her grandson's nature. The parish clergyman views the child "as hopeless" (176), having fruitlessly attempted to teach him Old Testament history.[8] Even the friend who relates the story to the priest finds his own faith "troubled" by the boy, for the boy seemed to him a sign of "the carelessness of God" (177).

Ultimately, the story's outcome challenges this facile assessment, for the friend experiences the presence of Christ through the boy's rudimentary form of worship. One day as the priest's friend stumbles upon a stone quarry during a long walk, he notices sounds and shapes that make him worry about tramps in the region. To his initial disgust, he espies "the mule-like head and tangled hair rising from the high shoulders of the village idiot" (180). What he discovers is a manger, made by the boy: "There was a kind of mud trough constructed against the stone, with a little straw sprinkled in it and holly berries and leaves in front of it" (181). Even more astonishing are the apparent traces of the Christ child: "Quite plainly marked on the soft edge of the mud-trough, in a place which the hobnailed boots had not touched, was the mark of a tiny child's naked foot, as if a baby had stood in trough or manger, with one foot on the floor and another on the edge" (182). Returning to the village, the friend questions the grandmother to ensure that there was not an ordinary child the grandson had been given charge of who might have left the mark. According to the grandmother, no such baby had been entrusted to the boy (182).

Despite the priest's friend's earlier dismissal of the boy, he comes away from his walking expedition convinced that the boy has been graced by the mystical presence of Christ. And as a testament to this Incarnational revelation, the priest's friend "went to the little church, already decorated for the festival [of Christmas], and there with the fragrance of the holly and yew in the air about him, and the glimmer of a candle near the altar where the church-cleaner was sweeping, he praised the Holy Child whose Birth-night it was, and who had not disdained to lie in a manger and be adored by the beasts of the stall" (182–83). Although he revisits the manger scene the next morning with a friend and finds nothing there, the story he recounts to the priest suggests three interrelated ideas: that the boy has received the sacrament of Christ's presence through the homely material of mud and holly; that the boy has been, for him, a vehicle of Christ's manifestation; and that the Christmas liturgical ritual he subsequently attends bears further witness to Christ's presence, not only through the material sights and smells of holly and yew, but also through the glimpse he might otherwise not have noticed of the humble church-cleaner's flesh-and-blood body sweeping near the altar, a further sign of the incarnate Love of Christ. Though many of Benson's chapters do not offer moralizations, here the priest draws the explicit conclusion from his friend's story that "the things which He hides from the wise and prudent He reveals to babes" (183).

The mystical reality of the Incarnation is drawn differently in another Christmas story, "Consolatrix Afflictorum," a chapter about a child who loses his mother, only to discover an unexpected "grace" through the mystical presence of the Virgin Mary (89). The story of this child was related to the priest via a letter from an anonymous, faithful parishioner in response to the priest's Christmas Day sermon. According to the priest, the letter was sent to him because of the writer's conviction that the priest shared his confidence in the reality of a supernatural realm of existence; the letter writer confided, "I thought I saw in you one to whom the supernatural was more than a beautiful and symbolical fairy-story, and one who held it not impossible that this unseen should sometimes manifest itself"(88). His response to the priest's sermon implies that the priest did not subscribe to the fashionable, but reductive "Higher Criticism" in vogue during the late nineteenth century, delivering instead a sermon about the actual human presence of God through the Incarnation. That conviction about the real intersection between the spiritual and material realms inspires the letter writer to share his own mysterious but no less real experience of the Incarnation.

The narrative that the letter writer relates to the priest conveys the writer's mystical experience of Christ's mother present to him in the time and space following his earthly mother's death. According to the story, the writer lost his mother when he was merely seven years old and endured excruciating grief in the aftermath of her death, waking repeatedly at night to "desolate emptiness" (89). Day after day, he tried all manner of mental gymnastics to believe she would return later in the day; alternately, he would force himself to confront her devastating absence. After weeks of such distress, one night, he sees his mother appear in his room, aglow with the light of the oil lamp outside his dark room and dressed as if for evening, but cloaked. When he cries out, she turns to the landing, "as if to someone waiting there, either of assent or dismissal"; as the story progresses, it becomes clearer that the woman must have come as a Christ-bearer, in response to angelic behest (92). Wordless and faceless, she lifts him in her arms, wraps him in her cloak, and rocks him beside the fire. These visits continue night after night, though only on nights when he awakens and cries (94). With the passivity characteristic of mystical experience, he receives the visits as an unexpected and unwilled grace, for they arise only "at night, when, I suppose, the will partly relaxes its control" (96–97).[9] On the final night of her visit, he has a mystical vision of her cloak, one that reveals its celestial character and the continuity between the spiritual and natural worlds, for he notices the "cloak which sheltered us both—of a deep blue, with an intricate pattern of flowers and leaves and birds among branches" (98). When he finally sees her face, he discovers with shock that "[i]t was not my mother, and yet was there ever such a mother's face as that? . . . I did not at the time know who she was, but my little soul dimly saw that my own mother for some reason could not at that time come to me who needed her so sorely, and that another great Mother had taken her place" (98–99). During this scene in which the boy recognizes the comforting maternal presence of the Divine, Benson stresses the physicality and sensuality of the boy's encounter. The boy's mystical encounter is deliberately not insubstantial, for when he kisses her hand, it "was strong and white, and delicately fragrant" (99).

Because the story of the boy's visitation may seem on the surface a mere supernatural ghost story, Benson anticipates the reader's potentially incredulous response by having the letter writer draw attention to how this scene represents that of the babe Christ lying at his mother's breast and of the need for all to have the receptivity of such a child. As the letter writer concludes his mysterious story, he reminds the priest that "our Saviour himself told us to be like children, and our Saviour too once lay on His Mother's breast" (100). In that sense, the Incarnation is, as Benson represents it, an ongoing reality, potentially made manifest in the time and place of all who are receptive to God's incarnate Love.

Christ the Man of Sorrows

While "Consolatrix Afflictorum" represents a mystical experience of God's love incarnated through the Virgin Mary's presence, the story's focus on affliction links it to several other chapters that give equal attention to the mystical connection between suffering life and the Christ whose Incarnation led to the Cross. Similar to *A Book of the Love of Jesus*, *The Light Invisible* makes Christ's passion—his very human suffering and pain—central to its theology. Such an emphasis is consistent with English Catholic writings of the period, wherein, according to Brian Sudlow, "the incarnate Christ cannot really be separated from the redeeming Christ who comes into the world to suffer and save" (205). And the Christ who suffers is as evident as Christ's Nativity in Benson's poetry as well as in his fiction. For instance, in a poem titled "In the Garden of a Religious House," he imagines "God Incarnate" (71) visible in the garden of some monks, but then departing and leaving his Cross. The poetic scene relates how "[t]he darkness broke,/ And, fair to see,/ The Garden shone—the priests went to and fro./ God has gone up, but left his Cross below" (72).

It is the Cross left below to which several sections of *The Light Invisible* turn, shedding a stark light on how both the natural world and the human world are scarred by pain. Even a *Christmas* chapter, such as "Unto Babes," includes details that suggest Nature itself is marked by the sorrows of the Cross, as with the description of the narrator and priest "pass[ing] under the pines that tossed their sombre plumes in the wind" (168–69). In other stories, such as "Over the Gateway," the green mass of lawn is cut through by a drive that "still showed plainly like a long, narrow grave across the grass" (65), and in "The Watcher," "thin patches of gossamer [dew] still hung like torn cambric on the yew shoots on either side" (29). Benson's subtle descriptive details of brokenness, mourning, and death hint that the natural world partakes of the pain and suffering of the Cross. That funereal feeling is amplified by specific scenes in which the narrator and priest come upon seemingly gratuitous death in the natural world—a dead mouse (29) or a fallen thrush (233). The details in these descriptions reflect Benson's sensitivity to suffering life, even, or maybe particularly, in the natural world.

The chapter called "The Watcher," for example, uses the death of the mouse to prompt an exploration of suffering in the natural world through a story that juxtaposes a sequence of deaths that ultimately lead to Christ's Cross. When the old man and narrator happen upon a dead mouse, the sight of the dead mouse prompts the priest's memory of an adventure during his teenage years, a period the priest describes with arresting ingenuity as "that terrible age when the soul seems to have dwindled to a spark overlaid by a mountain of ashes . . . and all tender things shrink back and hide from the dreadful noonday of manhood" (30–31).

At that peak of youthful energy, the priest ventured into the forest and, upon descrying a thrush singing its blithe song, cruelly shot it: "Every fibre of my life told me that the thrush had a right to live. Ah! he had earned it, if labour were wanting, by this very song that was guiding death towards him, but black sullen anger had thrown my conscience, and was now struggling to hold it down till the shot had been fired" (34). Though he rationalized his killing of the thrush in the moment, he later reflects that he killed it for naught, with "no excuse" (33), as if he were Augustine stealing a pear without reason or need.[10] In contrast to that youthful act of callousness, when the old priest encounters a small dead mouse on the path during his walk with the narrator, he picks it up with the "ready tears of old age," quickly regretting even that disturbance and replacing it to rest in peace (29). As the priest and narrator conclude their walk, they end up at the back of a path where "[o]pposite us hung a crucifix, with a penthouse over it that the old man had put up years before. As he did not speak I turned to him, and saw that he was looking steadily at the Figure on the Cross; and I thought how He who bore our griefs and carried our sorrows was one with the heavenly Father, without whom not even a sparrow falls to the ground" (38–39). The story thus juxtaposes the mouse's death, the teenager's callous shooting of the thrush, his mature and tender mercies toward the mouse, and Christ on the Cross. As readers follow this sequence of events, they glimpse for the first time how the old man's experiences have shaped his development, gradually inclining him to Christ's compassion for the sorrows of the world.

In the chapter "The Bridge over the Stream," Benson turns from the problem of suffering in the natural world to that in the human world, with a story that invites comparison to the Book of Job. Through the opening description, Benson uses natural images to sketch a kind of visual chiaroscuro that sets the stage for the story's apparent moral contradictions: "briar-roses" convey an incongruous image of beauty counterpointed by thorns, and "the sun throw[s] . . . the garden into cool shadow" (105). The chapter's story begins with Parker, the priest's servant, asking the priest to visit the family of Tom Awcock, a man who has been injured in a farming machine accident and is poised to lose his limbs and maybe his life. The narrator is shocked by the awfulness of the accident and expresses skepticism that any kind of religious consolation or atonement could suffice as an explanation of the event; such things, he feels, are nothing but terrible (106). The priest responds that he has come not to be shocked, saying, "It is the apparent purposelessness that distresses you: it is the certainty of a deliberate purpose that comforts me" (107).

Elaborating on his equanimity, the priest then relates an experience he once had of watching a driverless butcher cart accidentally run over and kill a young boy who had been playing at a stream with his two sisters and was about to cast a stone at a fish or blue flower (111). According to the priest, who was watching from afar and unable to halt the hurtling cart, the boy had space to move safely aside, but via a supernatural vision, the priest saw a figure of tender face and downcast eyes "looking upon the boy's head with indescribable love," as one hand covered the boy's eyes and the other pushed the boy in front of the horse to be "beaten down without a cry" (111–12). Like Job, the old priest nearly "cursed God and died" upon seeing the senseless death of this young child, whose death occurred at the hands of an inexplicably complicit divine being (112). Yet, as he reflects upon the face he perceived in his mystical vision, "It was as the face of a mother who nurses her first-born child, as the face of a child who kisses a wounded creature, it was as I think the Father's Face itself must have been, which those angels always behold, as He looked down upon the Sacrifice of His only Son" (112–13). The priest's story of Tom Awcock's accident and the boy's awful death is as provocative and rebarbative as the Book of Job, raising equally difficult moral questions. Was it the boy's desire to cast a stone at the fish and flower that led to his being pushed aside to his death? Did God whose concern is even for the fall of a sparrow care for those tiny creatures more than for the young boy? Did God cause the boy's accident due to some inscrutable beneficence toward him? And if so, does the tenderness of the face the priest sees offer assurance that what seems awful to the human eye may have a mercy human beings cannot fathom?

Several years later, in "The Life of Jesus Christ in His Mystical Body," a 1910 essay based on a lecture Benson gave to the Quest Society, he offers an answer to the problem of seemingly unjust individual suffering through an argument about the mystical body of Christ. Using the natural metaphor of a cell in relation to a whole organism, he lays out a "Corporatist" view of mysticism that frames the individual's well-being within the larger body of Christ. According to Benson's biological analogy, "There is no organic life that is not, in its lowest aspect, the sum of cell-life—though it also transcends it" (15); he continues, "So long as the cells are content to be lost in the unity of the whole, so long do the cells survive. The instant a cell asserts its independence, its doom is certain" (16). He extends this metaphor to the spiritual domain in arguing that "[i]ndividuals . . . are to occupy the same positions in the Mystical Body, which various cells occupied in the natural body" (22). For Benson, this Corporatist understanding of the individual in relation to the mystical body sheds new light on the problem of suffering. Using this mystical theology as a form of theodicy, he concludes,

> If we are no more than individuals, intended to be perfected as individuals, then the suffering of an innocent child who dies before reaching the age of reason, is exactly against all that we know as justice . . . But if the point of view is widened and we see the child not as a mere unit, but as a cell of a suffering and a blissful Body, whose corporate will accepts and welcomes suffering as a whole, we begin to see that the problem is soluble, if not solved. (25–26)

In this mystical theology, Benson adverts to the mystical body of Christ—the whole of which every individual is a part—as the only solution that would not render an individual child's senseless death a "hopeless state of affairs" (25). While his essay illumines the Corporatist theodicy he eventually adopts, *The Light Invisible* repeatedly resists the rational argumentation of theodicy. The priest accepts the consolation of mystical vision, and the story ultimately implies that there is no rational answer to the mystery of human suffering other than to trust in the purpose of the Divine being whose face of tenderness is mystically revealed to the priest.

If the uncomfortable "Bridge over the Stream" leaves readers with mystery rather than moral certainty, the chapter "Over the Gateway" explores Christ as the co-sufferer who answers human beings in their pain and enables them to bear their crosses. In this chapter's conversation with the narrator, the priest recounts how early in his career, not long after his ordination and when "sorrow was new" to him (68), he returned from London to his family's country home, having volunteered to bear "heavy news" to a lady staying with his family (64). The lady is unnamed in the story and the news is never identified, thus universalizing her plight and leaving space for the reader's imagination to deepen the "heart-breaking" nature of her predicament (64–65). In another chiaroscuro-like picture, after the priest delivers the news, he looks out upon his family's garden and perceives the incongruous contrast between the heavenly "garden full of peace and sweetness" stretching before him, and behind him the distraught and heartbroken woman, face down on a couch, absorbed in a private hell (68). Although he recognizes his priestly responsibility to offer her consolation, he feels impotent, longing for a "human person to pray and bear a little of that strife" (69).

Then, suddenly, he is gifted with a vision hovering at the garden's iron gate of a man "kneeling in the air," a praying man, who seemed oddly upright in relation to the tilt of the chestnut tree, with the angles of the natural world and the spiritual world creating a kind of cross, yet "[t]he true level was that of the man" (70). In Celtic lore, the chestnut tree has traditionally symbolized the place where the natural and spiritual planes intersect, but the tree also connotes the Cross of Christ. Through a kind of cosmic geometry, the imagery in the priest's vision suggests not only the intersection of the natural and spiritual planes, but also the crossing of the woman's suffering and Christ's prayer. As the priest recalls, "He [the man in the vision] was praying. I can say no more than that. He had opened his heart to this woman's sorrow. He had made it his own: and it met there" (71). As the pain on the praying man's face deepens, the woman's sobbing gradually ceases till she is able to stand and greet the priest again, with "the light of conquest . . . in her eyes" (72). The priest is left with the conviction that "I had seen her sorrow carried and laid before the throne of God by one greater than either of us" (72). This mystical vision of Christ praying and bearing the woman's cross offers a vision of the profound possibility of prayer as an act of substitutionary love.[11] And it illuminates the priest's own call to shoulder the sorrows of the world.

As the novel progresses, the old priest's visage gradually begins to reflect the sorrows he witnesses in the natural world and in the human world. In a chapter toward the end of the novel, for instance, the narrator observes that "[h]is eyes seemed larger than ever, and there was a sorrow in them that I had not seen before. They had been the eyes of a stainless child, wide and smiling; now they were the eyes of one who was under some burden almost too heavy to be borne" (169). The old man's passage toward death, we slowly realize, is a kind of Thomas à Kempis-like *imitatio Christi* (170). As we and the narrator listen to the stories he shares, we watch the slow, unfolding birth of his mystical union with Christ, the Man of Sorrows.

The Mystical Body of Christ

The movement toward the priest's mystical union with Christ begins in the novel's first chapter, "The Green Robe," with a story that offers a vision rather than an argument about the mystical body of Christ. It is a vision that begins to transform the priest's understanding of both religion and the nature of reality. When he was a young teenager, the priest recounts, morality was foremost in his mind; Christ, "ordinarily tender, sometimes stern," was in the "middle distance"; and beyond that "lay certain mysteries, sacramental and otherwise" and beyond that "infinitely far away, like clouds piled upon the horizon of a sea, was the invisible world of heaven whence God looked at me" (22). Life was divided according to the "tangible, enjoyable world" and "a misty picture" of "religion, claiming . . . my homage, but not my heart" (22–23). However, as he walks through a pine-bordered glade, he is suddenly struck by a vision:

> I stood on the border of a vast robe; its material was green. A great fold of it lay full in view, but I was conscious that it stretched for almost unlimited miles. This great green robe blazed with embroidery. There were straight lines of tawny work on either side which melted again into a darker green in high relief . . . I was conscious that this robe was vast beyond conception, and that I stood, as it were, in a fold of it, as it lay stretched out on some unseen floor. But, clearer than any other thought, stood out in my mind the certainty that this robe had not been flung down and left, but that it clothed a Person. (24)

The profound vision the teenage priest experiences is transient, and he does not see the vision when he looks again, but his individual experience presses him to wrestle with the disjuncture between the religious view he had inherited about the natural world as "vanity and unreality," separated from "Him who sits on the great white throne" and his experiential perception that the natural world is itself part of the mystical body of Christ—God's robe (25). It impresses upon him a sacramental understanding of Creation, helping to explain why Benson so frequently uses the word *mass* to describe a lawn or long stretch of grass.

Benson's explicit enfolding of the natural world within the mystical body of Christ is surely unorthodox in relation to traditional understandings of the Church as the mystical body of Christ. For instance, in a 1943 encyclical, Pope Pius XII summarized the Roman Catholic Church's longstanding definition of the mystical body of Christ thus:

> We desire to make clear why the Body of Christ, which is the Church, should be called mystical. This name, which is used by many early writers, has the sanction of numerous Pontifical documents. There are several reasons why it should be used; for by it we may distinguish the Body of the Church, which is a Society whose Head and Ruler is Christ, from His physical Body, which, born of the Virgin Mother of God, now sits at the right hand of the Father and is hidden under the Eucharistic veils; and, that which is of greater importance in view of modern errors this name enables us to distinguish it from any other body, whether in the physical or the moral order. (60)

In contrast to Pius XII's definition, which sets clear limits on the body of Christ and construes it solely as an ecclesiastical body, Benson's preconversion novel represents the mystical body of Christ idiosyncratically, with repeated images of nature itself as an extension of Christ's sacred body.

The priest's vision of Creation itself as of a piece with the mystical body of Christ parallels the introduction to "Consolatrix Afflictorum," wherein the anonymous letter writer names Creation as one of the additional ways Christ's presence makes itself known. Explaining this sacramental view of the natural world, he concurs with the priest that "the Religion of the Incarnation rests on the fact that the Infinite and the Eternal expresses Himself in terms of space and time; and that it is in this that the greatness of the Love of God consists" and "the Creation, the Incarnation, and the sacramental System alike, in various degree, are the manifestation of God" (88). This sacramental view of the natural world appears not only in *The Light Invisible*, but also in several of Benson's poems, illustrating the continuity of Benson's vision of the natural world. As Chad Stutz puts it, "The presence of God is revealed through an artistic rendering of His natural creation" (105). In a poem called "The Invitation," Benson singles out the many ways in which the natural world is a doorway through which Christ can enter and an invitation to grace: Whether the dawn's light or the sweet smells of evening breezes, all are "[s]o many doors, and all divine/ And every latch is loose to Thee" (42). Likewise, through the poem called "Christian Evidences," the poet wonders that people seek Faith's knowledge in faraway places and abstruse and recondite learning, when in fact "better the tale to teach/ Pebbles and shells, poor fragments of the beach" (64). He continues,

Nay, but with Faith, I saw my Lord and God
Walk in the fragrant garden yesterday.
Ah! how the thrushes sang; and, where He trod
Like spikenard lay
Jewels of dew, fresh-fallen from the sky,
While all the lawn rang round with melody. (64–65)

Benson's verse strongly echoes William Blake's mysticism, and, indeed, the "The Green Robe," which is the first chapter of *The Light Invisible*, opens with Blake's famous lines about the natural world as a gateway to human perception of eternity: "To see a world in a grain of sand,/ And a heaven in a wild flower;/ Hold infinity in the palm of your hand,/ And eternity in an hour" (16). As we have seen, the priest's story in "The Green Robe" meditates upon how the ordinary, natural world can reveal not only infinite life, but also the mystical body of Christ himself.

If the natural world of things manifests Christ's mystical body, so, too, do human bodies. The connection between individual human bodies and the mystical body of Christ is powerfully conveyed in the chapter "With Dyed Garments." That chapter opens with the priest's startling claim that one of his most holy friends was a stockbroker, a partner in his father's firm, who spent his life working for the Stock Exchange (154). The story the priest relates dramatizes how this man's vision of suffering humanity led from mystical illumination to fruition, resulting in the good works for which the priest came to admire him. On the stockbroker's way home one December afternoon, he witnesses a poor pedestrian whose feet are accidentally crushed by the omnibus the broker is traveling on (157). The next summer he witnesses a beggar whose hands were a shocking sight: "They were lying palms downwards on the beggar's knees, bandaged like his face, but in the centre of each was a dark spot, showing through the wrapping, as if there were a festering wound that soaked through from underneath" (158). The following autumn, he witnesses a servant girl who takes ill and requires an operation in her side, "And he would see the girl after it was over, with a bandage against her side, and the knowledge of the little wound beneath" (160). And, finally, one glorious autumn afternoon walk, he happens upon some children at play, only to see one of the boys emerge from a bramble thicket with a forehead marked by "a little thin red dotted line where a thorn had scratched him" (162). Taken together, these instances of human suffering or pain spoke to the stockbroker of "a design underlying them" (161): "And all seemed to concentrate themselves on one Figure—with wounded feet and hands and side—and a torn forehead." (162). Experiencing a kind of baptism of vision, he came to see each individual's suffering not only for the individual's unique pain, but for the way in which it participated in the suffering of the mystical body of Christ. That mystical illumination led the stockbroker to ask his priest friend for some "work to do in some poor district. And work of that kind he has carried on ever since" (163). "With Dyed Garments" illustrates, therefore, how a mystical awareness of the coherence of human life within Christ's body led one ordinary businessman to a life of compassionate action.

The Priest's Mystical Path: Purgation, Illumination, Union

The priest's story about his stockbroker friend directly connects to his own growth narrative in the novel, providing a paradigm for the priest's gradual union with the mystical body of Christ. The priest's growth narrative is one that few critics have attended to in their focus on the many complex and intricate stories he tells. But, as Zoë Lehmann Imfeld notes, "The stories of *The Light Invisible* . . . all come together to offer a dying priest a cumulative understanding of grace in the frame narrative" ("Decadent Horror" 63). The final three chapters of the novel shift from stories about the priest's past to the narrator's account of the priest's final days and eventual death. Taken together, the chapters follow the priest through the three major stages of the mystic's journey: purgation, illumination, and union. It is the epigraphs attached to each of the three final chapters that signal this movement from purgatorial suffering to illumination and finally to mystical union, with first a quotation from canto 11 of Dante's *Purgatorio*, then a quotation from Julian of Norwich's *Revelations* about seeing the light of Christ "[a]t the end of woe" (230), and finally an old prayer about calling Jesus to be at one with the individual person, "Jhesu! Jhesu! Esto michi, Jhesu!" (244).

The first of the three final chapters of *The Light Invisible*, called "The Sorrows of the World," uses Gothic techniques to represent via external means the old priest's spiritual turmoil and need for purgation as well as the narrator's fears about the old man's impending death. After a Christmastide celebration, a stormy night sets in, with wild gusts of wind and repeated descriptions of the forces of nature battering the windows. Even the ivy and leaves seem animated, as if they are "clamouring to be admitted to shelter" (214). Through such ghostly forces of nature besieging the house, the scene reverberates with echoes of Gothic novels like Brontë's *Wuthering Heights*. Within, the narrator is "anxious" (213); Parker the servant's face is "white and scared" (215); and spiritual gloom afflicts the priest (218–20). As the chapter unfolds, the priest's spiritual gloom becomes clearer, for he interprets the sighing sounds and guttering lights outside as the sounds and sights of all suffering things, confessing, "The sorrows of the world . . . they are crying at my window . . . and now they come crying for me to pray for them. How little I have prayed!" (218).[12] This awakening, brought about by the storm, moves him to pray to Christ to be mindful of all the sorrows of the world, and the priest's powerful prayer in turn gives the narrator "a glimpse into mysteries of which I had not dreamed; mysteries of the unity of Christ and His members, a unity of pain" (220). At first the old priest's gloom and spiritual disquietude lead him to lash out at the narrator in unexpected anger, asking whether the narrator has "borne [his share] in the Incarnation" by staying awake and watchful (220). Then, the priest sinks back into "self-reproach," tormented by the haunting of people and things whose pain he has not sufficiently shared (220–21).[13]

In the second of the final three chapters, "In the Morning," Benson shifts from the priest's purgatorial self-flagellation to his illumination. The narrator and Parker fear some sort of "shocking climax" to the terrors of the night before (232); even when the narrator leaves the house to walk outside, he still expects some sort of "climax," unable to judge "of what nature" (233). But, as the reviewer of Benson's late novel *Initiation* remarks, Benson's novels are "a drama of the spirit rather than a drama of action" (*Spectator* 574). As it happens, the climax is the priest's mystical illumination during the celebration of Communion in his oratory. Holding the body of Christ in his hands, the body suddenly disappears, as if in the climax of a dark night of the soul (238).[14] In the body's place, he perceives all of suffering creation sloping down from him, in a kind of inverted image of the beautiful green robe he had seen as a child. Whereas before he had seen all of created life in its glorious beauty, he now sees diverse and sundry created things in a state of suffering: a woman with a dead child, a crying blind child, beasts about to die, trampled flowers, a thrush shivering in a tree, and even purgatorial souls (238–39). At the height of this epiphanic vision, he says, "I remembered that I held in my hands the Body of the Lord" (240). Then, his vision overwhelms him and he falls back, as if in a seizure (234, 240). Curiously, at the time of the priest's celebration of Communion, there was a blow against the window-pane; only later when the narrator discovers a dead thrush beneath the chapel window does it become clear that a thrush seems to have hit the window and fallen to its death (233). The juxtaposition of the priest's fall and the thrush's suggests his union with suffering nature and his spiritual change from the youthful time when, alienated from the natural world, he shot a thrush. After what seems like a kind of "seizure," the old man is laid on the bed, with eyes that strike the narrator as having been transfigured, as if "all the pain was gone out of them, and they were a child's eyes again" (235). The climax of the novel, therefore, is not what Gothic terrors of the night before have led the narrator to expect but rather the celebration of Christ's body and the supernatural communion between the thrush that dies and the priest who is seized by mystical understanding of the sorrows of the world.

Even with this profound vision of all creation within Christ's mystical body, he says there is one more vision that remains for him to see (241). In the novel's last chapter, "The Expected Guest," children playing think they see "the master" at the gate, "under the chestnut" tree, apparently "looking out for someone" (246–47): thus, they seem to see the figure of the priest waiting and watching. When he is back in bed, "his eyes were full of expectancy" (249). At this moment of ultimate spiritual maturation and impending death, his face reflects youth rather than age, his wrinkles yield to a rosy visage, his eyes brighten like those in the face of a child (251), suggesting that he is finally being united with the renewing presence of Christ. And it is Christ whom the priest seems to see, exclaiming "He is here" and "Look!" (251).[15] The novel ends with mysterious footsteps on the stairs and a boy whispering news of the Rector's arrival (251), an arrival that hearkens back to the opening of the final three chapters. "The Sorrows of the World" had begun on Christmas Eve with the Rector "call[ing]" for tea (209), and the novel's last chapter concludes with the ambiguous announcement that "the Rector had come" (251). With that final ambiguity, readers are left to judge whether it is the ordinary human rector who has arrived for his visitation duties, or if, as the priest seems to believe, it is the arrival of the ultimate Rector, Christ himself. If the latter, then ironically, the falling action of the novel is the coming of the risen Christ.

Mystic Individualism, Ecclesiastical Authority, and the Reception of Benson's Work

The Light Invisible's focus on an individual priest's mystical experiences raises questions about the credibility of those experiences and the tension between individual mystical experience and other forms of religious authority. How ought one to know if the priest's—and by extension, the narrator's—experiential knowledge should be trusted? The title of the chapter "Under Which King?" broaches that very question. It is a story that directly reckons with problems of authority and, as Zoë Lehmann Imfeld puts it, "the possibility of error" to which mysticism lays one open ("Decadent" 64). In matters of religious knowledge, what authority is best to be trusted? Church dogma? Intellect? Intuition? In the introduction to "Under Which King?," the narrator draws attention to how the Spanish mystic Miguel de Molinos's quietist mysticism drew criticism because he neglected the Sacraments, but even with attention to the Sacraments, the problem of knowing when mystical intuition comes from an evil or ambiguous source and when it comes from God still remains. The priest in the story chooses to abandon the "study of mysticism" (148) because "no soul can be lost by following the simple and well-beaten path of ordinary devotion and prayer" (148). The *novel's* priest, however, withholds clear opinion about the experience that leads to his fellow priest's decision, leaving the narrator and the reader to make their own judgments (149). And this chapter about the dangers of error along the mystical path seems to be the exception rather than the rule, with the preponderance of chapters pointing to the educative or transformative potential of mystical experience, including for the priest himself, since his path seems to lead him face to face with Christ himself at the doorway to death.

Still, Benson anticipates readerly concerns about the subjectivity of mystical experience through the preface with which he introduces the novel. Throughout the preface, he speaks in the voice of the narrator who has recorded the priest's conversations, but he signs the preface with his authorial initials, R. B., suggesting that the fictional narrator is Benson himself. Therein, he notes that priestly protagonist, represented as R. B.'s friend, would make no claims to being an "accredited teacher" (xi). His friend's knowledge is simply a more developed form of the perceptive faculty that all human beings possess, but his perspective has been informed through "directly sensible forms" (xi). Benson the narrator hastens to add that if anything in the priest's experience would have "contravene[d]

Divine Revelation," the priest would not have shared them as his wisdom. In fact, Benson emphasizes the primacy of doctrinal teaching as a shaping influence on individual mystical experience in asserting that Christian teaching must undergird the individual's exercise of the "spiritual faculties" (xi). Not to adhere to that order of operations would result in "Protestantism in its extreme form" and "the extinction of faith" (xi). And as an assurance that the priest's experiences do not fall afoul of Christian doctrine, Benson claims to "have taken pains to submit the book before publication to the judgment of those whose theological learning is sufficient to reassure me" that no laws "ascetical, moral, mystical, or dogmatic theology" have been transgressed (xii). As Zoë Lehmann Imfeld rightly observes, Benson's *Light Invisible* reflects an "insistence on mysticism as part of religious experience, but with a loyalty to theological orthodoxy" ("Decadent" 72).

Benson's early thinking about mysticism thus combines a modernist interest in the individual's subjective spiritual experience and a conservative anxiety about preserving the Church's doctrines. This double perspective surfaces again in his 1907 lecture on mysticism. In that lecture, Benson embeds his definition of mysticism as "the art of Divine Intuition" within a modernist discourse on perspectivalism (19). This modernist embrace of perspectivalism suffuses the lecture, as Benson recognizes the perspectives of the past in relation to those of the present (11–14); one religion in relation to another (5); science in relation to art and spirituality (8–9); mystics in relation to theologians and pious people of prayer (41); and finally one major form of mysticism in relation to another (21). As a vivid example of this perspectivalism, he observes that a springtime field looks very different to the geologist, the farmer, and the poet: The geologist looks at it and sees ground to measure, the farmer looks at it and sees its land that will bear fruit, and the poet sees it for its beauty (8–9). But no one perspective means that the others are wrong, for "[i]t is God only who can see a thing absolutely as it is in all its aspects and relations" (10). Christian Revelation is complete, he says, but our perceptions of it are not. This consideration of perspectivalism helps to justify respect for the uniquely gifted perspective of the mystic.

At the same time, though, the preface to the published version of this lecture firmly anchors mysticism in institutional Christianity. He writes, "It is impossible . . . within the limits of this lecture, even to mention by name many of that great body of Mystics who at various times have been lights in the Catholic Church" (3). He highlights how the Church has "always recognised its value" (6), and theological dogma is not a contradiction of mysticism but rather a "correlative" (3). The picture he draws of mystical experience and ecclesiastical doctrine is of mutual support rather than contradiction; they are not "irreconcilables" but "necessary to the other" (41). He puts this relationship most powerfully in claiming, "If the dogmatic theologian needs the clear sight of the Mystic for encouragement in his work and for the discernment of truths which, if they are to be practical, must be reduced to form, the Mystic no less needs the dogmatic theologian to warn and correct him when his ardours begin to pass from the objective to the subjective plane" (41). Christian doctrine must undergird mystical experience, and mystical experience in turn is needed to illuminate and vivify Christian doctrine.

However, this mutually supportive balance seemed to Benson missing from *The Light Invisible* when he looked back upon the novel in subsequent years. Finding it to tilt too much toward mystical individualism rather than Christian orthodoxy, Benson retrospectively cast a harsh light on his novel. Years after his Catholic conversion, he decried the state in which he wrote it—a mood of "feverishness" and "sentimentality" (*Confessions* 81), claiming that he had been "largely insincere" (82). And he worried that the book is "rather . . . mischievous" because "it implies that what I then strove to believe was spiritual intuition—and what is really nothing but imagination—must be an integral element in religious experience; and that 'sight'—or rather personal realization—must be the mode of spiritual belief rather than the simple faith of a soul that receives divine truth from a divine authority" (82). By contrast, he says "For Catholics it is almost a matter of indifference as to whether or no [*sic*] the soul realizes, in such a manner as to be able to visualize, the facts of revelation and the principles of the spiritual world" (*Confessions* 82). Such an assessment, published almost a decade later in 1913, reflects the degree to which Benson shifted more and more during his career as a Roman Catholic priest toward a religious orthodoxy premised on reason, authority, and dogma. As a consequence of that shift, however, he alienated some of the very people who had initially been attracted to his spiritual counsel and thinking.[16]

Both Waite and Underhill eventually distanced themselves from Benson's doctrinaire Catholicism, evident not in *The Light Invisible* but in later works such as *The Lord of the World* (1907), an apocalyptic novel, and *The Dawn of All* (1911). For instance, although Waite claimed to have no quarrel with Benson the person, Waite objected to *The Lord of the World*'s pitting of Freemasonry against Catholicism in a kind of Manichean struggle of evil against good. To Waite, this seemingly reductive representation of Masonry contradicted his own research into Masonic ritual and his proclivity toward reconciling religion and its heterodox offshoots. In a review of Benson's work, he wrote, "I am a mystic, carrying as such in my heart an eirenicon for all the faiths, and I can recite with [Benson's] own sincerity every line and phrase of the *Pange lingua*" ("Latin Church" 147). He continues,

> I believe personally that the sacramentalism of the Christian scheme holds up the most perfect glass of reflection to the mystery of salvation, and in this sense that the Church contains the catholic scheme of the Mysteries, but I know, after another manner, which is also the same manner, that there are mysteries which are not of its fold, and that it is given unto man to find the hidden jewel of redemption in more than one Holy Place. I say, therefore, with the Welsh bards, that I despise no precious concealed mysteries, wherever they subsist, and above all I have not part in those Wardens of the Gates who deny in their particular enthusiasm that things which are equal to the same are equal to one another, since these Wardens are blind. ("Latin Church" 150)

Like Waite, Underhill developed objections to Benson's doctrinaire turn, despite seeking him as a spiritual counselor earlier in the decade. At the turn of the century, Benson was counted as one of Underhill's circle, along with J. A. and Alice Herbert (both "devout Roman Catholics"), Arthur Machen, Arthur Waite, Margaret Robinson, and Ethel Ross Barker (Greene 14–15). By 1907, when she herself was wrestling with whether to enter the Roman Catholic Church, she sought out Benson's advice; not only had she become familiar with him from her social circle, but she had also been able to hear his preaching at Kensington's Carmelite Church (Greene 26). She hoped, in addition, that Benson would help her in drawing her fiancé and future husband to Catholicism (Ramsey 274). As a spiritual counselor, Benson sensed a misguided Neoplatonic tendency in her thinking and tried to draw her toward his Christian sacramentalism, advising, "What I think therefore is your obstacle [to the relationship between matter and spirit] . . . is that while you have tight hold of the importance of the idea, and of the transcendence of God, you have not sufficiently firm hold of the dignity of matter, or sufficient sympathy with its limitations" (qtd. in Greene 26). Such counsel proved ineffective insofar as she and her future husband never converted to Roman Catholicism, but his sacramental thinking may have left its impress nonetheless. By 1908, the letters she and Benson exchanged seem to have fallen off (Greene 38). She resumed contact again in 1910 in the hope that he could arrange for her to meet the pope via a general audience, but "by 1911 she felt estranged; she said she was 'disgusted and pained' at the publication of his *The Dawn in* [sic] *All*, 'a mixture of childishness, intolerance and unspirituality' " (Greene 38). His strong allegiance to Roman Catholic orthodoxy alienated her, and she eventually traversed a different path by returning to the Anglican Church.

Yet, all of those differences in regard to degree of Christian orthodoxy do not overshadow the significant commonalities that linked Benson to Waite, Underhill, and Machen during the Edwardian mystical revival. Each held Benson's belief in mysticism as a spiritual faculty all human beings possess and are capable of developing. As Benson puts it in his preface to *The Light Invisible*, the priest's spiritual faculty is "no more than a particular development of a faculty common to all who possess a coherent spiritual life" (xi). And although Benson saw the Christian Eucharistic sacraments as the most profound vehicles for mystical illumination and union, he shared with his Edwardian peers a belief in the sacramental and mystical potential of creative life in its myriad "sensible forms" (xi). It is just such "sensible forms" that become the subject for Evelyn Underhill's first mystical novel, *The Gray World*, a novel that explores what it means to begin one's spiritual life not from doctrine, but from the "sensible" forms of art and craft. To that novel, we shall now turn.

Chapter 3

The Art and Craft of the Mystical Novel

Evelyn Underhill's *The Gray World*

> The spiritual life is not a special career, involving abstraction from the world of things. It is a part of every man's life; and until he has realized it he is not a complete human being, has not entered into possession of all his powers.
>
> —Evelyn Underhill, *Practical Mysticism* (14–15)

"God comes to the soul in His working clothes, and brings His tools with him"—that curious claim is one the scholar, mystic, and novelist Evelyn Underhill makes in *House of the Soul*, her 1929 guide to spirituality (38). So characteristic of Underhill's spiritual thinking is such a claim that iconographer Suzanne Schleck chose it as the textual accompaniment to her icon of Underhill (Dixon 653). That Underhill now has her own icon and even commemoration day within the Anglican church signifies the admiration her spiritual work has been accorded in recent decades, although she is still less well-known than her contemporary William James, despite her extraordinary contributions to the history and study of spirituality, mysticism, and religious ritual. In her own time, the editor, writer, and fellow spiritual seeker Arthur Edward Waite described her as a woman "whose repute as a mystical writer is at present second to none among living people" (*Shadows* 167). T. S. Eliot, another famous contemporary, read her work *Mysticism* while a student at Harvard, later met her, and was indelibly shaped by that "intellectual, personal, and spiritual acquaintance" (Childs 83). More recently, Gordon Mursell characterized her as "the most important scholar of mysticism in the twentieth century" (qtd. in Dixon 653).

During the first half of the twentieth century, Underhill wrote prolifically about spiritual topics. At the turn of the century, she collected a circle of friends with like-minded spiritual interests, including Arthur Machen, A. E. Waite, and Robert Hugh Benson (Greene 14), but her extensive study of and writing about mysticism has had a greater impact on the modern understanding of mysticism than that of any of her peers. Dana Greene notes, "In thirty-nine years she produced forty books, editions, and collections, and more than three hundred fifty articles, essays, and reviews" (37). As a result of those contributions to writing about spirituality, Underhill achieved some remarkable accomplishments: "In 1921, she was invited to deliver the first series of Upton lectures in religion at the Unitarian Manchester College, Oxford; in 1927, she was appointed the first woman fellow at King's College, London; in 1938, she received an honorary doctorate in divinity at the University of Aberdeen" (Dixon 653–54). She even served as religious editor for the distinguished *Spectator* magazine (Johnson, "Pneumatology" 114). And yet, despite recognition of her nonfictional spiritual writing by her peers and recent scholars, Underhill's fiction remains little read, and she still sits at the margins of scholarly study of early twentieth-century literature, although she wrote several spiritually inflected short stories, poems, and three novels during the first decade of the last century. Underhill's reputation rightly rests on *Mysticism* (1911), her major study of that topic, and the plentiful spiritual writings that issued from that seminal work.[1] However, Underhill's fiction, written in the decade prior to *Mysticism*, prefigures many of her most important spiritual insights and fits within the larger, underexplored movement of early twentieth-century writers like Machen, Benson, and Williams who test the boundaries of literary realism to explore significant spiritual and metaphysical questions, including the relationship between artistry and spirituality. In that respect, her fiction merits more scholarly attention.

Thus far, sustained scholarship about Underhill's fiction has been limited to criticism embedded within biographies about her, with the exception of an unpublished dissertation by Justine Scott McCarthy exploring the psychological implications of Underhill's modernist aesthetic and a splendid recent essay by Carol Poston on Marian devotion in her fiction and other writings. In analyzing Underhill's fiction, her most recent biographers, Christopher J. R. Armstrong and Dana Greene, have emphasized the degree to which she sees the mystic as what Greene calls "the artist of the infinite life," a phrase that serves as the title of Greene's biographical study of Underhill. In fact, in two of Underhill's novels—*The Gray World* and *The Lost Word*—artistic activity is central to the protagonist's mystic quest. Like Armstrong and Greene, Géza von Molnár also sees artistic activity as central to Underhill's conception of the mystic, arguing that she echoes Novalis's German Romanticism in conceiving of the "individual's evolution into a poet" as the "apex of human accomplishment" (70). Furthermore, because of Underhill's sustained attention to mysticism as an art, Kathleen Henderson Staudt claims that "her work lays the groundwork for a theological aesthetics" (116). Yet, underlying Underhill's obvious efforts to connect art and spirituality is the fundamental question: What *kind* of art?

I would suggest that a deeper understanding of the relationship between artistry and spirituality in Underhill's work depends upon examining how the Arts and Crafts movement, as a vehicle for translating and modernizing idealized aspects of medieval culture, shaped Underhill's novels and, ultimately, her unique spiritual ethos. So ubiquitous is the discourse of the Arts and Crafts movement in the aforementioned Underhill novels that it can only be called hidden in plain view. For her fiction is everywhere marked by medievalism and, more specifically, by the Arts and Crafts movement's distinctive reception of medieval culture. A study of Underhill's complex response to the Arts and Crafts movement illuminates why she sees God as a toolmaker and the human soul as a craftsman for whom the material things of this world—architecture, stained glass, jewelry, books—can become vehicles for making this life meaningful and for practically accessing the wild beauty of a divine Reality beyond. I shall argue, therefore, that key aspects of the Arts and Crafts movement's moral aesthetic define the practical mysticism in Underhill's novels, prefiguring the sacramental turn of her later theological thinking and writing.

Medieval Longings

Little about Underhill's early life would point toward a career as a spiritual writer, mystic, and scholar of mysticism. Underhill grew up with parents who were only nominally Anglican and inactive in the Church, though one of her uncles was an Anglican priest (Sauer 183). Although she prepared for confirmation as a teenager, her private notebooks were as full of doubts and questioning as of favorite prayers and hymns (Sauer 184). She seemed to have no special interest in theology while a student at King's College (Greene 12). Her major areas of study at King's College were botany, philosophy, languages, and art (Greene 11–12). Yet, Underhill's growing interest in art and religion—and, indeed her entire career—was directly indebted to her medieval longings, an admiration for things medieval that shaped her young adult life and set a course for all she was to write. At King's College, she encountered Dante (Greene 12), whose grand medieval narrative about a quest for God shaped her own fiction, even down to the Dantean quotations integrated within her novels' chapters.

However, Underhill's exposure to medieval culture was not limited to her college reading. Rather, her many trips to Italy, which began with her mother in 1898, immersed her in a world of medieval culture that enchanted her, making real what she had merely read about. Over a decade later, in a letter to Mrs. Meyrick Heath, she describes a recent trip to Italy during which she recounts: "I was *determined* to get to Camaldoli because there are still Hermits there, so we drove there: right over the Consuma Pass, and by Poppi and lots of other Dante places. The whole day was rather like being inside the *Divina Commedia*, and the whole landscape absolutely mediaeval" (Underhill, *Letters* 145). In the context of this letter and many others, Underhill's assessment of the landscape as "absolutely mediaeval" clearly connotes positive approbation, capturing the essence of her enchantment with Italy; time and again, she similarly praises the streets, architecture, and people of Italy for conjuring up the medieval past.

Her early letters from the 1890s and the first years of the 1900s, written mostly to her fiancé (soon-to-be-husband) Hubert Stuart Moore, give us an additional window on this love of medieval culture. For instance, she recounts from Perugia in 1902, "The more I see of this place the more I love it, every step one takes there is a fresh little medieval street, all narrow & steppy with great high houses with grated windows & carved doorways each side" (Underhill, *Making* 53). However, it is particularly the architecture of medieval churches that engages her, and many letters to Moore describe her sketching a church (Underhill, *Making* 50) or marveling at medieval craftsmanship, whether of church architecture or decorative objects within a church. "I do so wish you could have seen that 9th century metal work at Milan . . . It was a complete casing to the altar in the old church," she gushes to Moore in a 1903 letter from Padua

(Underhill, *Making* 58). From Firenze in 1898, she writes, "Oh! I did want you to see that monastery. I loved it so much. The whole thing was like a bit of the Middle Ages," anticipating her comment to Heath that for something to be like the Middle Ages was to be beautiful or lovely (Underhill, *Making* 27). Despite this admiration of medieval culture, she is notably quiet about medieval ideas or dogma; rather, it was the *artifacts* people had made and left behind that attracted her, even or maybe especially their practical arts. For instance, in a 1906 letter from Avignon, she notes to Moore, "What rather fetched one was the 14th century bakery with the oven, & at the oven entrance the device of the castle owner cut in the stone like a die, so that each loaf could be impressed against it before baking! So simple, & so efficient. We had a delightful old man to take us round who might have lived in the 14th century, he was so realistic about it" (Underhill, *Making* 87). Here we see that for Underhill, medieval art and culture were beautiful because they connoted simplicity and practicality.

On her return to England from various Continental adventures into the medieval past, Underhill found yet another entrée to the medieval world through her friend J. A. Herbert, keeper of manuscripts at the British Museum. She eventually collaborated with him on a 1911 book called *Illuminated Manuscripts*, published under his name (Whitlark 285). Thanks to his good offices, old manuscripts and books as much as churches became another window for Underhill on the medieval world. Greene notes that "it was he who introduced Evelyn Underhill to the treasure trove of medieval manuscripts in his keeping," thereby "open[ing] up the world of mystical literature to her" (15). Given this access, Underhill gradually immersed herself in a world of medieval writers who became her life's work as a translator, editor, and self-taught scholar of medieval mystical texts to which modern readers had previously lacked access. By 1905, this research had borne some of its earliest fruit, with her "translation of twenty-five medieval legends about the appearances of the Blessed Virgin Mary," called *The Miracles of Our Lady St. Mary* (Underhill, *Making* 3). As Michelle Sauer notes, her translations and editions of medieval texts, of which this text was an early foretaste, "continue to be important to today's medieval scholars" (183), meriting her a place in a 2005 study of women medievalists and the academy. For, according to Bernard McGinn, her contributions to the study of mysticism were "unprecedented in English scholarship" (22).

However, Underhill's attraction to medieval literature was not limited to mystical texts. In a 1900 letter to Hubert, she reports venturing into a bookshop to purchase Arthurian romance stories: "I investigated the new book shop which has set up in Kensington; it is full of the most delicious things & kept by two ladies—such nice girls, I went in & had quite a talk with them, & bought the new volume of those Arthurian Romance books, to match 'Gawain & the Green Knight'" (Underhill, *Making* 43). Carol Poston notes that this new volume may have been legends translated at the time by Jessie Weston (Underhill, *Making* 44). Although medieval mystics had a dominant influence on Underhill's subsequent writing, her acquaintance with Arthurian literature also surfaces in her three novels, particularly her final novel *Column of Dust*, in which the Grail myth is central.[2]

All in all, Underhill's attraction to medieval culture was complex and multifaceted, provoking new metaphysical, ethical, and aesthetic reflections. As Greene concludes, "For Underhill the medieval world intimately linked matter and spirit, the inner and the outer, the natural and the supernatural" (13).[3] Thus, in her appreciation of medieval manuscripts and their early book form, church architecture, and medieval decorative arts, Underhill shared with many nineteenth-century forerunners a passionate appreciation for the Middle Ages. Indeed, her reception of medieval culture both paralleled and was mediated by the Arts and Crafts movement that preceded her and dominated English culture during the years when she came to maturity.

From Medievalism to "Modernism": The Moral Aesthetic of the Arts and Crafts Movement

Born in 1875 in England, Underhill began her life during the heyday of the Arts and Crafts movement. Fired by the moral aesthetics of John Ruskin, Thomas Carlyle, and William Morris in the mid-nineteenth century, many key developments in that movement took place in the last decades of the nineteenth century, when Underhill was coming to maturity. In the year of Underhill's birth, William Morris took up a variety of handicrafts, ranging from painting and carving to furniture making, dyeing, and carpet weaving, and he reorganized his firm as Morris & Co. (Wilmer xiii). And many of his key works of literature were published a decade later: *A Dream of John Ball* serialized from 1886 to 1887 and *News from Nowhere* in 1890. In that regard, the Arts and Crafts movement constituted the modern culture of Underhill's developmental years. Not surprisingly, her own life came to be marked by Arts and Crafts ideas and artistic practices. That she was aware of some of the seminal figures of the Arts and Crafts movement early in her life is made clear when she highlights in a letter to Moore that she was able to have the very hotel room "that Ruskin used to have when he came to Lucca" (Underhill, *Making* 71). Ruskin and Carlyle subsequently appear multiple times in the epigraphs of her novel chapters, and their ideas are integrated throughout her novels in less explicit ways.

Inspired by figures like Ruskin, the Arts and Crafts movement had its roots in a love of medieval art and culture, similar to Underhill's. According to Elizabeth Cumming and Wendy Kaplan, "The architect and theorist A. W. N. Pugin . . . provided the foundation from which the moral aesthetics of Arts and Crafts evolved during the second half of the century. Pugin rejected the early Victorian vogue for Classical architecture in favour of a revival of medieval Gothic, which, he believed, reflected the order and stability of the Christian faith" (11). Cumming and Kaplan continue, "Pugin's dream of re-uniting designer and craftsman and, in broader terms, the spiritual with the everyday, was taken up by Ruskin and the designer and writer William Morris, the two main founders of the Arts and Crafts movement" (12). Their ideal of uniting spiritual ideas and ordinary life especially appealed to Underhill and shaped her thinking in myriad ways.

John Ruskin's ideas are particularly relevant to Underhill's middle novel, *The Lost Word*, which features a church architect, Paul Vickery, bent on a Ruskinesque quest to create the perfect Gothic church and find fulfillment as both designer and builder. To the broader Arts and Crafts movement, Ruskin was a seminal thinker, whose love of Gothic architecture was best articulated in his 1853 book *The Stones of Venice* in a chapter titled "The Nature of the Gothic." Therein, he identifies "certain mental tendencies of the [medieval] builders" that deserve admiration: "fancifulness, love of variety, love of richness," among others (Ruskin 159). And he makes a powerful argument in praise of Gothic architecture's sympathy with the natural world in contrast to classical architecture, which he regarded as slavishly conforming to artistic rules of symmetry (Ruskin 168–69). Yet he asserts that the natural variety evident in Gothic forms comes not from "love of change" for its own sake but rather from "practical necessities" (Ruskin 168), emphasizing a practical orientation that Underhill was to inherit and develop.

A generation later, William Morris and his friends adopted Ruskin's love of medieval culture and realized the ideal of making art out of the practical necessities of life by extending the craftsman's sphere of endeavor far beyond architecture. Morris's own love affair with the Middle Ages began in his youth, with the novels of Sir Walter Scott and adventures "riding his pony through Epping Forest" while "dressed in a miniature suit of armour" (Wilmer xi). He and his friend Edward Burne-Jones were later shaped by the Gothic revival afoot at Oxford, where he attended Exeter College, a place alive with medievalism in the form of the Anglo-Catholic movement. And he was subsequently influenced by Ruskin and Carlyle, whose rethinking of work and art hearkened back to models from the Middle Ages.

To some extent, the Arts and Crafts movement ushered in by Morris was loosely united by an interest in crafts such as bookmaking, jewelry making, weaving, and embroidery. The movement got its name in the 1880s, thanks to one of the most distinguished bookbinders of the era, T. J. Cobden-Sanderson: "When the bookbinder T. J. Cobden-Sanderson suggested 'The Arts and Crafts Exhibition Society,' he created a name that would thereafter be associated with the entire movement" (Kaplan, *Leading* 16). According to Kaplan, the decade of the 1880s "saw the formation of the first exhibition societies and the organization of guilds, inspired by the ideal of the craft associations that had maintained standards of workmanship in medieval Europe" (*Leading* 14). Although key leaders in these Arts and Crafts societies and guilds theorized idealistically about work and art, as is clear from William Morris's utopian philosophizing in *News from Nowhere*, the movement had a fundamentally practical orientation. Kaplan explains, "Crafts as a hobby was always an important part of the Arts and Crafts movement, since proponents believed so deeply in the spiritual benefits of work done by hand" (*Leading* 20).

Of the many ideas circulating among Arts and Crafts proponents, several stand out as influential for Underhill, and William Morris's writings provide perhaps the clearest and most succinct exposition of those ideas. First, Arts and Crafts thinkers developed ideals in strong sympathy with the culture of the Middle Ages. In Morris's utopian romance *News from Nowhere*, a Victorian-era protagonist named William Guest adventures into an ideal future society paradoxically premised on many of the values of the medieval past. As the utopian society's resident historian explains to William, "More akin to our way of looking at life was the spirit of the Middle Ages to whom heaven and the life of the next world was such a reality, that it became to them a part of the life upon earth; which accordingly they loved and adorned, in spite of the ascetic doctrines of their formal creed, which bade them contemn it" (158). Here Morris illuminates how an outlook rooted in a transcendent world beyond was connected to the art-making of this world. While Morris himself abandoned any belief in a transcendent world, he nonetheless lionized the individual craftsmanship characteristic of work in the Middle Ages and lost by the industrial processes of nineteenth-century mass production. In this regard the Arts and Crafts movement was fundamentally revivalist. As fellow designer Walter Crane summarized their movement, it was an effort "towards a *revival* of design and handicraft, the effort to unite—or rather *reunite*—the artist and the craftsman [emphasis mine]" (11).

Second, as Crane's comment makes clear, Arts and Crafts thinkers sought to elevate craft to the level of art. Morris directly justified ordinary decorative crafts as art in his 1877 lecture "The Lesser Arts," delivered to the Trades Guild of Learning. In that lecture, he asserts, "Our subject is that great body of art, by means of which men have at all times more or less striven to beautify the familiar matters of everyday life" (*News from Nowhere* 231–38). As Morris goes on to argue, it is not just the great arts—painting and sculpture—that are worthy of the artist's endeavor, but also book-making, enameling, carpentry, carving, pottery, and textile arts, among other traditional crafts. He explains that "[t]o give people pleasure in the things they must perforce *use*, that is one great office of decoration" (235). Crane echoes this sentiment in an essay written for the 1903 collection of *Arts and Crafts Essays*, published by the Arts and Crafts Exhibition Society: "[I]f Art is not recognised in the humblest object and material, and felt to be valuable in its own way . . . the arts cannot be in sound condition" ("Revival" 4–5). This democratizing of the arts, so to speak, opened the door to a democratizing of the artist. In other words, if one can create art by finishing a book or designing a jeweled pendant, then almost anyone can be an artist; one need not be a Michaelangelo or a Raphael. Morris's view reflects an egalitarianism and a practical utilitarianism that we will later see in Underhill's spiritual ethos, for she makes a similar argument about the ordinary character of the mystic's path in her book *Practical Mysticism* (1914).[4]

Third, Arts and Crafts thinkers inspired by Carlyle and Ruskin argued for the essential value of creative work. In *Past and Present* (1843), Carlyle had earlier lionized the sacred nature of work, writing, "there is a perennial nobleness, and even sacredness, in Work. Were he never so benighted, forgetful of his high calling, there is always hope in a man that actually and earnestly works" (202). Ruskin similarly saw work as central to human life, rooting his vision of work in the model of the medieval craft guilds. As Michael Alexander explains, "Ruskin and Morris dreamed of becoming working men. As adults, they lectured and wrote advocating the ideal of the craftsman. Ruskin founded the medieval Guild of St. George, and Morris tried to recreate a medieval workshop" (73). Morris, however, came to reject the argument that work per se is good for the soul. Instead, in his 1884 lecture "Useful Work Versus Useless Toil," he argues that work is central to human happiness, but it must meet certain criteria in order to be spiritually fulfilling. The work must, first of all, be pleasurable to the worker (288). It must be useful (a key justification for work at crafts like book making or textile weaving) (299). It must provide a livelihood and not merely supply the demands of the "profit market" (298). It must be performed in "pleasurable surroundings" (301–03), which Morris contrasts to the factory conditions increasingly typical of work in his modern era. And, finally, it must be performed with sincerity, reflecting authentic investment on the part of the designer, craftsman, and user. The authentic craftsman was imagined as a contrast to industrial workers, who were alienated from both the artistic conception and the final use of the products of their labor, manufacturing products only to fire a burgeoning mass market and increase profits (300–01).

Thus, many of the ideals laid out in Morris's writings—work as revival of medieval craft, the elevation of ordinary crafts to the level of art, the value and character of creative work—foreshadow ideals Underhill explores in *The Gray World* and *The Lost Word* as tools for a practical mysticism. In Morris's view, a revision of work as a creative endeavor not only provided spiritual contentment but also conduced toward the creation of a good society, which over time, became Morris's dominant concern. However, whereas Morris emphasized the craftsman's role in creating a good society, Underhill adopted such ideals with a focus on the individual and the creation of a healthy soul.

A Craftswoman's Spiritual Roots: Tools for the Soul

Prior to the publication of her novels, Underhill's early letters to her husband, Hubert Moore, offer ample evidence of her direct involvement with the Arts and Crafts movement, an involvement she shared with him. This shared marital interest in Arts and Crafts was not unusual, given how common husband-and-wife teams were in the movement (Kaplan,

Leading 24–28). They subscribed to magazines that would have kept people apprised of the latest Arts and Crafts trends. She subscribed to *The Artist* in 1902, was a reader of *The Studio* (an arts and crafts journal), and considered subscribing to *Architectural Review* because it used to have "lovely designs in it metal carving etc [*sic*]" (Underhill, *Making* 53–54, 64). As Rosalind Blakesley explains about *The Studio*, "The Movement as a whole was celebrated from 1893 in the pages of *The Studio*, which gave extensive coverage to the designs, plans and drawings of Voysey, Shaw, Ashbee and their colleagues, as well as publishing interviews with designers themselves" (75).

Underhill and her husband did not, however, simply read about the Arts and Crafts movement in the popular magazines of the day. They themselves practiced traditional crafts: Evelyn learned the art of bookbinding and Hubert developed a passion for the craft of enameling. Their devotion to craft-making was a significant shared bond, especially given Hubert's apparent lack of interest in spirituality or religion, the topic so central to Evelyn's heart. Consequently, Evelyn's letters to him are filled with discussion of Arts and Crafts topics. She often writes to him with ideas for or advice about jewelry making—for instance, an idea for an inlay or a description of a necklace design she has seen and admires (Underhill, *Making* 33, 56). So invested in craft-making is Hubert that one letter even records her chastising him for working in the workshop all day one Sunday without going out for exercise (Underhill, *Making* 60, 73). Sauer notes that "[t]hese practical pursuits led to a deepening of her relationship with Hubert Stuart Moore. He was the one who kept her binding knives sharp . . ." (185).

Underhill studied bookbinding with the famous Arts and Crafts bookbinders Johanna Birkenruth and T. J. Cobden-Sanderson (the latter a friend of William Morris). In one letter from S. Albans in 1895, she notes having to miss a bookbinding lesson with "Miss Borkenruth" because of the latter's illness but reveals her plan to attend a lecture "by Cobden Sanderson on Arts & Crafts for women" (Underhill, *Making* 15). The lecture, however, proves disappointing for reasons that are significant to understanding Underhill's response to the Arts and Crafts movement. In a subsequent letter, she explains to Hubert, "I don't think I shall get to the 1st day of term show this time, as the second Cobden Sanderson lecture [is] that day. The first was rather vapoury all about ideals of craftsmanship & revising the old trade guilds & stuff like that but next time he is going to bring his own tools & demonstrate" (Underhill, *Making* 17).

This remark suggests that she is less interested in the grandiose ideals behind the Arts and Crafts movement and, by contrast, more interested in the practical activity of making crafts, mentored by the masters of the various Arts and Crafts trades.

Her many letters to Hubert attest to how much time she devoted to improving her craft as a bookbinder. When in Italy, she takes especial advantage of lessons in bookbinding, reporting to her husband, "Now I am just off with one of the girls here to call on Miss Bailey the bookbinder & see her work which I will tell you about when I write next" (Underhill, *Making* 25). In Alessio, she receives "a lesson in a most delightful sort of old Italian bookbinding alone with vellum catgut & knotted leather, without the use of any paste or glue. I'm sure it will fascinate you" (Underhill, *Making* 65). She spends mornings doing bookbinding even as she chides her husband about his constant presence in the jewelry workshop at home (Underhill, *Making* 68). So skilled did Underhill eventually become as a bookbinder that one of her works was eventually "purchased by the Hungarian Museum for its collection" (Whitlark 286).

These bookbinding practices had a number of important effects on her life and work. On a personal level, her work as a craftswoman drew her closer to Moore, with his zeal for jewelry making matched by her commitment to the craft of bookbinding; these crafts served as the foundation of their early relationship. Her craft work also drew her closer to medieval culture, as she consciously sought to learn techniques from that distant past. For instance, writing to Moore, she notes, "I had two book binding lessons in Siena in the 15th century binding, & do hope I shall manage to make something of it with your help, as it's very pretty. I also drew a few designs for things at the exhibition" (Underhill, *Making* 72). Above all, though, Underhill's work as a craftswoman gave her concrete experience of the ideals touted by figures like Morris and firsthand understanding of the Arts and Crafts debates that were to unfold in her fictions and their link to her practical mysticism.

Arts and Crafts Ideals in Underhill's Fiction: *The Gray World* as Exemplum

That Underhill's interest in the Arts and Crafts movement influenced her fiction is evident in a number of ways. The most superficial evidence is reflected in the chapter epigraphs drawn from writers such as John

Ruskin and Thomas Carlyle. At a deeper level, the central characters in *The Gray World* and *The Lost Word*, her first and second novels, are, respectively, practitioners of the crafts of bookbinding and church building. Most importantly, though, both novels engage their characters in a spirited debate about art and spirituality that is interwoven with discourses drawn from Arts and Crafts thinkers. In these novels, we see a subtle shift in Underhill's aesthetic ideas, a shift shaped by the Arts and Crafts movement and responsible for defining her spiritual ethos and understanding of mysticism for decades to come. To be sure, Underhill's novelistic response to the Arts and Crafts movement is complicated and ambivalent. She is as wont to satirize distortions of the movement as to find kinship with its spiritual ideals. Still, the movement's moral aesthetic undergirds the practical mysticism evinced in her novels and shapes the sacramental direction her later writings take.

To illustrate this argument, I shall use her first novel, *The Gray World*, as my primary exemplum. Although Underhill's last novel *The Column of Dust* (1909) is often cited as her best novel (Armstrong 63), it does not reflect the aesthetic debates and preoccupation with Arts and Crafts found in her two earlier novels, *The Gray World* (1904) and *The Lost Word* (1907). Further, at the time of *The Gray World*'s publication, it was "widely and positively received" and has the added value of refracting aspects of Underhill's autobiography (Greene 15–16). Although her middle novel, *The Lost Word*, also invokes Arts and Crafts ideas in an overt, sustained way, I will reference it only in relation to *The Gray World* because its ideas are not as coherently developed and resolved; it is, as Greene and Armstrong bluntly put it, "not a good novel" (Greene 22) and "weak in construction" (Armstrong 62).

The Gray World marks a significant pivot in Underhill's thinking about art, as she turns to viewing it through the lens of the Arts and Crafts movement. Her earliest efforts at fiction took the form of several short stories published in *Horlick's Magazine*, a journal edited by A. E. Waite (Chapman 2). Of those stories, which were published during the same year as *The Gray World*, two focus on the role of art in human life. Yet, the picture those stories draw of artistic activity is very different from that drawn in her novels; indeed, the picture is a disturbing one. In "Death of the Artist," Father John, a saintly man on the verge of death, is discovered to have a cache of demonic art hidden away, expressive of the dark side of his nature. Given his saintly character, his disciples expect to find beautiful art featuring pious or ennobling images in his secret room, but instead they discover paintings of "the grotesque, morbid, unspeakable secrets of the world," with his last painting "personif[ying] all the dark, obscene secrets of our common nature" ("Death" 176). Upon discovering this art, one of the disciples, Cuthbert, dismisses Father John's accomplishments by remarking, "Our saint was only an artist after all!" (177). But the other disciple, Alban, seems to perceive that Father John's art was purgative and enabled him to return to life "purged of the stain of the earth and radiant with thanksgiving"; in fact, Alban goes so far as to speculate that "had he been less of an artist, he might not have been quite so much of a saint" (177). The story, therefore, portrays art as a vehicle for expressing the shadow side of human nature, furthering spiritual development only by serving as a canvas for collecting the dross of human life and purging the human soul.

"The Mountain Image" short story portrays a very different picture of art's relationship to spirituality, one that previews *The Gray World*'s interest in Arts and Crafts, but from a radically different interpretive perspective. In "The Mountain Image," the protagonist Nicholas practices the craft of carving to popular acclaim. His workshop is successful because of "the little figures of peasants and animals" that tourists find "wonderfully artistic" (375). Even his old mentor, the sculptor who had taught him his trade, praises his work for its practical utility, which will make him a "rich man" (376). The old man once feared that Nicholas would be consumed by dreams of being an "artist" at the expense of honing his craft. He says: "I am very glad to find you of so practical a mind. I was afraid, when you left me, that you were going to be a failure; you fancied yourself an artist, do you remember? Wanted to do big statues. Big statues don't come out of little villages. I see you have realized that. This talk of art has ruined many in our trade; but you are quite safe from that danger now" (376). In fact, Nicholas secretly scorns the old man's practical mindedness, and Nicholas feels he has betrayed his artistic inclinations by creating crafts for consumers. Instead, he has long dreamed of carving a perfect image of the Madonna.

To fulfill that dream, he leaves the village, a place of "solid common sense," for a remote cliff where he devotes himself to bringing his ideal image to reality in the stone (376). Yet the relationship Underhill figures forth between image and matter is a strained, oppositional one: "Steadily and quietly, from sunrise till dusk, he drove away the inimical rock, forcing the image of Our Lady out to the light" (378). The process of realizing the ideal image is framed here as a violent one, dependent on crucifying the matter that gives it form. In the end, the artistic process results in his own crucifixion: "He lay dead at the feet of the mighty, but lifeless Madonna, whose carven knees had received the impact of his head" (380), an image of the futility of idealism. In this story, Underhill presents a set of stark oppositions premised on a philosophical opposition between matter and spiritual ideal. Nicholas's artistry is opposed to mere craft; his idealism is contrasted to crass materialism; the ideal can only be realized by doing violence to matter; and the human being cannot survive the effort to make an ideal real in the material world. This sharp division between the practical and the artistic, the material and the spiritual, unresolved in "The Mountain Image," constitutes the philosophical dilemma *The Gray World* opens with and, I would argue, ultimately resolves.

By contrast to Nicholas's story of alienation and artistic defeat, *The Gray World* traces its protagonist's progression from a state of alienation and meaninglessness to a state of mystical contentment as an artist who is a craftsman. The novel recounts the story of a young slum child named Willie who dies from typhoid fever, hovers in the "gray world," and then, after expressing a passionate prayer to return to life, is reborn in a bourgeois English family.[5] Willie is forever haunted by his memory of that immaterial world—the gray world—as he seeks meaning and spiritual orientation while growing into his new life. In the course of that new life, his education often turns out to be miseducation, for his material experiences often prove good for the body but bad for the soul. Anxious to find a spiritual home in the material world, he tries first one dead-end path, then another and another. For instance, over the course of Willie's coming of age in this spiritual bildungsroman, he tries a society of the occult and finds the "searchers of the soul" there banal and pretentious (83). He tries platonic friendship with a fellow society member, Stephen, but that friendship proves a "false beacon" (115). He tries romantic love with his friend Mildred and his elder mentor Elsa (a kind of Beatrice manqué), and then grows disillusioned with each.

Finally, though, he finds inspiration in the beauty of medieval art and meaning in the medieval craft of bookbinding, achieving final contentment at the end of the novel by retreating to the remote countryside to practice bookbinding in the company of a fellow hermit. Extraordinary as this bildungsroman seems on the surface, it chimes with notes from Underhill's own life story, particularly as it traces Willie's encounters with an occult society (a distant echo of Underhill's membership in the Order of the Golden Dawn), his enchantment with Italian medieval architecture, and his devotion to the art of bookbinding. Even more importantly, the novel charts Willie's evolution from the kind of philosophical dualism Underhill explored in "The Mountain Image," where matter opposes spirit, to a vision of art as the practical mediator between matter and soul.

A Philosophical Dialectic: Materialism, Idealism, and Their Limits

The novel opens by establishing a strict opposition between the material and spiritual world, creating an existential problem Willie must resolve in the course of the novel. Willie's brief sojourn into the "gray world" of the afterlife, akin to the Greek Hades, cuts him off from ordinary material objects like the hospital door's brass knob, which he perceives while dying as "getting very hazy" and "float[ing] uncertainly in the air" (8). Once dead, he looks back on those "ten years of aggressively material life" (10), only to perceive of that material world as a shadowy one. He finds himself "converted into a pure spirit to whom the material universe was no more actual than the air and other invisible gases are to living men" (10). In his new form, material things are insubstantial, for he can pass through rooms, walls, and buildings without resistance (12). This unique perspective creates consternation for him, as he tries to live in the material world while questioning its reality.

As a result of his sojourn in the gray world, Willie returns to ordinary reality perplexed by the many family members and family friends who are materialists of one kind or another and who seem to regard material things as the only reality. One sort of materialist, Mrs. Steinmann, is to be found in his mother's social circle. Mrs. Steinmann is hopelessly narrow-minded in her view of reality: "For her, life held but one thing—the domestic interior" (30). Willie's mother, Mrs. Hopkinson, rivals this triviality in focusing on domestic details such as his sister Pauline's dirty pinafore and having "all her sense tuned to the level of her best tea-set" (31). Throughout these scenes of social satire, practical attention to such material comforts is affiliated with superficiality—an inability either to apprehend a transcendent world beyond material reality or to engage in the kind of imaginative thinking derided as "fancy" by Willie's father. In such a home environment, Willie finds himself an outsider, for even his sister Pauline seems to have been "[b]orn a materialist" (22).

Another form of materialism equally disconcerting to Willie is represented by his father, Mr. Hopkinson. Willie's father—a wholesale tailor and worshiper of modern science—loves to anatomize the world, reducing its "magical clouds" to transactions of force and matter (41). Later in the novel, he dismisses any view that emotion or soul lives on after death as "medieval nonsense about future states" (281), invoking modern biological theories about brain-cortex, consciousness, and protoplasm to support his skeptical perspective (280). Furthermore, Willie's practical father tends to dismiss as insignificant anything unrelated to business; Willie laments that his father "thinks that nothing is of serious importance that has not some bearing on practical affairs" (94). In this instance, "practicality" has a clear negative connotation, suggesting a world view bereft of any transcendent or imaginative richness. Underhill thus satirizes several kinds of materialist world views as different forms of reductive thinking: the women's materialism driven by social proprieties and the father's driven by science and business. Both are shown to be inadequate responses to a more complicated reality.

Surrounded by this materialism, Willie's imaginative spirit leads him to take refuge in medieval romance stories, especially of the Grail. In his "second" life, Willie is early on enchanted with those old stories:

> He loved to read the old romances and tales of King Arthur's knights, for a peculiar inarticulate joy that they gave him: but when he tried to find out the source of his fascination, he could not. Specially the story of the Holy Grail attracted him. Though his reason told him that it and the others were as untrue, as shadowy, as the rest of life, his soul found in them some secret element which nourished it and gave it peace. (39)

The Arthurian legend is recognized by Willie as fiction—something made up, but its Grail story nonetheless adumbrates an elusive Reality beyond, and such transcendence symbolically conveyed is temporarily consoling. Given Willie's transcendental intimations and longings, he becomes friends with an older woman, the middle-aged Elsa Levi, whose idealistic inclinations are satirized just as sharply as are the materialisms of Mrs. Steinmann and Mr. Hopkinson, even though Elsa eventually becomes a bridge to the world of Arts and Crafts and, thereby, a character who is instrumental in forwarding Willie on his spiritual path.

Elsa's idealism takes the form of aestheticism. As Staudt notes, in Underhill's Edwardian England, "Aestheticism was in fashion—the pursuit of experience for its own sake in the arts and in human relationships" (116). This aestheticism derives in part from Walter Pater, who espoused the "necessity of dying with a faith in art" (Bloom, "Introduction" 13). In several ways, Elsa tries to conform her ordinary experiences to ideals drawn from art. For instance, inspired by Arthurian legend, she has named her two sons after Tristram and Geraint, but both boys fall far short of the legendary people after which they are named: They "did not incarnate the Arthurian legend to the extent that their cultured mother had hoped" (*The Gray World* 54), and she was disappointed to "see her sons, in spite of romantic names and picturesque dresses, become more uncompromisingly Hebraic day by day" (55). Their very appearance, more like her "Hebraic" husband than akin to figures from Celtic legend, offended her "esthetic sense" (55). Elsa's antisemitic perspective here is the most morally rebarbative aspect of her so-called idealism. Underhill illuminates how that idealism is driven in this case not only by her quixotic temperament, Paterian aestheticism, and reading of romance stories, but also by an undercurrent of antisemitism.

Elsa's aestheticism is further satirized insofar as all the ordinary things connected to rearing children are antithetical to her artistic spirit: She had no practical interest in family linens or airing the drawing room or even in keeping her children's hair cut or their teeth doctored (55). And at one comic moment in the story, as Willie and Elsa are about to have a romantic encounter, Geraint, despite his Romantic name, flips on the lights, abruptly disrupting their drama with his blundering, prosaic action. In these scenes, Elsa's appropriation of medieval romance as a lens for interpreting her life illustrates the complex way in which Underhill represents medieval romance within her novel. On the one hand, it gives Willie spiritual intimations of a world beyond, but on the other hand, the idealism therein leads characters like Elsa to derogate ordinary life and create an illusory world comically at odds with the prosaic realities of family life.

Elsa's idealism pertains not just to her children; it is also evinced in her self-fashioning. In her dress, she attempts to epitomize ideal beauty. Her apparel is often artfully arranged, making her appear like a figure out of a Pre-Raphaelite painting, "looking exactly like Rossetti's 'Astarte Syriaca' " (94). Her hands even reflect her artistic ideals, as Willie notices her "soft and manicured hand with its strange rings of olivine, chrysoprase, and enamels" (96). Clearly, they are hands unaccustomed to the kind of craft work she later promotes to Willie. Her house, too, reflects her high-minded artistic aspirations. For instance, her drawing room eclectically blends Renaissance religious art, impressionist Degas painting, and an Arts and Crafts frieze by Walter Crane: "But with two such works of art, a little fumed oak, and the poems of Emile Vehaeren in a Niger morocco binding, any room, she considered, was adequately furnished" (91). Here Underhill's allusion to the Belgian surrealist poet Vehaeren is no doubt ironic because the book merely symbolizes Elsa's interest in art, seeming more a decorative object than literature she actually reads. Echoing the carver Nicholas's high-minded aspirations about art, Elsa proclaims, "It is [art] which raises us from the market-place, and leads us to the skies" (92). Beauty trumps all, she tries to convince Willie, as she tries to beautify her life in service to that ideal.

Elsa's idealism takes another form in her relationship with Willie, but her efforts to become his ideal lover are similarly satirized. Namely, she sees herself as a kind of Beatrician courtly lady, whom Willie should worship. She would rather not have an ordinary, humdrum relationship with him, preferring instead that he serve as her courtly lover: "She reflected on the superior habits of the middle ages [*sic*], when young men were content to worship at the feet of married beauty without any hope of reward. 'In those days,' she said, 'life was really beautiful. An engagement, I think, is almost indelicate' " (190). Initially, she attempts to idealize their relationship and keep it free of sordid practicalities. That her idealism represents a tantalizing illusion is emphasized through the impression she makes on him when he visits her drawing room. Late in the novel, as Willie and Elsa approach the consummation of their romantic relationship, Willie suddenly recognizes Elsa's artistic idealism within their relationship as an illusion. Nature rescues him from the sexual temptation prompted by Elsa's aesthetic displays—the beclouding curtains, perfumes, and clothing. The sun's rays cut through. He sees plants and trees outside "in a sort of gay revel of perfection which was piety and daintiness in one. It drew his thoughts abruptly to the ordered and exquisite places unsullied by human grime, where life could be beautiful, temperate, ideal" (315). By contrast, Elsa's room is described as "artifice" (315) and Elsa as a character who "was tempted to add artifice to art" (309). At the end of the encounter "her acting broke abruptly" (318), leaving Elsa crestfallen and Willie revolted. She laments, "I thought for a minute that it could have been beautiful; oh, indeed I did. With us, because of the artistry we could have put into it" (318). Here Underhill uses Elsa's character in part to illustrate how egoistically driven artistry can be degraded by artifice and lack of sincerity. As we shall see, Elsa is eventually juxtaposed to the artist and bookbinder Hester Waring, whose art of bookbinding epitomizes the authentic artistry celebrated by Arts and Crafts thinkers.

Elsa is, therefore, the complete antithesis of Mr. Hopkinson. Where he values science, she exalts art; where he prizes practicality, she inhabits a romantic sphere above practical realities. Ultimately, both the unreflective materialism of characters like Mr. Hopkinson and the quixotic idealism of Elsa are satirized and shown to be of limited value, in the father's case because he naïvely rejects the reality of a transcendent world beyond and in Elsa's because she rejects the practical realities of the material world.

The Use and Abuse of Arts and Crafts Ideas

Despite Elsa's imperfections, it is she who first introduces Willie to medieval art and particularly to the renovation of medieval art represented by the Arts and Crafts movement, ideas that become crucial to Willie's spiritual progress and the resolution of the dialectical conflict established between materialism and idealism in the first part of the novel. In that regard, Elsa is a character akin to what Underhill's friend and novelist Arthur Machen called a "Muddy Companion," in a phrase directly invoked in one of the novel's chapter epigraphs (*The Gray World* 304). According to Machen in *Hieroglyphics*, his short book of literary criticism, a "Muddy Companion," in contrast to a "Shadowy" one, is "a being often of exquisite wit and deep understanding but given to evil ways if one does not hold him in check" (Machen 104). As illustrated in the previous section, Elsa's romantic idealism is often misguided and liable to misdirect Willie, but it is also illuminating for him, making her a spiritually ambiguous "daimon" in Willie's life. For instance, when Willie's father proposes an ill-fitting life of factory work to Willie, Elsa intervenes and argues for handicraft instead. Introducing Arts and Crafts work to Willie's father and Willie, she explains, "bookbinding, you know, or jewelry, or metal-work—something of that kind. The creation of really beautiful things, as the medieval craftsmen used to do. That's so very delightful, and all the most cultivated people are taking to it. It's paying, too, I believe. They get enormous prices for these things" (130). Thus redirecting Willie from factory work, she even fancies herself as a figure from Arthurian romance who will rescue Willie from mortal danger, for she "wished to deliver the boy from the dragon which awaited him; seeing herself in the position of a strong-minded princess coming to the rescue of some helpless and neurotic St. George" (127).

Therefore, Willie first encounters Arts and Crafts ideas thanks to Elsa's "heroic" intervention. Like Underhill herself, Willie begins "to read the 'Studio' and the 'Artist,' and to pay secret visits to the National Gallery. From these he returned ill-tempered and disconsolate, tired out by uninstructed efforts to appreciate medieval art," which apparently challenged "his preconceived idea of the beautiful" (*The Gray World* 105). Later in the novel, however, he returns to the National Gallery and his appreciation for medieval art matures, assisted by Elsa's religious attitude toward art (237). Although Elsa is an equivocal figure in the novel, she introduces to him her "dictum that prie-dieux ought to be placed before the masterpieces of devotional art" (237), thereby making a positive impact on his spiritual development through a reverence for art. While Elsa's recommendations for Willie are often worthy ones, they sit comically at odds with her own reception of the Arts and Crafts movement. For she herself is only a consumer of crafts, not a creator. She has no labor to take joy in. And, in contrast to the Arts and Crafts movement's insistence on simplicity, she is complex and full of artifice rather than simple. In the satirizing of Elsa, Underhill highlights the ideals Elsa espouses and preaches but does not practice, characterizing her as a woman "who pointed so persistently the way she did not go" (305).[6] Due to Elsa's prodding, however, Willie begins not only to appreciate art but also to practice an artistic craft. At her prompting, he starts work at a bookbindery, which precipitates the novel's extensive examination of Arts and Crafts ideas.

Here and throughout in the novel, Underhill does not present a monolithic view of the Arts and Crafts movement. Instead, she satirizes distortions of the movement even as she makes its ideals central to the novel's vision of spiritual maturity. Underhill's satire is evident in the reader's first glimpses of the bookbindery. For instance, the bindery does not frankly call itself a bindery for fear of being "too obvious" (136). Instead, the narrator notes, "Above the doorway, a sign swung on wrought-iron hinges. It bore two pierced hearts, and said, in Kelmscott-Gothic characters, 'Atte ye Signe of ye Presse and Ploughe.' Underneath, in case the public might not understand this cryptic phrase, there was added in English type the information, 'Books bound Artistically and Inexpensively.' " (136). The narrator characterizes this door, with its faux medieval text, as "feeble estheticism," akin to the aestheticism satirized earlier in connection to Elsa.

At the bindery, Willie becomes romantically entangled with a young bookbinder, Mildred, who, like Elsa, illustrates how Arts and Crafts ideas can be superficially romanticized and, thereby, misappropriated. Mildred, however, subjugates those ideas not to aestheticism, but to careerism. Mildred is smitten by the Arts and Crafts movement and has developed idealistic aspirations for her life based on the Arts and Crafts ideals she has read about in magazines. As the narrator observes: "She hated gray walls and monotony and the mingled art and commerce of the bindery. She longed to escape to those higher circles of handicraft which are celebrated in the art magazine. . . . Picturesque dress was only possible to her in the best materials. She had two ambitions—to become a member of the Arts and Crafts Society and buy her clothes at Liberty's" (160–61). Like Elsa, Mildred is a romantic, discontented with humdrum life. Unlike the bindery's elder workman, Carter, she seems less interested in the joy of the work and more interested in the romantic life to which it might lead. Mildred is hobbled in her ability to fully enjoy either work or love by her cynical disregard for the ordinary, worldly things that seem vulgar to her. This is as evident in her attitude toward the bookbindery as it is in her attitude toward lovemaking with Willie. No sooner do she and Willie begin to kiss than "[a] sudden loathing of love and its vulgar accessories overcame her. It seemed to her that it was very like bookbinding—full of poetic charm when seen from outside, but made up, for those who chose to investigate its technic, of ordinary, sticky, even unpleasant, materials" (188). In this way, Mildred's romanticism prevents her from being able to see the ordinary things of this world as material that can be made holy through creative work and joyful regard.

Mildred's real intention for pursuing Arts and Crafts work becomes clearer later in the novel in her conversation with the fellow bookbinder Tiddy, who eventually replaces Willie as her romantic partner. Mildred seeks reputation; she wants to be recognized for her work by exhibiting it at the Arts and Crafts exhibition (221), thereby gaining access to other movers and shakers in the art world. Mildred views this as a "practical" attitude (229), but her practicality echoes Mr. Hopkinson's careerism and differs from the kind of practicality Underhill ultimately espouses. Tiddy likewise wants to be impressive, especially before Mildred. To her, "He spoke with vague grandeur of his theories of art, and hopes of their future success" (220). Mildred and Tiddy scorn Carter's traditionalism and seem to want to update the bookbinding business to be "successful" (223). Tiddy claims, "[Y]ou must be arty, and you must be up to date" (223). These sentiments distort the founding fathers of the Arts and Crafts movement, who sought to do something new, but only by integrating their original inspiration with past visions and practices.

Aside from Mildred and Tiddy, however, other aspects of the bookbinding workshop present a positive paradigm for Willie. The "flavor of past ages" about the workshop, which he recognizes as he is jolted back into "a less peaceful century" on the modern tram ride home from work, is exactly what Willie prizes (143). Furthermore, the elderly workman Carter, who is described as the "mainstay of the bindery" (137), serves as exemplar of a more authentic reception of Arts and Crafts ideas. Admittedly, he, too, has become caught up in some of the conventions of the movement; for instance, he wears "the collarless shirts of coarse blue linen which the example of more celebrated craftsmen compelled him to wear" (138). Still, Carter emerges as a wisdom figure, who models for Willie the creative work and authentic investment in craft idealized by the Arts and Crafts movement.

Upon first encountering Carter, Willie is initially unable to perceive the "higher life" Elsa had promised in all the "noise and muddle" of the workshop (138). However, Carter's words and example pierce through the muddle and help him to better understand the value of bookbinding. Willie perceives this wisdom in Carter's attitude toward his craft:

> This was the first happy and honest workman whom he had met—the first who extracted the soul of labor from its outer shell by his attitude of steady reverence toward his craft . . . there was a sincere and beautiful connection between Carter and his work. With him it was a manual religion, faithfully followed without any sordid thought. He felt slovenly work to be a sin toward his material as well as toward the master who paid him. (140)

Here the language of religion cloaks Willie's perception of Carter's work, emphasizing the holy nature of his simple work. Notably, too, Carter is critical of facile aestheticism, either in craft-making or in craft reception: "He hated the showily finished bindings of cheap polished leather and facile tooling which visitors to the bindery thought so very artistic" (140), aiming instead for "good toolin' " and work that's "solid" (142). Although

Mildred and Tiddy dismiss Carter as "a puritan" (179) and too much of a traditionalist, caring more for craft than for art (212), Willie appreciates Carter's devotion to the lifelong process of good craftsmanship, forging a connection with Carter that Underhill characterizes as the "the reaction of homely intuition on convinced idealism" (141). When Willie later describes Carter's loving, honest attitude toward labor, Elsa perceives his attitude as "medieval," for she observes, "He has quite the medieval tone of mind" (144).

Willie's own rationale for choosing bookbinding as his craft relates partly to the pursuit of giving ideas permanence: He "adored books for a permanence of thought which they possessed, and extended his love of literature with odd inconsequence to the leather which dressed it" (135). He inherits from Carter the idea that education in a craft is a lifelong endeavor, not something to be picked up in a few months (139). Most importantly, though, he comes to see the craft of bookbinding as creating a spiritual equilibrium he had long sought; his work in the bindery has the salutary effect of joining soul and body in balance. As the narrator observes: "He learned there for the first time in his life the meaning of his hands, and discovered their use. They gave his soul a new and inexplicable pleasure. Regular manual occupation steadied him, drawing off his earth energies and leaving his spirit clearer. As he sat at the sewing-press, or mechanically pared the edges of leather for the covers of his books, he meditated. *Busy hands and dreaming soul balanced one another, and he felt sane, alive, untrameled* [emphasis mine]" (143). This moment represents a pivotal stage in Willie's spiritual bildungsroman. Insofar as he has been caught between two worlds—matter and spirit—and has long sought to reject the former to fulfill the latter, he discovers that the manual work of craftsmanship enables him to reconcile matter and spirit. In fact, through his work as a craftsman, his view of the material practice of art-making reshapes his view of the material world beyond art. He notices, "The symbolic rightness of the quiet work justified to him the existence of his body, and sometimes allowed him a glimpse of the gateway which leads to the heaven of the industrious" (143). Furthermore, Willie's work in the bindery has the salutary effect not only of repairing the matter-spirit division that has so bedeviled him, but also of changing his mental disposition toward the world at large. The narrator observes, "Since Willie entered the bindery, he had become more patient, less assertive toward existence" (146). This description of Willie's disposition aptly captures the symmetries between artistry and mysticism. To become a true craftsman is to develop habits of mind and hand that restore the soul to right relationship with the world.

Although Willie subsequently experiences a period of additional errantry after his first experiences in the bindery, it is to the practice of bookbinding that he returns at the novel's climax. For, at the end of the novel, he discovers his spiritual ideal in a widowed artist, Hester Waring, who lives as a hermit in the woods and practices the crafts of painting and bookbinding. Willie finds in Hester's life a refined version of Arts and Crafts ideals, not perverted by ambitiousness, conventionality, or social posturing. Even Hester's workshop, nestled in the natural world away from urban life, captures a dimension of the ideal Arts and Crafts life. Cumming and Kaplan explain that for some Arts and Crafts designers, "belief in the restorative power of craftsmanship and the search for a 'simple life' led them to establish workshops in idyllic, rural surroundings where art was promoted as a way of life" (7).

As Willie surveys Hester's attic artist's space, "Willie, one part craftsman, felt his heart going out to those clean, well-tended tools: knives, brushes, size-and color-pots, all disposed with a loving touch which spoke of happy and deliberate labor" (*The Gray World* 334). Hester's advice to Willie aptly articulates key facets of the novel's Arts and Crafts ideals:

> [T]he joyous, significant life is so easy to get! So cheap! It's only to live beautifully, laboriously, and austerely; in the air, with the light and color to remind you of the hidden beauty behind. And to work with your mind, soul, and body . . . You must love everything, don't you see, because everything in the whole world is being offered to you as a symbol of an adorable idea that is beyond. It's only when you've entered into loving alliance with the universe that you are making the most of life. Because flowers and trees live beautifully for you, it's your duty to live beautifully for others. That's the only law. You've got your moment of self-expression, and if you use it for ugliness you will die. (335–36)

Willie ultimately heeds Hester's advice, and, much to the consternation of his family's social circle back home, chooses to spend the rest of his life in the woodland refuge crafting beautiful books and making the divine image real through his knives, brushes, and color pots. In this way, he lives into the ideal of creative work once imagined by Morris, finding pleasure in his work, working on useful products designed and created with integrity, and living in the pleasurable surroundings of the countryside, at one with the natural world. For, as Willie concludes, "*I think the honest artist is very near to God*" (350).

The Soul as Tool Maker: Craft as the Sacramental Reconciliation of Matter and Spirit

Underhill's concluding vision of Willie as craftsman and artist offers important insights about her intellectual and spiritual development and the relationship between her early fiction and her later writings. The novel illuminates her views of art, her early efforts to reconcile the two worlds of matter and spirit through the art of craft-making, and the seeds of her practical spirituality.

Earlier I noted that one of Underhill's biographers, Dana Greene, calls her "the artist of the infinite life" because Underhill imagines the mystic as an artist. To say that she regarded mysticism as analogous to artistry gives us valuable insight, but it takes us only part way toward understanding her thinking about mysticism and art. Her novels do not present a monolithic picture of art or its relationship to spirituality. Instead, she presents a novelized debate about that relationship, as she shifts between satire and idealization, challenging the reader to discern between true and false, authentic and inauthentic art. She is critical of certain kinds of artistry, with the aestheticism in vogue during her era subject to particularly keen derision. Likewise, she highlights the comical ways in which people err in their appropriation of Arts and Crafts ideals when they are driven by egoism, careerism, or otherwise callow consumption of art. Yet, she simultaneously shares Arts and Crafts ideals and draws upon them to forge her own model of spiritual fulfillment.

Of course, many of the key Arts and Crafts leaders were Socialists as well as artists, with a distinctive vision of transforming society through art (Cumming and Kaplan 7). The designer Walter Crane articulated this ideal connection between art and society when he asserted, "[C]laiming for man this primitive and common delight in common things made beautiful, [the Arts and Crafts movement] makes, through art, the great socializer for a common and kindred life, for sympathetic and helpful fellowship, and demands conditions under which your artist and craftsman shall be free" (14). Living that creed, William Morris promoted such ideas through word and action in his vigorous efforts on behalf of the Socialist movement. As the scholar of Victorian literature Clive Wilmer notes about Morris, "Probably aestheticism had never satisfied him. What he wanted was the real world with its prelapsarian glow restored to it . . . It was in his work as a decorative artist that Morris first achieved this blend of the actual and the paradisal" (xxvii).

Underhill clearly shared Morris's dissatisfaction with aestheticism. But she differs from her Victorian forerunners in at least two key ways. First, unlike Morris, who gravitated away from any religious orientation or interest in a world beyond this one, Underhill remained anchored in a transcendent view of the universe, one in which art—even ordinary art—could be a connection to divine Reality.[7] Second, her vision in *The Gray World*, and indeed all of her fiction, was fundamentally individualistic rather than social. As Michael Stoeber observes, "She was not a socio-political activist" (132).[8] Unlike Morris, whose *News from Nowhere* renovates a medieval world view in order to redeem the social order, Underhill represents lost medieval arts as a way of redeeming individual souls: Willie, retreating to the natural world, finds full flourishing by making books in the company of only one other like-minded soul, whereas Paul Vickery in *The Lost Word* spends most of that novel finding spiritual fulfillment through church building with a small coterie of like-minded craftspeople.

Still, Wilmer characterizes Morris in a way that illuminates Underhill's indebtedness to him and others in the Arts and Crafts movement, for Wilmer's characterization of Morris as aiming to "blend . . . the actual and the paradisal" through his decorative art aptly captures the central point of connection between Underhill's novel and the ideas she inherited from Arts and Crafts thinkers. Early in the novel, Willie confesses to Mildred, "I live in two worlds" (172). He is immersed in the "actual," material world, but constantly remembers a transcendent world beyond. Over time, though, Willie's craft enables him to reconcile those two worlds: The material substance of handcrafted books becomes a vehicle for him to experience God (350). In that regard, Willie's bookbinding experiences serve as evidence of Underhill's early sacramental thinking.

Indeed, Underhill explicitly uses sacramental language in discussing the effect of craft-making on Willie's soul. For instance, during his induction to the mysteries of bookbinding, she explains that "Willie, learning slowly—almost unconsciously—to treat his work as a sacrament which bore some mystic relation to truth, lost the constant itch to step from his path and hunt for solutions to the great conundrum. He had an inner content, equally removed from piety and despair, which anesthetized his spirit" (146). Much later he has a similar revelation after meditating upon an Italian painting of the Madonna and Christ child. In response, Willie "had a new vision of the world. He saw it as a shadow cast by divine beauty—a loveliness of which material beauty was the sacrament, the faint image thrown by God on the mirror of sense" (239). And he perceives art as a place where one experiences a "penetration of the visible by the real" (238). No doubt it is significant that Willie experiences this incarnational revelation while viewing a picture of the Madonna and Christ. Art, therefore, becomes the dialectical resolution of Willie's matter-spirit dilemma, a resolution Underhill signifies by quoting Hegel at the head of the chapter where Willie views the Italian painting. "The Beautiful," she quotes, "is essentially the Spiritual making itself known sensuously" (231).

Willie's growing appreciation of material things as sacraments is echoed many years later in Underhill's discussion of the term *sacramental*. In a 1925 letter addressed to W. Y., she counsels one of her spiritual students to adopt a "more sacramental type of religion," pausing thereafter to define *sacramentalism* in a particularly expansive way (Underhill, *Letters* 168). She notes that she does not use sacramentalism to denote just "music, beauty, and liturgy," which she calls the "chocolate-creams of religion" (168). Instead she explains, "By sacramentalism I mean the humble acceptance of grace through the medium of *things*—God coming into our souls by means of humblest accidents—the intermingling of spirit and sense. This is the corrective—one of the correctives—needed by your tendency to 'loftiness' " (Underhill, *Letters* 168). This view of sacramentalism, offered almost twenty years after the publication of her first novel, is prefigured in the story of Willie's journey from the lofty heights of ghostly experience in the gray world to the humble level of a bookbinder's work.

To suggest that the seeds of Underhill's sacramental thinking were sown in the early 1900s in response to her Arts and Crafts work runs counter to the typical narrative offered about her spiritual development. In Todd Johnson's "Evelyn Underhill Primer," a review of her life and work, Johnson recounts how her spiritual mentor in the early 1920s, Baron Friedrich von Hügel, tried, at first unsuccessfully, to draw her to a sacramental theology: "Where von Hügel could ground his sacramentality in the incarnation of Christ, Underhill's avoidance of the preexistence of the Word left her no mooring for a sacramental principle. Underhill had yet to complete her theology" (408). In his review, Johnson pays scant attention to her fiction and makes no mention of her intercourse with the Arts and Crafts movement.[9] Like Johnson, John R. Francis describes her spiritual development as a "movement from . . . Neoplatonism toward an incarnational and sacramental life . . . " (283–84), with Neoplatonism defining the decade during which she wrote fiction and with sacramentalism emerging much later in her career. Based on his assessment of her fiction between 1902 to 1905, he describes her spirituality in this early stage as "esoteric, spiritistic, and neoplatonic," suggesting that her Christian journey does not begin until 1907 (285), three years after the publication of *The Gray World*. Like Johnson and other interpreters of Underhill's career, Francis attributes Underhill's sacramental shift to her work on Jacopone da Todi in 1918 and to the mentorship of von Hügel (284). These accounts have become standard for scholars charting the trajectory of Underhill's spiritual development.[10]

Certainly, there is ample evidence in the correspondence between Underhill and von Hügel of his attempts to attract her to a "more incarnational, Christocentric, and sacramental spirituality" (Kripal 83). And there is no question that her early thinking is marked by Neoplatonism as much as by other philosophical and theological inspirations. However, Jeffrey Kripal raises a crucial question about her theological shift when he wonders, "But perhaps such a 'descent' from the mystical heights, cats and all, was there all along in Underhill's person and writing" (83). For Kripal, whose analysis focuses on Underhill's conception of mystical love, it is her ordinary marriage with Hubert that prompts this question and suggests an earlier rootedness in sacramental theology. For Michael Stoeber, it is her early interests in Hermeticism and magic that "play a significant role in the developments of her mystical and sacramental theologies" (135). I argue, however, that there are traces of her sacramental theology in her earliest novel in her presentation of art as mediated by the Arts and Crafts movement, for there she imaginatively explores how the practical things of this world can serve as vehicles for experiencing the Divine. In that regard, Armstrong is right to identify Underhill's life process as one of "progressive incarnation" (xv), and he even concedes, "Not that the incarnational and sacrificial idea is not present from near the beginning: it is, and strongly" (xv). Indeed, it is there in her early fiction, catalyzed by the Arts and Crafts movement.

However, an understanding of the Arts and Crafts movement as a shaping influence illuminates far more than the development of Underhill's sacramental theology; it also sheds light on the distinctively practical nature of her spirituality.[11] Much has rightly been made about Underhill's "practical mysticism." This practicality must have derived in part from her temperament. But I would suggest that Underhill's contact with the Arts and Crafts movement, with its emphasis on creative, useful work, significantly shaped the practical orientation of her mysticism. That practical emphasis remained with Underhill throughout her career. It is obvious in the denouement of *The Gray World* as well as in her other novels. In *The Lost Word*, Paul Vickery substitutes devotion to domestic marriage for life as an architect at the end of his quest, and in *The Column of Dust*, Constance ultimately abandons occult experimentation and sacrifices her life for her dirty, messy daughter, Vera. Underhill's practicality emerges even more explicitly in her 1914 book *Practical Mysticism*, a how-to guide in which she aims to "suggest the practical conditions under which ordinary persons may participate in [the mystics'] experience" (16). And years later, her practical orientation is evident in the counsel she offers to her spiritual followers. For instance, in a letter written on May 5, 1930, Underhill advises her correspondent to "be a tool" for God and to pray primarily "to be *useful* to Him first and always" rather than to "*see* Him" (*Letters* 188). Given the many instances of such advice in Underhill's writing, it is not surprising that, of all the characteristics Annice Callahan enumerates to define Underhill's spirituality, she lists first practicality: "meeting God in daily life: seeing the spiritual in the practical" (230).

Not all readers have recognized this strong practical dimension. For instance, in Nadia Delicata's analysis of Underhill's concept of holiness, Delicata suggests that Underhill privileged "intellectual prowess" as a path to holiness, leading her "to neglect other channels to holiness—her feelings, her intuition, her body, and the people whom she encountered" (521).[12] No doubt Underhill's novel *The Gray World* illustrates her character Willie "trying on" different intellectual paths to holiness and often finding fragments rather than wholeness or holiness. However, as Underhill's "growing-up" story about that mystically inclined bookbinder illustrates, holiness comes as much through the practical work of one's hands as through the mental gymnastics of the mind. Ultimately, I would suggest that Underhill's love of the bookbinding craft, which she inherited from medieval tradition and bequeathed to her protagonist and alter ego Willie, kept returning her from intellectual rejection of the material world, opening a path toward the reconciliation of worlds once perceived as opposed. If, then, as Underhill came to claim, God comes to us a toolmaker, ready with his work clothes and tools, she even earlier envisioned the soul as craftsman—a craftsman who experienced God through the homely tools of everyday trade, uniting matter and spirit, life and art, the heavenly world and the human one.[13]

Chapter 4

Grail Prosaics as a Mode of Mystical Fiction

Arthur Machen's *A Fragment of Life*

> Oh, a mystic, someone may say dismissingly. Yes, but his mysticism was no escapism, but a transmutation.
>
> —Norah Hoult, *Arthur Machen: A Farewell* (qtd. in Valentine and Dobson 53)

"I will write a 'Robinson Crusoe' of the soul," Arthur Machen observed, in recollecting the composition of his now-famous novel *The Hill of Dreams* (Danielson 39). That statement, merging as it does a literary endeavor that is both material and spiritual, quotidian and metaphysical, aptly captures the complex and contrasting strands within Machen's literature. For, the literary work of Arthur Machen (1863 to 1947) is a study in surprising contrasts. His novel *The Great God Pan* was tweeted by Stephen King in 2024 to be one of the two best horror stories ever written (@StephenKing). His many other stories from the 1890s are often categorized as occult, Gothic, or weird fiction. He joined his dear friend A. E. Waite in an occult society, the Hermetic Order of the Golden Dawn, in 1899. And, in the years leading up to that initiation, he worked at cataloging and annotating a wide variety of occult literature in the Catherine Street garret of a secondhand bookseller and publisher—all strong evidence of his affiliation with the world of the occult.

Yet, this same writer is known to have regarded occult practices and activities as so much stuff and nonsense, or, as he put it, "rubbish, not worth a moment's consideration" (*Things* 17). He maintained lifelong loyalty to the Christian faith of his father, a Welsh Anglo-Catholic rector. And he even asserted that one must be at least "subconsciously . . . Catholic" in order to write literature (*Hieroglyphics* 163). Despite these and other religious avowals, his explorations of the occult and demonic have loomed largest in the popular imagination. As Mark Valentine observes, "The lurid early horror stories have probably stopped his later, more spiritually-charged work, such as *A Fragment of Life* and *The Secret Glory*, from receiving appropriate attention from students of mysticism" (136).

Consequently, Machen's position within the world of occult literature has had extensive scholarly attention. In *Talking to the Gods: Occultism in the Work of W. B. Yeats, Arthur Machen, Algernon Blackwood, and Dion Fortune*, Susan Graf, for instance, positions Arthur Machen's work within the context of occultism, though she acknowledges that "[a]n interest in the Holy Graal and the Celtic Church replaced occultism of the 1890s," noting that "[f]or most of his life, Machen was a High Church Anglican" (78). Glen Cavaliero's analysis of Machen's fiction emphasizes his earlier, "preternaturalist horror" fiction in noting how his early fiction "crudely" but "effectively" explores the "eruption of pagan occult forces in contemporary society" (*Supernatural* 72), though Cavaliero concludes that "his best work exhibits a refreshing delight in substantial things, not only landscape and weather but also food and drink . . . presenting a view of the world that is basically Christian and sacramental" (*Supernatural* 79). More recently, Alison Milbank has examined Machen's use of terror within the context of spiritual Gothic fiction, illustrating how "horror and the abject are theurgically raised to holiness by a mode of mystical Gothic" (9). This attention to Machen's horror and Gothic writing has led Nicholas Freeman to concur that "Machen's spiritual writings have been largely overlooked by academic commentators who have preferred to concentrate on his Gothic fiction or, latterly, his treatment of urban life" (243). In Freeman's assessment, "Machen occupies an uncertain position in the religious literature and culture of the early 20th century, being a radical yet traditional Anglo-Catholic" (243).

Indeed, the strong traditionalist currents within Machen's life and work suggest that he was neither opposed to orthodox Christianity nor, by his own lights, an occultist.[1] His admiring American contemporary Vincent Starrett identified him as an Anglo-Catholic theologian and medievalist, boldly proclaiming in his 1924 preface to *The Glorious Mystery*, a collection of Machen's work, "In the history of religion, I believe no more arresting and challenging theological work has appeared than the present volume, in which a great mediaevalist, still living, sets forth his quest of the Graal, and finds a symbol of that sacred vessel in less holy cups; in which a High Church theologian of the first importance triumphantly asserts and perhaps proves his conviction that Protestantism is a revolt against Christianity and the industrial blight and a curse on civilization" (Starrett "Foreword"). In that same vein, H. P. Lovecraft, notwithstanding his regard for Machen's "powerful horror-material," highlighted both the medievalism and Catholicism that mark Machen's thought: "He has absorbed the mediaeval mystery of dark woods and ancient customs, and is a champion of the Middle Ages in all things—including the Catholic faith" (88). Yet, in 1924, the reviewer R. Ellis Roberts noted that "our brethren of Rome make more than the most of such novelists as Hugh Benson . . . but Mr. Machen, who has never made any secret of his devotion to British Catholicism, has been as neglected by church-people as was Mr. Chesterton" (353). Only in the last few decades have the Christian religious dimensions of Machen's writing been pursued in a more extensive way by Charles Coloumbe, Geoffrey Reiter, and others.

In Machen's fiction, however, his religiosity manifests itself particularly through the exploration of mystical experience. Reiter has recently gone so far as to claim that "[i]f there is one thing all scholars of Arthur Machen can agree on, it is that he was, at least in some manner, a mystic" ("Through" 225). Although the borderland is fuzzy between Machen's early and late work, Machen's literature takes a turn from horror fiction to mystical literature, or from what one of his biographers calls "sorcery to sanctity" at the turn of the twentieth century. In Valentine's words, "The philosophical Ambrose seems to return in the guise of 'the Hermit' in Machen's next book, *Hieroglyphics*: and his later fiction all aspires to convey sanctity, not sorcery" (63). This pivot is important not only for what it signifies about the course of Machen's own career, but also for what it reflects about the Edwardian literary movement of which he was a part. Though Machen's mystical inclinations seem to have arisen from a profound personal experience in 1899, he participated in and contributed to a *zeitgeist*—what Reynolds calls the Edwardian-era "heyday" of the mystical revival (17), for, Machen's religious sensibility and mystical novels show a kinship with other writers within the Edwardian mystical revival, including R. H. Benson and Machen's friends A. E. Waite and Evelyn Underhill. The kinship Machen shares with Underhill, as well as with the poet and novelist Charles Williams, is the subject of a short section in Alison Milbank's 2018 book, *God and the Gothic.* Therein, Milbank argues that all draw upon the Gothic tradition as a way of "narrat[ing] descents into the material and the abject to raise it to full participation in a transcendent reality" and to "give convincing accounts of hidden levels of spiritual reality" (270). Milbank is certainly right to see these writers as participating in a common movement and sharing a tradition. I argue, however, that the family resemblance they share is not limited to experiments in the Gothic tradition because their novelistic experiments are more variegated, especially in their use of medievalism. For this reason, I believe that the term *mystical novel* rather than *spiritual Gothic* or *mystical Gothic* is a more inclusive and capacious way of categorizing the kind of fiction about mysticism that Machen and his peers sought to write during the Edwardian era and that evolved from the Victorian-style mystical novels MacDonald popularized and Waite imitated.[2]

The chapter to follow will explore how Machen participated in an Edwardian movement, shared by friends, colleagues, and peers, that was both medieval and modern, an experiment with the novel of literary realism as a way of representing mystical experience for the middlebrow reader. By hybridizing medieval mythology and literary realism, as he does in *A Fragment of Life*, Machen developed a novelistic mode that carved space for profound spiritual experience within the prosaic world of the novel of literary realism, reflecting his distinctive approach to aligning mysticism with the Christian sacramental tradition and, like Waite, distinguishing it from popular understandings of *the Occult.*

Arthur Machen and the Company He Kept

If manuscripts, books, art, and crafts were Evelyn Underhill's entrée to the Middle Ages and its mystical traditions, the Welsh landscape initially served that end for Arthur Machen. Machen's religious and spiritual orientation was set from his earliest days. It has often been noted that Machen was the son of Welsh priests and scholars; this religious, spiritual, and intellectual tradition was one he himself frequently alluded to in his essays and autobiographical writing. Growing up in Wales, Machen also absorbed the sensuous impressions of the Welsh landscape and the land's Celtic mythology, both of which intertwined and imprinted themselves on his memory (Valentine 9). Machen recounts being "convinced that anything which I may have accomplished in literature is due to the fact that when my eyes were first opened in earliest childhood they had before them the vision of an enchanted land. As soon as I saw anything I saw Twyn Barlwm, that mystic tumulus, the memorial of peoples that dwelt in that region before the Celts left the Land of Summer" (*Far Off* 8–9). This homage to the Welsh landscape and countryside reflects how "he was deeply steeped in Welsh hagiography, history and legend," though Valentine believes that "his revitalising of the images and motifs of these ancient national sources, especially in the Grail novels and essays, has not been properly recognised" (138).

Upon moving to London to make a living, Machen fell into working for the publisher and secondhand bookseller George Redway, assigned to sort and write about the occult literature increasingly popular in the second half of the nineteenth century. Machen's assignment in the summer of 1885 was to "compile a 48-page catalogue of *The Literature of Archaeology and the Occult*" (Gilbert, *Magician* 77). In later recalling this work at Redway's, Machen mocked many of bizarre texts and outré genres he encountered while according others only the status of curiosities, as when he urged readers, "Dip then, and read and wander in the Kabbala; but do not become a Kabbalist" (*Things* 23). In his reflections on such occult literature, he playfully imagines the possibility of an Aryan Kabbalah and pokes fun at the idea that so much "nonsense" could arise from time spent in cramped rooms full of dusty occult books (24–25). In 1887, he further lampooned this library by publishing a sixteen-page pamphlet advertising the library through parody of the famous library episode in Cervantes's *Don Quixote*.

Nonetheless, he himself joined the now-famous Hermetic Order of the Golden Dawn in November of 1899, hoping that it would give him "light and guidance" following the painful and profound events he experienced in 1899, but it "shed no ray of any kind upon my path" (*Things* 154), and he judged that the "society as a society was pure foolishness concerned with impotent and imbecile Abracadabras" (*Things* 152). Given those impressions, it is not surprising that his membership lasted little longer than twelve months (Gilbert, *Magician* 67). Yet, even though Machen's view of occultism was consistently skeptical, he drew broadly upon his knowledge of occult practices in the literature he wrote during the 1890s. This growing knowledge resulted in works such as *The Great God Pan* (1894), "Novel of the White Powder" (published in 1895 within

The Three Imposters) and "The White People" (written in 1899, but published in 1904), all of which have become cult classics within the literature of the occult.

It was, however, the difficult, life-changing loss of his first wife that seems to have redirected Machen's literary career. His first wife, Amy (Hogg), died in July of 1899 after just over a decade of marriage and months of decline from cancer. Machen recounted that he had fallen into a state of desolation following her death, leading him during that time to engage in a certain process to assuage his pain. The "process" to which he alludes is unclear, and different interpreters have suggested everything from drugs or occult practices to self-hypnosis and prayer. Machen's language is oblique, for he refers only to making "my experiment, expecting, very doubtfully, almost incredulously, certain results" (*Things* 134). The consequence was a total rearrangement of his sense of reality, and a "peace of the spirit that was quite ineffable, a knowledge that all hurts and doles and wounds were healed, that that which was broken was reunited. Everything, of body and of mind, was resolved into an infinite and an exquisite delight; into a joy so great that—let this be duly noted—it became almost intolerable in its ecstasy. I remember thinking at the time: 'There is wine so strong that no earthly vessels can hold it' " (137). Valentine interprets Machen's account as an almost classic description of "mystical experience," noting how its characteristics align with Happold's description of mysticism (drawn from William James) in his classic 1963 anthology *Mysticism* (72). This experience marked the beginning of a turn toward authoring novels and essays devoted to a different form of ecstatic experience—not the shock and awe of horror fiction but the awe and wonder that came to define his understanding of mystical experience.

Machen's first wife, Amy, played another significant role in his engagement with the Edwardian-era mystical revival, for it was she who introduced him to A. E. Waite in 1887, the year of Machen's marriage to Amy (Gilbert, *Magician* 60; Valentine 36). As a result of that momentous meeting, Machen and Waite developed a rich, lifelong friendship, during which their life, work, and intellectual interests came to intersect in many ways. They interacted through the Hermetic Order of the Golden Dawn, and Machen later joined Waite's Independent and Rectified Rite of the Golden Dawn, "an offshoot of the original order, having an emphasis on mystical Christianity" (Graf 62). During these years, each published the other's work, Waite as the editor of *Horlick's Magazine* and the *Unknown World* (Gilbert, *Magician* 64) and Machen as the de facto editor of *Walford's Antiquarian Magazine* (Gilbert, *Magician* 28; Sweetser 25). Waite was particularly instrumental in bringing Machen's work into print. *The Hill of Dreams*, for instance, was repeatedly rejected by other publishers and first appeared in serial form in *Horlick's Magazine*, from July to December 1904 (Valentine 57). Not only did Waite and Machen publish each other's work, but Machen and he also collaborated on a mystery play, "The Hidden Sacrament of the Holy Graal," published in Waite's *Strange Houses of Sleep* in 1906 (Gilbert, *Magician* 74–75). Wood observes, "Machen's enthusiasm for the Grail and its meaning was shared by his friend and onetime associate A. E. Waite. Like many of the intellectuals, artists and writers interested in occultism at the time, Machen and Waite sought to counter the growing secular materialism in modern life with a revival of mystical and spiritual values" (80). While he and Waite differed on many topics and had nuances of difference in their understanding of mysticism and the origin and nature of the Holy Grail, both gravitated toward a sacramental understanding of mysticism and a sense of its opposition to popular occultism. For, they also "shared a mutual interest, though a mutual disbelief, in occultism" (Sweetser 25). These common interests were often the subject of the many letters Machen and Waite exchanged over the course of their long friendship. After fifty years of friendship, Waite recalled, "[W]e were friends and great intimates from the beginning" (*Shadows* 106), and when Waite died in 1942, Machen wrote of his loss to Oliver Stonor: "To lose Waite is for me to lose a considerable part of life," even though they were "utterly at variance on fundamental things, and yet with a strong underlying sympathy" (qtd. in Gilbert, *Magician* 61).

When Machen joined Waite's Independent and Rectified Rite, he also met fellow member Evelyn Underhill, who had joined in 1903 (Greene 17), and they knew each other "fairly well" by 1904 (Armstrong 33). She and he, along with Waite, shared an interest in magic and mysticism as well as a love for writers such as John Ruskin and Coventry Patmore (Machen *Things* 97). Over the next decade, Machen and his second wife, Dorothie (Purefoy), a Bensonian actress he married in 1903, deepened their friendship with Underhill in ways that were manifested both in Underhill's writing and in Machen's. A 1904 letter from Underhill to her husband records her request that he send "proofs" back to Machen (qtd. in Armstrong 33). In fact, some passages in Underhill's celebrated 1911 *Mysticism* may owe a close debt to passages from Machen's work (Valentine 136). For instance, Wesley Sweetser notes that the main character in

The Secret Glory demonstrates the five stages of the mystic way, described in fictional form prior to the publication of the first edition of *Mysticism* (83). *Mysticism* was a book that Sweetser claims Machen may have "edited unofficially" (64), and in a review essay Machen claimed that it "will always be essential to the student of mystic thought" ("Middle Ages" 708). Machen was apparently less enthusiastic about Underhill's fiction, confiding to Colin Summerford that her 1909 novel *Column of Dust* was "not very good" (*Selected Letters* 93), though the novel bears the mark of their friendship, for Underhill dedicated it to Arthur and Purefoy Machen as "friendship's offering."

While Machen shared with Waite, Underhill, and R. H. Benson a personal mystical experience and an inclination to conceive of mysticism as distinct from occultism, Machen was more self-consciously literary than Benson, who wrote little about the art of novel writing, or Waite and Underhill, who subordinated novel writing to the writing of nonfiction essays and books. Indeed, Machen had strong opinions about the art of the novel. At the time he was conceiving of his first mystical novel, *A Fragment of Life*, he was simultaneously writing a manifesto about what literature can and should do. That manifesto, *Hieroglyphics: A Note upon Ecstasy in Literature*, outlines the assumptions that underlie his experiment in mystical fiction. It is a literary theory that captures what his friend Morchard Bishop saw as Machen's quiddity, "From his earliest years, he had been in love with the splendour and the mystery of ordinary human life, with its miraculous beauty, the sacramental wonder of the world that we inhabit. . . . To a man so constituted, boredom, cynicism, indifferentism were impossibilities. He lived his mortal years in a rapture of thanksgiving which, when one considers the worldly hardships, the cruel disappointments, that he encountered, is in itself sufficiently a miracle" (v). It was a life lived with a sense of the ecstasy potentially evoked by everyday existence, and he believed that good literature should conjure experience of that character.

Hieroglyphics: The Letter of Literature as Sacrament

In a 1937 BBC interview, Machen crystallized some of his key views about literature. The best literature, he asserts, ought not to recreate characters whom we can meet in everyday life, but to create characters like Sancho Panza, Don Quixote, and King Arthur who have been hitherto "unmet" and "unseen" in ordinary life. This view is one he elaborates on in a more nuanced way in *Hieroglyphics*, a work of literary theory and criticism that Machen playfully represents as the literary views of an old hermit, as recorded by the book's narrator.[3] Through the lens of this "hermit," he skewers Thackeray as "nothing but a photographer" (41) who never "realised the mystery of things" (42). He scorns the work of authors like George Eliot, whom he perceives of as drudges (58). And he lionizes the work of Dickens and Cervantes (*passim*). Literature is not good, he has his hermit opine, because it is mimetic, structurally deft, or possessed of stylistic grace. Rather, fine literature is good because of how it enables readers to stand outside of common life and, thereby, to see common life transmuted into something rich, strange, and wonderful.

Central to the hermit's argument is his claim that "ecstasy" is the defining feature of good literature (18). He asserts, "If ecstasy be present . . . there is fine literature; if it be absent, then, in spite of all the cleverness, all the talents, all the workmanship and observation and dexterity you may show me . . . we have a product (possibly a very interesting one) which is not fine literature" (18). Illustrating how much he and George Eliot espouse opposite views of literature, he instances her fiction as the kind of art that focuses readers only on millstones and, by contrast, Cervantes's *Don Quixote* as art that leads one out of the material and to the mystery beyond. He says, "read a chapter of *Don Quixote*; you will not be aware of the existence of the mile-stones, since your gaze is fixed on the mystery of the woods, and you are a pilgrim to the blissful shrine beyond" (162). "Ecstatic literature" thereby envisages both the human and the universe with an eye to their transcendent potential. Criticizing literature such as George Eliot's as a literature *manque*, he asserts that "when we find not only the consciousness but also the subconsciousness permeated by the impression that man is a logical, 'rationalistic' creature and nothing more, when the total impression of the human being gathered from the book is of a simply demonstrating and demonstrable animal; then we may be perfectly assured that we have not to deal with literature" (161). In Eliot's literature, according to Machen, material things are nothing more than material things. What one sees on the surface of things is all there is, resulting in a materialist worldview that reduces the metaphysical potential within both the story and the world it represents.

In developing this theory of fine literature, Machen boldly and unabashedly connects ecstatic literature to the Catholic imagination—by which he means a sacramental imagination. He claims, "It is the subconsciousness . . . alone that matters; and (to put it again theologically) you will find that books which are not literature proceed from ignorance of the Sacramental System. Thackeray was an unconscious heretic, while George Eliot was a conscious one, but each was ignorant of the meaning of Sacramentalism" (161), and from each, he thought, we gain a life that "is substantially the same, and entirely false" (162). He elaborates further on what he means by the Catholic imagination in suggesting that "from the literary standpoint, Catholic dogma is merely the witness, under a special symbolism, of the enduring facts of human nature and the universe; it is merely the voice which tells us distinctly that man is *not* the creature of the drawing room and the Stock Exchange, but a lonely awful soul confronted by the Source of all Souls, and you will realise that to make literature it is necessary to be, at all events subconsciously, Catholic" (162–63). In a different fashion, he dismisses as profoundly "melancholy" "the book which has the body of fine literature without the soul, which uses literary methods without understanding" (164). The letter of literature is not mere etchings in stone. For Machen, it is a hieroglyph, visible and tangible as a material mode of communication, but also significant for the hidden glory it can make manifest.

When Machen came to write his own fiction, he, unlike his dear friend and colleague Waite, whose fiction imitated Victorian fairy stories, but like Underhill, Benson, and Williams, gravitated toward fiction set within the context of literary realism. This remained true whether Machen was writing horror stories or mystical fiction. In early works like *The Great God Pan* and *The Hill of Dreams* as well as *A Fragment of Life*, *The Great Return*, and *The Secret Glory*, Machen's settings and people are recognizable from his attention to the ordinary details of the human and natural world. At first glance, such a propensity may seem strange for the man who wrote so derisively about Eliot and other writers within the tradition of literary realism. But a book must have "accident as well as essence" (65), he concedes in *Hieroglyphics*, using the language of medieval scholastic theology. Further, Machen's literary realism enables him both to critique a materialist worldview and to encourage a revision of the ordinary in light of his perception of how the natural world can be shot through with intimations of a transcendent world beyond. For him, the literary world and the ordinary world are chock full of hieroglyphs, hidden in plain view and poised to translate perceptive "readers" of literature and life to a glorious mystery beyond.

Sancho Panza Meets Suburbia: Satire and the "Bliss" of Prosaic Life

Mark Valentine has drawn attention to the presence of "hieroglyphics" elsewhere in Machen's writing, noting that "[t]he metaphor of the hieroglyphic, used as a sigil signifying the high and hidden nature of everyday things, of even the most mundane lives, recurs in Machen's . . . *A Fragment of Life*" (67). This short novel stands as a pivotal work in Machen's oeuvre because it was begun during the year of his wife's death and his subsequent mystical experience; as Sweetser notes, "[t]he element of mysticism enters his work extensively after 1899" (131). It signals Machen's shift from writing about occultism to writing about mystical experience, and it was published concurrently with Underhill's first mystical novel, *The Gray World*. In S. T. Joshi's view, it is the novel that "captures the essence of Machen's whole worldview" (27).

The first section of Machen's *Fragment of Life* was written in June of 1899, but a completed version did not come into print till 1904, when it was serialized in *Horlick's Magazine* under A. E. Waite's editorship. Machen later came to view this early version of the novel as having a "false ending" (Sweetser 28; *Arthur Machen Selected Letters* 227). A final, significantly rewritten version of the novel appeared in a collection of Machen stories called *The House of Souls*, published by Grant Richards Publishing in 1906, and then finally as an independent whole in 1928 by Martin Secker Publishing.[4]

Machen linked *A Fragment of Life* to an earlier story, "The Resurrection of the Dead," which he had published in a weekly paper (Danielson 35). But the idea for the novel apparently arose in March of 1899, during his first wife's final months, as he was out walking on a "bleak" March Sunday. Machen recalls that the origins of the story came from passing by a monotonous row of houses, architecturally similar and all set for Sunday tea. He saw then, ascending the tram

> [a] colourless, mildly whiskered man, and a foolish-looking young woman, his wife, in her foolish black satin Sunday dress, holding the simple baby on her knee, and I thought, glancing at them: 'These, silly as they look, limited as they doubtless are, these two also have been initiated in the ever-lasting mysteries and have partaken of the great secrets, and have known

> what is concealed under the barley in the sacred basket of the holy procession of Eleusis.' That, then—Sunday tea-tables and Sunday people—was the fount of what became 'A Fragment of Life': the formless impression which comes before any plot or designed succession of circumstances. (Danielson 35)

As Machen reflects on the family's humdrum lives, he uses surprising analogues to the bread and wine of the Christian Eucharist—in this case, barley and tea—to represent the sacramental mystery hidden within ordinary life. They are "Sunday people" in a double sense: In one sense, by being wedded to the deadening customs of conventional Sunday routines, but in another sense, by having access through the homely vehicles of barley and tea to the resurrecting presence of divine grace. As Machen's recollection shifts from satire to wonderment through the antique and defamiliarizing language of pagan ritual, he pushes himself to see the deeper mystery of their existence. Machen's fascination with the mystery hidden within ordinary life is not unique to *A Fragment of Life*, for it was evident even in a poem, "Eleusinia," that he wrote as a seventeen-year-old. In "Beneath the Barley," his note about the origins of that poem, he explained, "I chose the mysteries first and I chose them last: seeking always that secret which is hidden beneath the barley—to use the phrase of Eleusis—the one secret which is concealed beneath the various assemblage of sensible appearances" ("Eleusinia" n.p.).

In the novel *A Fragment of Life*, both the "barley and tea" and the transcendent mystery are equally evident. In that work, Machen experiments with juxtaposing two starkly different ways of experiencing the world, the one indebted to a Robinson Crusoe-esque preoccupation with "sensible appearances," the material minutia of everyday life, and the other drawn from the medieval mythic imagination and aimed at re-baptizing the reader's vision of everyday things. Though Machen's characters are figures drawn from ordinary life, their story seems to suggest, to borrow a mythic lens Machen frequently invoked, that Sancho Panza's propensity to tread the earth is insufficient and needs Quixote's visionary eye to fully animate life.[5] In the first two sections of the novella, Edward Darnell and his wife, Mary, have a Sancho Panza-like existence, spending much of their time together discussing practical matters, such as how to use the hundred pounds they receive as a gift from Mary's aunt, who has been enriched by her marriage to a coal merchant. After allotting the lion's share to investment in government securities, they deliberate endlessly about using the remaining ten to decorate a spare room in their house and possibly purchase a new stove—ironically named the Bliss (149, 167). Machen's satire on their obsessive attention to allocating ten pounds becomes clear, for their deliberations "gave rise to legends and discourses as interminable as the disputes of the schools" (149). Even at this early moment, Machen hints at an ironic contrast between the medieval theological disputes of old and the length and gravity of the discourse accorded even to this mundane domestic concern.

Machen's narrative in these two sections is marked by a laborious exercise in mimesis, chronicling the couple's most trivial and insignificant vexings about material comforts. Some of Edward's reflections about his interior-decorating dilemmas recall similar scenes of misguided attention in Tolstoy's 1886 novella *The Death of Ivan Ilych*. Even Edward's relationship with Mary, close as it is, betrays some elements of the Tolstoyan "comme il faut," for, section one both opens and closes with the repetition of Edward kissing his wife "seriously and dutifully" (148, 170), though as the first section closes, Edward perceives in Mary's eyes, something more, something beyond (170).

In addition to the unduly decorous nature of the couple's relationship, Edward's distraction by things qua things is represented as a kind of living death. Describing Edward's dreary existence, Machen writes:

> So, day after day, he lived in the grey phantasmal world, akin to death, that has, somehow, with most of us, made good its claim to be called life . . . so went forth Darnell, day by day, strangely mistaking death for life, madness for sanity, and purposeless and wandering phantoms for true beings. He was sincerely of opinion [*sic*] that he was a City clerk, living in Shepherd's Bush—having forgotten the mysteries and the far-shining glories of the kingdom which was his by legitimate inheritance. (170)

Even as the reader is enticed into the familiar world of novelistic realism, with its married couple, its conventional conversations about financial matters and family members, the novel early on strikes an Augustinian note, with "death in life" recalling the opening of Augustine's *Confessions*. On the novel's first page, when Edward awakens from a dream, distant in place and time, he awakens to the "varnish of the new furniture," with the varnish implying something superficial, the mere surface of things, and the fleeting detail of "his wife's place vacant" hinting at an emptiness in their domestic space (148).

Machen becomes even more explicit about the deadness of Edward's world in turning from their suburban home to Edward's urban work as a clerk. For ten years, his work life had consisted of "the routine of the City, the counting of coupons, and all the mechanical drudgery" (148). London itself seems condemned to death in life as section three opens with a view of urban London as a toxic and suffocating milieu: "The foot passengers struggled wearily along the pavements, and the reek of the summer's end mingled with the breath of the brick-fields made Darnell gasp, as if he were inhaling the poison of some foul sick-room" (170). Insofar as London seems a kind of sick room, Machen's presentation of it mirrors the searing urban critiques of Dickens, one of Machen's favorite writers. As with novels like *Oliver Twist*, *Great Expectations*, and *Bleak House*, Machen emphasizes the city's mechanization, emptiness, and deadening effects. Edward Darnell is not initially cognizant of being unhappy, but this living death is the reality to which he is wedded.

However, unlike Dickens's Wemmick, whose work life in the city is banal and routinized but whose suburban homelife is full of wonder and joy, Edward's and Mary's marriage, while not portrayed as explicitly unhappy, bears marks of the same mechanization and mundanity. Their relationship seems one of "placid affection" rather than laughter, joy, or shared passion (162). They talk frequently, but mostly of getting and spending and decorating; as the narrator notes, they "got on excellently, rarely sitting silent for more than an hour" (148), yet their initial conversations repeatedly recur to the gift money and the "unseemly emptiness of the spare room" in their house (149). Ironically, the more they try to fix the emptiness of the room, the more they are shown to be trying to "fix" an empty existence with money and more furnishings.

Edward's friend Wilson exemplifies in an even more exaggerated fashion the reductively materialist views Edward and his wife share. Seeking advice about "the laying out of money to the very best advantage" (150), Edward visits his friend Wilson's house and garden, finding Wilson's talk to be all about a new door opening he considers clever and the gardening suit he sports. However, the unnaturalness of Wilson's preoccupations becomes clear through the narrator's description of his gardening clothes: "The jacket hung about his body like a sack, the knickerbockers drooped lamentably over his calves, and in prominent positions the bloom of the heather seemed about to fade and disappear"

(151). Here, the fading heather offers a first intimation that Wilson's world is one of degeneration rather than growth and life. The friend's garden itself, which Edward tours, reflects order and control but not growth or abundance of life: "There were hardly any blossoms, but everything was neatly arranged" and Wilson showed "a rigid row of stunted plants" (151), though he proudly recounts their names. Edward's thoughts seem to wander in the direction of "vague recollections . . . of an old, wild garden" (152), as if to emphasize how this suburban garden has fallen away from the archetypal garden of perfection, mythic Eden.

Wilson's children at play in the garden further foregrounds the fallen state of the family's temporal garden in relation to the mythic garden of Eden from biblical tradition. Wilson admires his children for "playing at being Gawd" on a small piece of turf at the back of the house, but this admiration is misplaced according to Machen's world view, for their "play" is more political than it is religious, characterized by an ordering sensibility, not a numinous one (152). The eldest child Havelock plays at sending the other children "to the bad place" (152), leading Wilson to remark, with pride, that the Sunday-school "think[s] a lot of" his child (152). The Sunday-school's view, however, is quite contrary to Machen's. For, the child's understanding of religion as being about political and moral order rather than wonder or awe is one Machen satirized in works such as *Dr. Stiggins* (58–90). Therein, Puritanism and Protestantism were subject to particularly lacerating satire because, as Sweetser explains, "they were too immersed in the moral aspects of religion to leave room for faith" (58). To highlight this contrast between a Protestant religious sensibility and a Catholic one, Machen returns again to the antithesis between Sancho Panza and Don Quixote. In an essay called "Sancho Panza in Geneva," Machen suggests that Protestantism has left the world with practical religion absent mystery, with meals, shelter, and money but "contempt for all enchantments, magic balsams, faery barks, thaumaturgic sages, and the whole universe of mystery and wonder. It is an extravagant notion, but it is no bad analogy of what has happened in the field of religion" (*The Glorious Mystery* 124).

So, throughout the early sections of *A Fragment of Life*, in place of mystery and wonder, Edward and Mary typically see things as things: Aunt Marian's money, the stove, the spare room. And these things initially hinder more profound intimacy between Edward and Mary, a predicament Machen conveys through a fireside scene. After the trip to Wilson's, Edward and Mary are sitting at a fireplace. Notably, though, the fire is not mentioned or described, only the things that occlude it, for the grate "was concealed by a pretty cardboard screen, painted with landscapes" (154). In other words, something artificial blocks both the warmth and the light, and something physical separates rather than unites the couple. Though Mary's eyes naturally seem like they should be gifted to behold "strange visions" at this fireside conversation, "[i]n reality she was thinking of Darnell's plan [for furnishing the spare room]" (154). The word dreaming used in a degraded sense, alluding to egoistic fantasy, "She dreamed again, calculating the cost of all the necessaries" (155). Machen thus introduces a contrast between the dream of an ancient wood that Edward recollected at the start of the story and the dreams, in the sense of misguided or distracting fantasies, that preoccupy his characters daily and hinder their apprehension of deeper realities. Even after Edward's first disclosure of his transformative walks through Hampstead and London, the next morning, they "spoke of common things," and "avoided one another's eyes" (185). Only gradually do Edward's imaginative adventures conduce to a recuperation of the transcendent mystery that portends resurrection of life for him and Mary.

The Mystical Picaro: A Common Clerk's Quixotic Adventures

If Edward is, from one vantage, a benighted Sancho Panza, he is at the same time the novel's Quixote. But for Machen, the Quixote character is not a naïve dreamer, innocently detached from reality, as connoted by the adjective *quixotic* that has entered into our ordinary lexicon from Cervantes's novel. In Machen's view, "No one remotely resembling Don Quixote ever stepped the earth, but Don Quixote lives in each of us, and, in a sense, is more real than any of us—is by far more real than the mere 'imitations' of the so-called realists" ("Aristotle" 368). Consequently, true realist literature follows its characters' wandering along strange paths and by ways after the fashion of that paradigmatic wanderer, Don Quixote; in Machen's words, genuinely realist literature is "the literature of wandering . . . the literature that symbolises a sense that we all have at times, the sense that we are bound on a journey of strange adventures, that marvels lie beyond the bend of the road, that we have but to go on and on and wonders will be manifested to us" ("Realism and Symbol" 110).[6] In that regard, the figure of Don Quixote is an important mythic type for Machen not only because of his propensity to wander, but also because of his ability to perceive the hidden wonders within the world of common things through which he wanders. That ability to see the world as infused with divine mystery is for Machen the essence of mystical experience. For Machen, Quixote is not only a picaresque adventurer; he is the archetype of the mystic as visionary.

Machen never explicitly mentions Don Quixote in *A Fragment of Life*, but there are several ways in which Edward Darnell is as Quixote-like as he is Pancha-esque, for he carries within him a propensity to dream and an adventurous longing for a divinely wild world beyond the bend of the brick walls confining his suburban home. This form of dreaming is significantly different from egoistic fantasies of blissful stoves or lucrative investments. Dreaming in the novel is also shown to be imaginative vision, through memory, mental peregrination, or actual sleep. For Machen, it is sometimes an intimation of mystical experience because it connects the dreamer to transcendent reality.

This second, fruitful form of dreaming often appears in bits and fragments, as when Edward awakens to his daily routine from "a dream of an ancient wood" (148) or when, on a Sunday, Mary awakens and finds her waking life shadowed by "the quick moment of a dream, another world where rapture was wine, where one wandered in a deep and happy valley, and the moon was always rising red above the trees. She was thinking of Hampstead, which represented to her the vision of the world beyond the [suburban] walls" (157). Yet, the further she awakens to the day, the more the "chains of common life" (207) bind her to "the grey phantasmal world" (170). Thenceforth, she resumes debates about the spare room, the stove, her servant Alice's relationship woes, and her Aunt Marian's plight.

A contrapuntal contrast between her immersion in the common world and Edward's more persistent dreaming of another characterizes the novel's second section. Whereas Mary regales Edward with a long-winded, banal story about their servant Alice's run-in with Mrs. Murray, her beau's mother, and Mrs. Murray's disdain for Hampstead Court, Edward counters Mary's story with a meandering one about his first sight of Hampstead Court, with digressions detailing a suburban sojourn and a walking tour of London—both common adventures that nonetheless prime his visionary eye. At first glance, Mary's story seems merely one of the story's seeming "digressions and irrelevances," to use John Howard's phrase (335). Speculating about the purpose of Mary's story, Howard suggests that it "highlights the capricious nature of families and relationships" or possibly figures forth what the couple's relationship was like at an earlier stage

(337). There are, however, two more specific and substantive reasons for including Mary's story about Alice. On the one hand, Edward's response to the profusion of tedious detail from common life in Mary's story provides an early glimpse of his mystic inclinations. For, he responds to the story not according to its ordinary meaning but rather to its spiritual sound. Machen writes,

> He had not been attending very carefully to the subject-matter of her story, but he loved to hear a voice that was incantation in his ears, tones that summoned before him the vision of a magic world . . . His ears were charmed, ravished with the grave, supernal melody, as of antique song, rather of the first made world in which all speech was descant, and *all words were sacraments of might, speaking not to the mind but to the soul* [emphasis mine]. (172–73)

This is the first of many instances of Edward's ability to see common things as possessed of a sacramental grace.[7]

This proclivity to perceive in the experiences of ordinary life something magical becomes even clearer when the two compare Mrs. Murray's perception of Hampton Court to Edward's. Though this story focuses on Alice's abuse by Mrs. Murray, it is the contrast between Mrs. Murray's perception of Hampton Court and Edward's that is most significant. Mrs. Murray finds it far less interesting than Kew Gardens and hardly worth visiting; Edward finds it transfiguring. On holiday in July, he'd read "bits from a queer old book that had belonged to my poor dad" (177) and then took a walk, which represents the beginning of a process of mystical awakening. The fact that the book is described as queer, old, and beyond understanding foreshadows the ancestral manuscripts he later reads, which similarly prepare him for an experience of mystery and transformation. He first walks eight-some miles in his suburban area, and it is significant that the experience comes during a "wonderful night" (177). Like Nicodemus and in a kind of inversion of Platonic imagery, Edward frequently finds the darkness of night occasion for mystic revelation. "I don't know why, but the sky or something made me feel quite queer; everything seemed changed in a way I couldn't understand" (177), and when he tries to relate his experience to others, the impression is as if he were talking "about fairyland" (178). The world around him, to his shifted senses, was imbued with a holy quality, such that "the air seemed to smell sweet, like the incense in Catholic churches" (178). Significantly, the ordinary things of his suburban environment are transmuted into something strange and wonderful, for "that little back street was beautiful, and the noise of the children and the men in the public house seemed to fit in with the sky and become part of it" (178). In other words, he comes to see his small fragment of the world as of a piece with all of reality in a kind of mystic union. As a consequence of this unitive experience, he not only perceives the external world as transmuted, but he also senses a shift in his own identity. He explains, "It was all so different . . . to what I had been doing all my life, particularly for the year before, and it almost seemed as if I couldn't be the man who had been going into the City every day in the morning and coming back from it every evening after writing a lot of uninteresting letters" (178).

This suburban walk prompts him to take a walking tour of London, which Machen describes in language evocative of a "Robinson Crusoe of the soul." Recollecting tales from boyhood, Edward tells Mary he was "fond of reading of great travellers . . . and of sailors who were driven out of their course and found themselves in latitudes where no ship had ever sailed before" (179). After the fashion of those stories, he perceives of the walking adventure he embarks upon as a "voyage of discovery" (179), aimed at "feel[ing] that I was going where nobody had been before" (179). He resists any maps and tour books he had read like *London and Its Surroundings* because their stock, conventional details "seemed to take the life, the real heart, out of everything, making it as dry and stupid as the stuffed birds in a museum" (180). Moreover, he seems bent on discovering something never before seen or experienced, "imagin[ing] that [he] was going to discover a new world" (181).

And discover a new world he does. Edward's walking tour results in one of his earliest experiences of mystical transmutation: a growing awareness that the world of common things is enchanted in ways he had not realized. He describes to Mary entering an almost rapturous state, recalling how "some enchantment had informed all common things, transmuting them into a great sacrament, causing earthly works to glow with the fire and the glory of the everlasting light" (183). Yet, there is something about this stage of his mystical awakening to a transmuted London that is more akin to Robinson Crusoe's adventure than to Quixote's. Like Crusoe's solitary island adventures, this episode is marked by isolation and individualism. Edward goes it alone. He rejects other books as informing his experience. He records his sights and insights through personal, idiosyncratic hieroglyphs, "signs—things like queer letters . . . Nobody but myself could understand it" (184). And notably, when he tries to draw a picture, including houses and a "great church, all spires and pinnacles, and above it, in the air, a cup with rays coming from it," "it wasn't a success" (184). He does not believe he can share his experience with others, nor does he think he should, perceiving that "the trees that were like dark low clouds were all mine, and mine alone, that I was living in a world that nobody else knew of, into which no one could enter" (183). His initial mystical awakening results in a mystic individualism that keeps him separated even from Mary, despite the story he shares. For, it is the next morning when "[t]he Darnells avoided one another's eyes as they sat at breakfast" (185). While his poetic sensibility enables him to encounter a transformed world, he remains on a spiritual island. Thus, he experiences the capacity to access a transcendent reality, but finds himself only in a magical, enchanted world, bereft of the religious communion that might enable him to bind his experience to Mary, to other readers, and to past pilgrims who have traversed the same paths.

Medievalism, Mystical Orthodoxy, and Machen's Grail Prosaics

As Edward Darnell's story progresses, so his spiritual experiences continue to evolve. At the end of the novel's third section, after Edward stumbles upon a fragment of "prophecy" in his garden, he finds that the night again proves fertile for illumination and prompts another profound mystical experience, springing from the "Daystar that had risen in his heart" (202).[8] The state created by this illumination fills his heart with "great joy" and "great peace" as he lies down to sleep next to his wife (202), and Machen describes the climactic scene leading up to this peace in such elevated spiritual language that, like the previous illumination, it seems as if it should conclude the novel. Strangely, though, the novel continues on. It does so both to communicate Machen's understanding of ordinary time and sacred time and to suggest that the mystical illumination of the individual is insufficient alone and needs a shared religious framework for fulfillment. Despite the inward light that illuminates what Waite sometimes calls the "interior church," Edward's mystical vision leaves him marooned within that interior space. As Machen describes Edward's illuminated vision in this section, "from a great and unutterable height [he] looked on the confusion of the mortal pageant, beholding mysteries in which he was no true actor, hearing magic songs that could by no means draw him down from the battlements of the high and holy city" (202). Illuminated as he is, he still stands apart from the common run of humanity and lies down to sleep "beside" but not *with* his wife Mary (202).

However, the language of evolution during this experience is significant. Machen notes that "[the Daystar] had dwelt there all his life, and had *slowly shone forth with clearer and clearer light* [emphasis mine]" (202). Here and elsewhere, the novel moves at a slow pace, with a recursive quality, to suggest that Darnell's spiritual development is indeed a process of incremental growth due to repeated experiences over time rather than a single, momentous occasion of revelation. This narrative approach is consistent with what Gary Saul Morson, drawing upon Mikhail Bakhtin's theory of the novel, has identified as the novel's "prosaic" ethos. In contradistinction to poetics, Morson describes *prosaics* as the novel's characteristic way of capturing the "ordinary, messy, quotidian facts of daily life" (516), but prosaics also implies a distinctive understanding of time insofar as within prosaic novels "lives generally are saved or ruined by innumerable prosaic moments" rather than single, dramatic, cataclysmic ones (522). Whereas other genres, such as the epic and romance, tend to pare away the dross of everyday life, Machen's use of time and narrative, as in the prosaic novel, preserves those ordinary moments and things. He does so because they are central to his sacramental mysticism—a sacramental theology in which the most ordinary things can manifest extraordinary divine revelations. As Machen articulates that sacramental mysticism in another story, "The Novel of the White Powder": "The whole universe, my friend, is a tremendous sacrament; a mystic, ineffable force and energy, veiled by an outward form of matter; and man, and the sun and the other stars, and the flower of the grass, and the crystal in the test-tube, are each and every one as spiritual, as material, and subject to an inner working" (80). Thus, Edward Darnell's illuminations come from daily experiences of ordinary life. He does not have a single, climactic transformational moment, nor do his transformations arise from grand, dramatic events. Rather, he dreams, he remembers, he goes on walks, he finds a torn page in his garden, he digs among books in his storeroom—and all of these ordinary things, repetitive to read about, conduce to changes in his self and his perception of the world.

At the same time, though, Machen's novel contradicts other fundamental aspects of the prosaic novel, such as its typical erasure of deep structures underlying individual human histories and time. Drawing upon examples from nineteenth-century realist novels, Morson continues, "[P]rosaics assumes that the natural state of the world is mess, and that it is order, not disorder, that requires an explanation. Order does exist, of course, but it is always the result of work. *It is never given, but always made* [emphasis mine]" (516). While Machen acknowledges the apparent messiness of human life histories through the interpolated stories of Alice, Aunt Marian, and even Edward and Mary's domestic affairs, he subordinates that understanding of temporal life to a mythic sense of divinely patterned time. It is primarily Machen's fascination with the medieval past and its mythic traces that gives rise to this *layering of time* in *A Fragment of Life.*

Machen's affection for the medieval past is evident everywhere in his larger oeuvre, from one of his earliest literary efforts, *The Chronicle of Clemendy* (written in his twenties), to his Grail stories, including *A Fragment of Life*, "The Great Return," and *The Secret Glory*. He frequently mused on medieval times and customs in essays such as "St. George and the Dragon" and "The Dark Ages." Even works that are less thoroughgoingly medieval are peppered with allusions to the Middle Ages, as in *The Three Imposters*, *The Hill of Dreams*, and *The Green Round*. And his lacerating 1906 satire, *Dr. Stiggins*, showcases his propensity to savage modern people for their disparagement of the Middle Ages and concomitant lionization of the so-called landmarks of modern progress—industrialism, Protestantism, and Puritan moralism. As Sweetser notes, he often used medievalism "to display his contempt for the modern material standards characterized by an obliviousness to the glories of the past" (68).

In *A Fragment of Life*, Machen hints at the losses occasioned by time's passage from the Middle Ages to the modern world. One of several instances of this loss appears in his representation of the church Mary attends, a church that, from outward appearance, seems to have the "correct" Gothic features (161). On closer inspection, however, its modernizations have created an "elaborate blasphemy" (161). Among those modernizations, Machen singles out the way "[t]he canticles were sung to Joll in B flat, the chants were 'Anglican,' and the sermon was the gospel for the day, amplified and rendered in the more modern and graceful English of the preacher" (161). Especially rebarbative, though, is the "substitution of a low 'chancel wall' with iron gates for the rood screen," a seemingly minor modern adaptation that Machen sees as a desecration (161), destructive of the sweet mystery the old medieval church architecture evoked. Significantly, in the scene featuring this church, Edward departs from his usual Sunday routine and declines to attend the service because of "some bitterness in his heart," preferring nature to religion and opting to "lounge under the shade of the big mulberry tree" instead of attending the service (161). Although Mary attends, Machen describes her response to the service in perfunctory terms, saying merely, "And Mary came away" (161). The contrast between this laconic description of Mary leaving church compared to the elaborate descriptions of Edward's spiritual responses to the landscape is notable, emphasizing how modern religious reforms have stripped churches of their power to evoke experiences of holy mystery.

It is in fact the evocation of religious mystery and his Welsh background that drew Machen to medieval Grail mythology. Sweetser observes, "One of the lasting interests of his life was the Holy Graal, which, for him, was the most satisfying symbol of faith; and through his research on the subject, he gratified his religious being and fulfilled the mystical qualities of his Celtic heritage" (51). Machen's fascination with Grail mythology grew and deepened over his many conversations with A. E. Waite and his own months of research at the British Museum, research he used for a series of articles in *The Academy*, later reprinted in *The Glorious Mystery* (Reynolds and Charlton 104). In his own view, the Graal, as he spelled it, had "Celtic and Sacramental origins" (*Glorious Mystery* [*GM*] 12) and its legend hearkened back to the "Graal Service," a ritual called "going to Grace" through which "worshipers were rapt into an ecstasy" (*GM* 25). It was through a wonderful process of literary transformation, he thought, that these early Celtic ritual traditions were transformed, "rough literary materials into the great temple of the Graal Romances" (*GM* 32). Machen researched these views about the Holy Grail and wrote about them so much that he once half-seriously, half-jokingly proposed to the American poet and novelist Robert Hillyer that he deserved an honorary degree for his labors (Sweetser 51). Summarizing the significance of the Grail in Machen's writing, Charles Coulombe says that he "returned to it again and again," for it "[s]ymbolis[ed] at once the Eucharist, the Crucifixion, and the ecstasy Machen believed was at the heart of Christianity" (351).

It is not surprising, then, that Machen introduces fragments of Grail lore as a way of deepening Edward's encounter with sacred life and dilating the mystery of his protagonist's mystical experience. The novel's Grail poem, which is represented as Edward's own composition, serves as the climax of the novel's fourth and final section. That final section of the novel allows Machen to connect ordinary time and deep time, Darnell's individual mystical experience and the mystical body of Christ, adding a final evolution to his spiritual progress from mystic individualism to mythopoetic mysticism.

The positive impact of medieval myth on Edward's modern life emerges gradually during his annual holiday. One rainy day, Edward, like a medieval hermit, begins cloistering himself day after day in the box-room of his house, sorting through his ancestral history, going back "far into the dim past, beyond the Normans, beyond the Saxons, far into the Roman days" and to the Welsh ancestral home, now owned by his great-uncle (213), a place that becomes for him like an "Avalon of the soul" (Valentine 163). The time spent among these "musty rolls" of manuscripts is described as leaving its trace upon his face like "the blazonry of some great adventure," intimating that his research and studying is another kind of adventure of the soul (212).

Edward's contact with these old manuscripts occasions significant changes in his life—changes to his perception of himself, of the city of London, and of his relationship with his wife, Mary. The manuscripts he discovers ignite his mythic imagination such that he comes to perceive the interconnection between his time and deep time, between his identity and that of his ancestors, including Adam, and between his place and the holy city of Zion ("Syon"). In that sense, the mythic manuscripts become a kind of "mystic well," overflowing into his life from the past (217). When he returns to work from his holiday, some of his coworkers notice that "he was in some vague manner changed in appearance" (210). And indeed, the book he subsequently writes reflects his conviction, expressed in Latin script, that the histories, legends, and Scripture are about him (220). He thereby becomes "aware of the enchantment that was transmuting all the world about him, informing his life with a strange significance and romance. London seemed a city of the Arabian Nights" at first, but then his visionary imagination passes beyond even that fictional, magical association as he perceives a religious correlation to his place and time: "There must be yet another transformation: London had become Bagdad; it must at last be transmuted to Syon, or in the phrase of one of his old documents, the City of the Cup" (217).

Machen implies that the mystical illumination occasioned by Edward's encounter with Grail lore lights the way to closer union between him and Mary. Though Machen acknowledges the impossibility of capturing the full story of their mystical consummation, he claims that their story "seems to put on the semblance of the stories of the Graal. It is certain, indeed, that in this world they changed their lives, like King Arthur, but this is a work which no chronicler has cared to describe with any amplitude of detail" (220). Accordingly, Machen leaves us not with literal details, but rather with a poem and a dream. The earlier images of a grate separating Mary and Edward, or of the two "dutifully" kissing each other, are replaced by traditional mystical bridal imagery of union, for the novel ends with a fragmentary passage from Edward's book, recording how "a form came towards me from the hidden places of the wood, and my love and I were united by the well" (222). The form here is clearly Mary, and the lowercase *f* reminds readers that the flesh-and-blood Mary is the incarnation of love, seen and recognized as such, within his transmuted vision. This conclusion leads Graf to argue that the novel is "really about the alchemy of marriage" and "the realization that even the most normal, unenlightened couples experience the mystical secrets of sexuality, the whispering in the darkness known only to each other, the joyous alchemy of man and woman becoming one" (Graf 67).

I would suggest, however, that the novel's representation of mysticism is about more than the union of Mary and Edward; it is about the place of mystical experience within the eternal communion of Christian faith. In an essay on the theological character of Arthur Machen's work, Zoë Lehmann Imfeld argues that Machen, like his contemporary R. H. Benson, counters the late Victorian trend toward "individualist mysticism" by representing "a mysticism that must subordinate itself to the authority of the Church—for Machen, Anglo-Catholicism" ("Decadent" 59). Imfeld's analysis focuses on Machen's "horror fiction," but her keen insight helps to explain a key conundrum about the structure of *A Fragment of Life*: the earlier question of why the novel does not end with Edward's ecstatic responses to the landscape or even with the Daystar rising within his heart. Instead, it ends with his re-embrace of the Christian Church's ritual Mass. In the final section, he and Mary discover a different church, "a little church of another fashion in a back street, and Darnell, who had found in one of the old notebooks the maxim *Incredibilia sola Credenda*, soon perceived how high and glorious a thing was that service at which he assisted" (215). This moves the narrator to remark that those who seek wisdom must not "read 'science' books, but mass-books" (215). And Edward does exactly that. In a passage so significant that it is worth quoting in full, Machen writes that Edward came to see

> the whole world is but a great ceremony or sacrament, which teaches under visible forms a hidden and transcendent doctrine.

> It was thus that he found in the ritual of the church a perfect image of the world; an image purged, exalted, and illuminate, a holy house built up of shining and translucent stones, in which the burning torches were more significant than the wheeling stars, and the fuming incense was a more certain token than the rising of the mist. His soul went forth with the albed procession in its white and solemn order, the mystic dance that signifies rapture and a joy above all joys, and when he beheld Love slain and rise again victorious he knew that he witnessed, in a figure, the consummation of all things, the Bridal of all Bridals, the mystery that is beyond all mysteries, accomplished from the foundation of the world. So day by day the house of his life became more magical. (215–16)

Thus, Edward's excavation of Grail lore leads him back to the holy Church and its ritual Mass, as "instruments" not to be neglected in his spiritual growth (215). The fruit of that growth is figured forth in a poem the narrator attributes to Edward and includes near the end of the novel. Capturing Edward's own spiritual journey, the poem progresses from a picture of the solitary individual to the individual perceiving his relationship to the natural world and finally to the individual recognizing, via the Grail myth, his relationship to the holy Church. The poem concludes with the poet's sight of

> . . . a great city all ablaze
> With burning torches, to light up
> The pinnacles that shrine the Cup.
> Ever the magic wine is poured,
> Ever the Feast shines on the board,
> Ever the Song is borne on high
> That chants the holy Magistry—(221)

The word *Magistry* here offers especially important clues to the mystical orthodoxy that shapes Edward's mature mystical vision. In the nineteenth century, the word had chemical and alchemical associations, connected to the power to transmute one substance into another. However, the *Oxford English Dictionary* (*OED*) illustrates the ecclesiastical connotations of the term with the following sentence from 1899: "The Church alone possesses supreme doctrinal magistery in fact and in right" ("Magistery"). The *OED* explains that this 1899 use of the term referred to the "teaching function of the Church." Combined with other Christian images such as the wine and the feast laid out on a table, the poem exemplifies Machen's efforts to link Edward's mystical vision to the mystical revelation of the Christian Church. For Machen, the Grail itself was rooted in Celtic Christian ceremony, a key point of controversy between him and Waite, and so, too, does he link mystical vision to the mystic revelation of the Christian Mass. What Imfeld rightly observes about Machen's weird tales holds true also for his mystical fiction: "Christian orthodoxy is the *only* framework which provides the clarifying lens for grace, giving man to himself, as it were" (*Victorian Ghost* 71).

By introducing the medieval Grail myth in the final section of *A Fragment of Life*, Machen ultimately challenges the view that human life is nothing more than a fragment afloat in a chaotic sea and that Edward's mystical vision is merely an idiosyncratic illumination. By yoking his prosaic novel to the medieval myth of the Grail, Machen preserves his understanding of mysticism as an individual experience of ecstasy, but he does so by bringing Edward's mysticism into accord with the larger community of Christian faith, past, present, and future.

Shipwrecked Fragments and the Mythic Ship to Far Paradise

Over the decades since *A Fragment of Life*'s first publication, scholars and critics have differed about whether the novel proved to be an artistic success or failure. S. T. Joshi considers the novel to be Machen's "most finished and satisfying work" (29). Howard characterized the novel as an "impossible history," though one that successfully coalesces as a "self-contained and intelligible story" (335). By contrast, Reynolds and Charlton thought that its pieces remained fragmentary, with the whole never achieving the caliber of the individual parts (77). Insofar as the novel as a whole does seem an impossible story, Valentine remarked that "sustaining a conventional novel at such a sacramental level is hardly to be expected and so the novel ends rather abruptly," with the novelist conceding that further history would be "impossible" (70). Valentine's characterization accurately identifies the difficulty Machen confronted in trying to capture ecstatic experience within the prosaic narrative of a novel. Ordinary words fail. Glyphs can translate but not fully reveal. As the novel's penultimate paragraph puts it, "From documents such as these it is clearly impossible to gather any very definite information" (222). And thus, from one vantage, this Robinson Crusoe of the soul, a mythopoetic prosaics, could be said to end in a kind of epistemological shipwreck.

But that may well be as Machen liked it, given his conviction that human knowledge must yield to mystery. After all, knowledge was not, to his mind, the true fruit of mysticism. In this, Machen felt he differed from Evelyn Underhill. As he wrote in a two-part, generally admiring review of her 1911 book *Mysticism*,

> I must . . . dispute with Miss Evelyn Underhill over her definition of mysticism. The mystic quest, she says, appears to be "the finding of a 'way out' or a 'way back' to some desirable state in which alone they [the mystics] can satisfy their craving for absolute truth." And, no doubt, absolute truth does enter into the mystic purview; but I should prefer to say that the real aim, the true and final end of the great adventure and perilous quest of mysticism is Absolute Life. ("Great Quest" 352)

And "Absolute Life"—in the sense of the fullness of existence—he did believe everyone to be capable of realizing (Reynolds and Charlton 76). For, Edward's mystic union was one Machen felt was available to all who could see the world's prosaic details with the poet's transfiguring eye.

From that vantage, while *A Fragment of Life* may purport to be only a fragment, in effect it is a fragment that works to reconnect readers to the whole fabric of existence—to "Absolute Life." In other words, it does what Machen thinks good literature ought to do. As he put it in *Far Off Things*, "the whole matter of imaginative literature depends upon this faculty of seeing the universe, from the aeonian pebble of the wayside to the raw suburban street as something new, unheard of, marvelous, finally, miraculous. The good people—among whom I naturally class myself—feel that everything is miraculous; they are continually amazed at the strangeness of the proportion of all things" (124). By following a common clerk's adventures in "continual amazement," Machen anchors readers in ordinary life and transports them within and beyond. And through that process of mythopoetic prosaics, his novel bears the fragile shipwrecked fragments of our ordinary life to the transfiguring place of far Paradise.

Conclusion

Mysticism for the Modern World, or, All True Pathways Lead Beyond Themselves

This book has examined the literary flowers of the Edwardian era's mystical revival, arguing that the Edwardian heyday of interest in mysticism, seeded in the final decades of the nineteenth century, featured the development of a distinctive genre, the mystical novel; it was cultivated by a loose fellowship of British writers who were inspired by the medieval past, inclined to distinguish mysticism from magic, and interested in engaging the modern middlebrow reader with Christian mystical experience in ways not previously explored in the English novel's realist tradition. To say that their literature was "popular literature" is not to say that it was "best-selling" literature. As Clive Bloom notes, "[P]opular literature is a broader concept than the more narrow one of the bestseller," and it "defines a perceptual arena, a field out of which the bestseller emerges" (82–83). That this literature was intended to popularize mystical insights for ordinary people, as Underhill seeks to do in her book *Practical Mysticism*, is undeniable. In other words, it had a popularizing intention. And it was written in an era in England of expanding popular audiences, when compulsory elementary education had produced a "vast new pool of readers" and "a huge new market for literary entertainment and printed information" (Bloom 76). Just as Machen's story "The Great Return" fictionalized how "the Holy Grail was manifested to the common people, to common modern people, to Welsh tradesmen and farmers," which seemed "very low" to one critic but simply true to life to Machen (*Things* 141), so the novels he and his peers wrote were published for and read by an increasingly "common" audience who might never have chosen to read Julian of Norwich's *Revelations* or Richard Rolle's work.

But that such literature achieved widespread popularity in its own day, in the sense of selling mass numbers of copies to the popular public, was decidedly not the case for the fiction of Waite and Underhill. Machen's horror fiction sold better and found a wider reading audience than did some of his later mystical literature. Theorizing about Machen's uneven success, Carl Van Vechten mused in a 1923 review, "[O]ne would attempt to explain the long-drawn-out obscurity of Arthur Machen by remembering that he is a mystic, and that the man in the street, the idle bystander, the ecstatic reader of 'This Freedom,' cannot be expected to find delight in the reading of mystic books" (36); but no sooner does Van Vechten offer that theory about the barriers to Machen's appeal than he rejects it, observing that Machen is finally achieving recognition, possibly even due to his mysticism. Van Vechten concludes, "Machen is indubitably a mystic and . . . in spite of (or because of) this fact, he is no longer an obscurity" (36). Since Van Vechten's day, Machen has had periodic celebrations as a master of genre fiction, particularly by practitioners or aficionados of the horror genre, such as Lovecraft and King. However, of the four writers in this study, Benson stands alone as a writer who both wrote for a popular audience and achieved popular success; he was, without doubt, "vastly popular in his day" (Griffiths 61), perhaps because Catholic readers provided a critical mass of followers. And yet, despite that Edwardian-era fame, his popular readership has all but vanished today. As Bloom observes, "Genres were, and still are, rapidly modernized or 'reinvented' whilst authors once central to such genres are forgotten" (81).

The challenge of writing spiritual fiction for a popular audience was articulated with canny insight by the best-selling novelist Marie Corelli, an author whose prolific output and popularity outshone that of any of her Victorian or Edwardian peers. In the prologue to her novel *The Life Everlasting*, published in 1911, the same year as the first edition of Underhill's *Mysticism*, Corelli recounts how her publisher looked askance at what he considered "spiritualistic" fiction (18). She had early on tried her hand at it with *A Romance of Two Worlds* (1886), but her publisher, George Bentley, thought she would "lose the public hearing [she] had just gained" (18) if she were to write more in that vein; in a desire to "please him . . . and to please the particular public to which he had introduced [her]," she accepted his suggestions for writing a melodrama and then what he called "a love-story, *pur et simple*" (19). But her authorial conviction led her to believe that she was called to write fiction that pushed readers beyond their "merely material Selves" (19). Toward that end, she produced *Ardath* (1889) and eventually others like *The Life Everlasting*. Corelli's account suggests that writers who sought to address spiritual and even metaphysical matters within the novel achieved more popular success by first establishing a readership as writers of romance or melodrama, or, as Machen did, through the horror genre, which drew writers to him and thenceforth interested them in his mystical fiction. And in fact, Benson, whose popularity as a novelist in his own era far exceeded that of Waite, Underhill, and Machen, developed his novelistic craft in a variety of modes—historical novels, romance novels, apocalyptic thrillers, with one of his novels, *The Necromancers*, now classified as "occult fiction" and even made into a dramatic script and, posthumously, a major motion picture (the 1941 British film *Spellbound*, directed by John Harlow). That early success, of course, did not save Benson for posterity, nor did the passion Corelli's fiction inspired in "ordinary shop girls" (Bloom 70) as well as "Nonconformist ministers and purity campaigners" (Waller 217), secure her fiction for the future. Corelli's Victorian sentimentality and strict Christian moralizing left her fiction a mere "Victorian curiosity" after her death in 1924 (Bloom 71).

Like Corelli, Machen was himself aware of the challenges of writing successful mystical fiction, not only in terms of its attractiveness to the reading public, but also in terms of the artistic challenges it presented to the author. In a review of Underhill's 1909 mystical novel, *The Column of Dust*, he acknowledges that Underhill is attempting something new and untried, praising her novel as "one of the most daring experiments that have been made in literature" and claiming that "she has found a secret path leading to an undiscovered country," especially through her treatment of the Grail ("A Great Experiment" 627). Despite these initial comments, he moderates his praise as the review continues, finding fault in Underhill's attempt to do in novel form what he deems impossible: "We can hint at the unseen world, we can symbolise it . . . but—and this is a very great but—we cannot incarnate the unincarnate. Miss Underhill has done her very best; she has done, indeed, exquisitely; but being mortal, she has not succeeded in putting on immortality" ("A Great Experiment" 627). Having in his own work struggled with the limits of the novel's form as a vehicle for conveying the transcendent through the finite—which is the fundamental challenge of representing mystical experience in any linguistic form or genre—he seems to have perceived with especial acuity the limitations of his and his fellow mystical novelists' aspirations to yoke the practical and the spiritual, the mundane and the mystical, the immanent and the transcendent. It may have been those self-identified shortcomings that led to lackluster critical assessments of their mystical fiction in the decades to follow—critical assessments that even went so far as to ignore the popular interest in spirituality that their work reflected. For instance, in a 1982 study of Edwardian fiction, Jefferson Hunter concluded that G. K. Chesterton stands alone in "demonstrat[ing] that one Edwardian novelist at least could treat religion in an imaginative and intelligent way. Chesterton was an exception in a prevailingly secular decade" (57). Such an assessment raises questions about the literary and cultural legacy of this literary movement within the Edwardian mystical revival, given that none of these writers has become a canonical author and the mystical revival itself was, for a long time, eclipsed by a narrative about Edwardian secularization. Is Hunter right that "[m]inor writing lives and dies wholly within one period, of which it is therefore representative. A Baedeker gone out of date, it is the best guide to monuments which have now been swept away or seem inexplicable" (46)? If so, is the Edwardian mystical novel now only an antiquarian curiosity, a mere guidebook to other dusty relics of a bygone age? Has the genre of the mystical novel itself been "swept away" with the Edwardians themselves?

Despite Underhill's conviction that mysticism would be as important as ever during the impending time of world war, her confidence proved too optimistic. The kind of mystical fiction she and her peers developed seems to have appeared only sporadically after 1914, and without the anchoring in Christian tradition characteristic of their work. Underhill's friend May Sinclair's autobiographical novel *Mary Oliver* (1919) could be said to take the genre in a psychoanalytic direction by "examin[ing] the relationship between mysticism and the unconscious" (Neff 87), but Sinclair's fiction is shaped by philosophical Idealism rather than Christian sacramentalism. E. M. Forster's *Passage to India* (1924) clearly plays with the possibility of mystical experience through the characters of Mrs. Moore and Professor Godbole and the mystery of the Marabar caves. However, this and other explorations of "the mystical" in Forster's fiction ran counter to the tastes of his Bloomsbury friends: Virginia Woolf apparently poked fun at Forster for being a little "mystic, silly" (Kane 328), and Roger Fry wished Forster "weren't a mystic, or that he would keep his mysticism out of his books" (qtd. in Trilling 44). While some scholars such as Michael Roeschlein have interpreted *A Passage to India* to mean that Forster "rejects mythopoeia for mysticism's silent, incommunicable promise" (96–97), Craig Woelfel argues that mysticism for Forster "amounted to a further set of problems, not a solution" (52). Suggesting that Forster was "cross-pressured" by the different claims of liberal, humanist skepticism and religious experience (36), Woelfel notes that Forster both disavowed any belief in belief (50) *and* claimed to have had "(at least) four visionary experiences" (29), resulting in a cognitive dissonance that manifested in the irresolvable tensions within his fiction. Consequently, in novels such as *A Passage to India*, Forster seems to treat mystical experience with an ambivalence not evident in the fiction of Underhill and her peers.

Woolf herself, like George Eliot whom she admired, had significant scruples about "combining religious belief with literary endeavor" (Gough 57). Yet, in her now-famous 1919 essay "Modern Fiction," she criticized Edwardian practitioners of the realist novel for being shortsighted "materialists" and, by contrast, lionized James Joyce and those of her generation for finally writing "spiritual" fiction (Woolf 158): "It is because they [Arnold Bennett and other Edwardian realists] are concerned not with the spirit but with the body that they have disappointed us, and left us with the feeling that the sooner English fiction turns its back upon them . . . and marches, if only into the desert, the better for its soul" (158). Such comments, along with Woolf's personal writing and the epiphanic or ecstatic episodes in her fiction, have led to several decades of scholarly interest in Woolf herself as a mystical novelist. In *Religion Around Virginia Woolf*, Stephanie Paulsell observes that "[the] most-studied aspect of the religious dimension of Woolf's work is the mystical. Although understandings of the term range widely in this scholarship, the word 'mysticism' is often used to keep Woolf on the secular side of a perceived secular-religious divide" (4). Martin Corner claims that Woolf was both "an atheist" and "also a mystic" (408); Val Gough considers her an "agnostic mystic" within the apophatic tradition (75). Elaborating on such assessments, Julie Kane claims, "If one were to catalogue the various types of 'mystical' experience appearing in the writings of Virginia Woolf, the list would be virtually indistinguishable from the topics of interest to the Theosophists and spiritualists of her day: telepathy, auras, astral travel, synesthesia, reincarnation, the immortality of the soul, and the existence of Universal Mind" (328). Kane's use of the term *mystical* here clearly reverts to the more fluid understanding of mysticism prevalent in the Victorian era and diverges from the "rectified" definition Waite and Underhill sought to popularize. To the extent that mysticism is evident in Woolf's fiction, particularly after 1928, Woolf creatively plumbs the depths of the mystical novel's individualism and subjectivity, but without any mooring in religious tradition or orthodoxy. The vertical dimension of the novel for Woolf is not God, Christ, or a Platonic ultimate Reality; it is, rather, multiple, individual psyches. As Erich Auerbach has argued, she uses multiple consciousnesses as her measure of "objective reality" (536); by representing the internal state of multiple individuals in single moments of time, she thereby inverts conventional realism and, he suggests, creates a new form of mimesis (552).[1]

In the wake of these Modernist trends toward increasing subjectivity, skepticism about religious orthodoxy, and rejection of conventional realism, Charles Williams, friend of C. S. Lewis and J. R. R. Tolkien and the "oddest Inkling,"[2] is the clearest example of an inheritor of the Edwardian's era's Christian mystical novel, though he did not publish his own mystical novels until the 1930s and 1940s. Living between 1886 and 1945, he had significant contact with Waite, Underhill, and Machen as a result of meeting them directly or reading their work. Williams may have first learned of Waite's mystical poetry as an editor charged with seeking authorial permissions for the Oxford University Press's 1917 publication of the *Oxford Book of English Mystical Verse*, a book that included Waite's work (Lindop 55–56). Williams had also read Waite's *Hidden Church of the Holy Graal* and *Mysteries of Magic: A Digest of the Writings of Éliphas Lévi* in doing research for his creative projects (44). Consequently, in 1915, he sent Waite a copy of his own poetry collection, *The Silver Stair* (56), and so began their long acquaintance, with meetings at Waite's house in West London as well as at the Imperial Hotel in Russell Square, the locale of Waite's Fellowship of the Rosy Cross, which Williams joined in 1917 (59). Williams was also aware of Machen's writing, for, Williams's "Commonplace Book" records that he had read Machen's *The Great God Pan*. And Williams seems to have read Underhill's *Mysticism* (44) and directly conversed with her, "though we know only that they discussed *Descent into Hell* and substitution" (369). He eventually became a speaker at the Pleshey Retreat House, a spiritual retreat with which Underhill was affiliated (347). And shortly after her death, he accepted a job for Longman as the editor of the first collection of her letters, published in 1943, just two years after her death (369–70).

With these and other shaping influences, Williams pursued his own passionate interests in mysticism and the occult, while remaining a devout Anglican who wrote extensively about Christian theology. Like his Edwardian predecessors, he authored a series of popular novels that sought to marry the traditional form of the realist novel with metaphysical speculation, often exploring the occult in relation to a mysticism marked by Christian sacramentalism. Two of his novels, *War in Heaven* (1930) and *The Greater Trumps* (1932), attempt to represent mystical experience within the ordinary, everyday world of the novel of literary realism, with the former embedding Grail lore within the narrative after the fashion of Arthur Machen. In *Charles Williams: Poet of Theology*, Glen Cavaliero outlined the impact Machen, Benson, and Underhill had on Williams's thinking and novel writing. He notes that "the diverse but broadly Christian novels of Arthur Machen, Evelyn Underhill and G. K. Chesterton" had a significant shaping influence on Williams's thinking and writing (*Poet of Theology* 55). And about Benson, Cavaliero adds that Benson "anticipates Williams in his resolute outflanking of [the claims of spiritualism] with the more powerful rituals of orthodoxy" (56). Williams's theological idea of "mystical substitution" was anticipated in Benson's *Light Invisible* and *Mirror of Shalott*, and, like Machen, Waite, and Underhill, Williams drew upon the Arthurian legend as a spiritual and literary resource. In many ways, Williams represents the culmination of this mystical literary revival in the realist tradition, enriching the metaphysical potential of the English novel and illustrating the interconnectedness of the writers in this study.

Among post-World War II novelists, however, Iris Murdoch is likely right to argue that the Existentialism that took root within the novel mid-century sharply contrasted the mystical novel by figuring the individual in the context of a random, contingent world rather than a divinely ordered or objectively Real one—a world made only by the individual's will and ingenuity rather than discovered by mystical revelation (*Existentialists* 223, 225). Perhaps Murdoch might even have argued that the Existentialist novel supplanted or at least overshadowed those one might call mid-century mystical novelists. Many of the authors whom Murdoch adduces—Graham Greene, Patrick White, Muriel Spark, and William Golding in the English tradition—hardly have the recognition of Existentialists such as Sartre and Camus. In even more recent times, one thinks of John Fowles's *A Maggot* (1985), Ben Okri's *The Famished Road* (1991), Ian McEwan's *Black Dogs* (1992), Murdoch's *The Green Knight* (1993), and Susan Howatch's Starbridge series (1987 to 1995) as examples of mystical fiction. However, of the novelists who have explored mystical experience in recent decades, few would align themselves with institutional Christianity in the way that Waite, Benson, Underhill, and Machen did. For instance, Murdoch called herself only a "Christian fellow traveler" (*Metaphysics* 419) and Fowles, notwithstanding his surprisingly sympathetic treatment of the Shaker Ann Lee, considered himself an atheist. To the extent that these writers have popularity, in most cases it is because, as Marie Corelli recognized, they established their readership in another mode. Since the end of the twentieth century, realist novelists have been even less inclined to focus on mystical experience, and realist fiction itself has, in the last two decades, often ceded ground to the rage for dystopian fiction.

As we consider the relatively thin literary legacy of this Edwardian genre, which is at once realist and Realist, one might ask why relatively few novelists have imitated the Edwardian mystical novel and sought to represent mystical experience with the tools of literary realism. Is it because, as Machen suggested, the artistic challenges to successful mystical fiction are too difficult for realist novelists to surmount? One might be tempted to say yes, except that Dostoevsky's *Brothers Karamazov*, the consummate example of a mystical novel, albeit in the Russian tradition, would surely argue against the impossibility of such accomplishment. Is the dearth of mystical fiction due to a cultural zeitgeist, the winds of which have increasingly blown toward the social and political rather than the spiritual and theological? Is it connected to our culture's increasing emphasis upon particularized identities rather than common humanity and union with the Divine? Or is it because writers and readers drawn to realist fiction are less metaphysically inclined from the outset and typically gravitate toward it out of interest in social, political, or secular topics, rather than spiritual or theological ones?

If the latter is the case, Waite may have been right after all in seeing MacDonald's fairy-tale tradition as having the most potential for popular metaphysical exploration of mysticism. While Waite's own attempts to extend the "MacDonald" fairy tradition of spiritual literature were unsuccessful, others adapted that tradition and extended it in ways that exceeded the popularity of almost any other literature in the twentieth century. The literature of Williams's fellow Inklings—Tolkien and Lewis—stands as a paradigm of that popular success. As John Milbank observes in his provocative article "Fictioning Things: Gift and Narrative":

> Theologians today exercise almost zero public influence. And yet, through the medium of children's literature and fantasy literature generally, a public theological debate of a kind continues to be conducted. From George Macdonald in the Victorian era through G. K. Chesterton to the Inklings, an attempt has been

> made to re-present Christianity in the mode of what Macdonald already called the fantastic imagination. If one judges by book sales, the avid readership of this literature must extend well beyond the numbers of those who go to church, although the latter group also have been perhaps much more profoundly shaped by this literary mode of reflection than by the work of conceptual theologians. (1)

Milbank goes on to propose that there are special synergies between the nature of the Christian narrative and the fairy tale that make the latter a "truer re-imagination of Christianity" (30). He argues, "[I]f the Christian narrative can be taken as a fairy-tale that centrally concerns the proper use of material things and their sacramental nature, it remains truer than we have suspected to the magical nature of the fairy-tale sign-object which is gift (and then supremely the eucharist as grail), just as it takes more seriously than we have suspected the immanent mediation of valuation than can be identified as 'the fairy realm'" (30). And it is "[t]he new tellers of fairy-tales to children and adults" that "open out just this real horizon" within the "grown-up, disenchanted cosmos" (31).

Yet, even if the so-called MacDonald tradition ultimately succeeded in producing popular mystical fiction in ways that forays into mystical fiction within the realist mode did not, the impact of the Edwardian writers in this study transcends their experiments within the mystical novel as a genre. Energetic and prolific on the topic of all matters mystical, they variously wrote poetry, scholarship, and magazine essays; they edited journals and books, did translations or adaptations, lectured, led ritual societies or spiritual retreats, and kept up a vigorous epistolary correspondence with spiritually inclined readers and fellow writers. Taken together, their fiction and other work related to mysticism left a significant mark on their own generation and the generations that have ensued, although some of the ways in which they have left a mark may seem paradoxical, with the potential both to strengthen institutional, collective religion and to undermine it.

Most notably, their work in both fictional and nonfictional modes popularized mysticism by revitalizing study of it as an academic concern and as a topic of interest for the mainstream public. In this effort, they participated in a movement shared by several other key figures who lived during the Edwardian age. In a scholarly vein, the work of Waite and Underhill was counterpointed by William Inge's *Christian Mysticism*

(1899), a seminal account of mysticism from the vantage of an Anglican dean. In the Catholic tradition, Baron Friedrich von Hügel, who later became Underhill's spiritual counselor, published *The Mystical Element of Religion* in 1908, a study that was both sympathetic to mystical philosophy and critical of its dangers. And the scholar Caroline Spurgeon authored an academic study called *Mysticism in English Literature*, published by Cambridge University Press in 1913.[3] The historian Dana Greene, Underhill's biographer, speculates that the reasons for this turn-of-the-century interest in mysticism are "various and complex," with mysticism arising in the interstices between orthodox belief and spiritual longing (41). She argues:

> In England orthodox Christianity, both as an institution and as an intellectual system, had been shown to be deficient. Church attendance, particularly in urban areas, was minimal. The Modernists, who were tinged with mysticism themselves, attempted to save Christian doctrine by accommodating it to secular and scientific thought. Their condemnation by the papacy showed the inflexibility of Roman orthodoxy to accommodate to modern intellectual developments. It was precisely in the gaps created by the dissolution of Christianity in England that interest in mysticism flourished. (41)

Thus, the scholars who studied mysticism both responded to an increasingly popular movement and contributed to its legitimacy as a topic worthy of academic inquiry.

In a literary vein, the mystical poetry of Underhill, Waite, and Benson was coupled with new efforts to make mystical poetry available to the reading public. For instance, in 1910, Adeline Cashmore, the anchoress of All Saints' Church in York, published a collection of mystical verse called *The Mount of Vision*, with a preface by Alice Meynell and poetry ranging from well-known figures such as Blake, Browning, and MacDonald to lesser names like Frederick Faber. Just a few years later, in 1917, D. H. S. Nicholson and A. H. E. Lee, both members of Waite's Independent and Rectified Rite, edited *The Oxford Book of English Mystical Verse* for the Clarendon imprint of Oxford University Press; their book included selections of poetry by Underhill and Benson as well as Waite (Lindop 55). Notwithstanding the contributions of Inge and these other figures, the impact Underhill, Waite, and Benson had in resurrecting an earlier era's mystical literature cannot be overstated. Each in their own way helped to give a new generation of readers access to medieval mystics whose work had hitherto been the province only of intrepid visitors to remote and dusty archives. Their work recuperating and publishing earlier traditions of mystical reflection ultimately led to the wide availability of medieval mystical texts through publishing houses like Paulist Press—texts that for decades have been sold in mainstream bookstores like Barnes & Noble and subsequently via mass online merchandizers like Amazon.

Not only did the Edwardians in this study build bridges between modern spirituality and medieval spiritual traditions, but they also built bridges between the individual's mystical experience and institutional Christianity, helping to carve a more hospitable space for mystical spirituality within both Catholic and Protestant churches. The fact that Paulist Press, a major Catholic publishing house, now has a "Classics of Western Spirituality" series featuring the mystical texts of writers such as Julian of Norwich, the *Cloud of Unknowing* author, and Hadewijch (among many others) attests to a deepened relationship between mysticism and institutional Christianity. Indeed, mystical writers, including Underhill herself, are now regularly found in church libraries, discussed in mainstream Christian publications and church reading groups, and increasingly regarded not as the texts of heretics, but as "spiritual classics." In that regard, a genuine rapprochement between mysticism and institutional religion seems to have issued from the work of the Edwardian mystical revival.

On the other hand, the interest that Edwardians such as A. E. Waite showed in exploring esoteric traditions and their relationship to Christianity has also taken root in surprising ways within contemporary Christianity, as illustrated by several recent issues of *The Christian Century*, a liberal and progressive, but mainstream Christian publication, whose head editor is a Midwestern Lutheran pastor. For instance, the cover of the May 2023 issue featured a vivid image of the Fool tarot card from the famous Rider-Waite tarot deck, with a lead article about Pamela Colman Smith's collaboration with Waite on the deck's design and her eventual conversion to Roman Catholicism (Mesman 42).[4] No more than a half year later, the January 2024 issue highlighted an essay by Mordechai Beck called "The Jewish Kabbalah Tradition Offers a Way of Understanding God in the World—One That Has Profoundly Influenced Christianity." While the Jewish journalist who authored this *Christian Century* piece makes no mention of A. E. Waite's deep and thoroughgoing exploration of kabbalistic teaching in *The Holy Kabbalah* (1929), the long arm of

Waite is nonetheless evident in the magazine's effort to juxtapose Jewish mysticism and Christian theology.

This new propensity for mainstream Christian publications to embrace esoteric spiritual topics is unambiguously a sign of the Edwardian mystical revival's impact—and of twenty-first-century Christianity's recognition that it may need the spiritual adventuresomeness of Waite and his peers to speak to new generations. In *The Spiritual Revolution*, a 2005 study of religion and spirituality in England at the turn of the twenty-first century, Paul Heelas et al. describe how increasing numbers of people are turning toward individual forms of spiritual life and away from traditional forms of institutional religion as a result of the "subjective turn" in modern Western culture (5).[5] They contrast what they call "life-as" forms of the sacred, based on conformity of one's life to a transcendent source of authority, with what they call "subjective-life" forms of the sacred, "which emphasize inner sources of significance and authority" (6). Their research has correlated "subjective-life" forms of spirituality with movement growth and "life-as" religious forms with movement decline (9). For them, this shift toward increasingly subjective forms of spirituality constitutes a spiritual revolution, one, in my view, clearly adumbrated by the early twentieth-century's mania for mysticism.

The American journalist Tara Isabella Burton has even more recently studied the modern Western turn toward subjective spirituality and the concomitant embrace of esoteric, occult, or heterodox forms of spirituality. In her 2020 book *Strange Rites: New Religions for a Godless World*, Burton has noted that "traditional—which is to say, organized and formal—religion in America is in a free fall" (239) whereas "[e]clectic spiritual and magical practices—from astrology to tarot to yoga to crystals to sage cleansing to meditation—are now integral parts of millennial culture" (240). If Burton is right, then despite the efforts of the writers in this study to draw boundaries between Christian mysticism and esoteric or magical practice, the Edwardian era's exploration of mysticism side by side with forays into occultism may have seeded a buffet-style approach to religion and spirituality, in which seekers like Underhill's character Willie Hopkinson experience Buddhist-like rebirth *and* Christian union, sojourning among the psychics, the Freemasons, and the art aficionados until ultimately finding their own solitary spiritual niche, separate from formal religious community. As Burton asks, with evident reservation, "We curate and render bespoke everything else about our lives. Why should our faith not be similarly fluid?" (242). Paradoxically, therefore, even as the Edwardian mystical revival may have prompted a rapprochement between mystic individualism and Christian orthodoxy, the revival may also have unleashed a new freedom to pick and choose one's own spiritual tools, accelerating the current exodus from institutional religion and firing the growth of the "Spiritual but Not Religious" movement, whether for better or worse.[6]

Although Burton, like Bellah and his colleagues, seems to see in this trend toward religious eclecticism and spiritual individualism a worrisome erosion of our communal lives, the British historian and Anglican priest Jane Shaw evaluates the rising interest in personal spirituality then and now with more optimism. In *Pioneers of Modern Spirituality: The Neglected Anglican Innovators of A "Spiritual but Not Religious" Age*, Shaw explores how Evelyn Underhill and a different set of Edwardian figures, the Anglican priests Percy Dearmer and Reginald Somerset Ward[7] along with the Anglican-agnostic novelist Rose Macaulay, paved a way for the deeper cultivation of spiritual life, leaving a legacy of spiritual reflection that speaks especially well to the increasing number of people who identify as "spiritual but not religious" (2). Their work arose within Edwardian religious trends that Shaw describes thus: "The usual expression of Christian faith—going to church—began to decline, both as a habit of spiritual being and a societal expectation, but this did not mean people were no longer searching and questing after some form of ultimate meaning. Faith was being revitalized in other ways: through the cultivation of an individual prayer life, in retreats and a great flourishing of interest in mysticism, and through the arts" (2). For that reason, she sees the spiritual writing of Edwardians like Underhill as having a special "resonance in our own 'spiritual but not religious' age" (2). She concludes that the spiritual pathways these Edwardian figures forged may be just what today's seekers want and need (105). And even if such pathways do not lead people back into church, she argues, "they may well result in transformed lives—which is what faith, in the end, is about" (105).

However one may choose to regard the legacy of the Edwardian mystical revival, particularly its impact on institutional religion, it is surely true that Underhill saw its legacy as giving ordinary people a sense of their share in a spiritual tradition uniting people of the past, present, and future with a Reality in and beyond the world we see with our eyes. Today, the Anglican Church's 2018 *Book of Lesser Feasts and Fasts* asserts that

"Evelyn Underhill's most valuable contribution to spiritual literature must surely be her conviction that the mystical life is not only open to a saintly few, but to anyone who cares to nurture it and weave it into everyday experience" (272). Attesting to this goal, she wrote in the conclusion to her magnum opus, *Mysticism*:

> We are, then, one and all the kindred of the mystics; and it is by dwelling upon this kinship, by interpreting—so far as we may—their great declarations in the light of our little experience, that we shall learn to understand them best. Strange and far away though they seem, they are not cut off from us by some impassable abyss. They belong to us. They are our brethren; the giants, the heroes of our race. As the achievement of genius belongs not to itself only, but also to the society that brought it forth; as theology declares that the merits of the saints avail for all; so, because of the solidarity of the human family, the supernal accomplishment of the mystics is ours also. (446)

Notwithstanding the individual subjectivity of mysticism, it was just this hope for spiritual unity—past and present, things near and far—that Waite, Benson, Underhill, and Machen spoke to in their literature about mysticism and tried to convey through concrete images such as the radiance of a rainbow, the green mass of grass, the artfully bound book, or even the aeonian pebble. R. H. Benson acknowledged as much in his 1907 lecture on mysticism, suggesting that his era's passion for mysticism reflected a hope "that the road to the restoration of broken unity lies along these lines" (*Mysticism* 4). After all, what most moved Waite in his search through so many disparate spiritual traditions was unity. According to his biographer, "For Waite the end of the mystical quest was not union but Unity; his last word could only have been 'Unitas'" (Gilbert, *Magician* 160).

And it may well be that this hope for unity is the most important legacy Underhill and her peers have bequeathed to our fractured, modern world. Nearly one hundred years after King Edward's reign, at the turn of the twenty-first century, Queen Elizabeth II delivered a Christmastide address that echoed their spiritual aspirations. During that broadcast, in December of 2000, she addressed her nation with words not of Christian nationalism, but of spiritual unity, expressing faith that "[w]hether we believe in God or not, I think most of us have a sense of the spiritual, that recognition of a deeper meaning and purpose in our lives, and I believe that this sense flourishes despite the pressures of our world" (qtd. in Heelas et al. 1). That was the hope of these spiritual writers over a century ago. Whither it will lead is a path yet unseen.

Notes

Introduction

1. In addition to the aforementioned books on mysticism and modern fiction, George M. Johnson has also recently published a book titled *Mourning and Mysticism in First World War Literature and Beyond: Grappling with Ghosts* (Palgrave 2015). Johnson, however, construes mysticism as broadly as possible, taking it to mean "an experience of the spiritual life" (4) and including within that definition occultism and spiritualism as well as mysticism in the narrower sense. Mysticism in this broad sense, he argues, arose as a response to mourning following the losses occasioned by the Boer War, World War I, and the ensuing influenza epidemic (3), and it served a therapeutic purpose (26). Though Johnson's study mentions Underhill's nonfiction book *Mysticism* in its introductory discussion of mysticism, his psycho-biographical history focuses on writers such as Arthur Conan Doyle, Woolf, and Wilfred Owen for whom "mysticism" was a response to grief (26), and it ignores the mystical fiction written by Underhill and others in her literary constellation who sought to better define mysticism and exemplify it in their fiction.

2. Machen is the exception to this claim, for only his early literary career links him to Graf's group of occult writers. His fiction and theology developed significantly over the course of his lifetime, so that by the Edwardian era he had shifted from focusing in his fiction on forms of magical or occult activity, about which he harbored great skepticism, to writing about Christian mysticism. In the argument to follow, I shall show how he evolved to become affiliated with the group of writers who, in my view, are responsible for developing the "mystical novel" and distinguishing mysticism from occultism.

3. In recognition of this affinity, Glen Cavaliero has offered a sweeping history of *The Supernatural and English Fiction* (1995) that positions Christian apologists like George MacDonald, G. K. Chesterton, and Charles Williams within a larger tradition of supernatural fiction dating back to the Gothic novel and extending forward to Peter Ackroyd's *Hawksmoor*.

4. Here and henceforth, I shall use the term *middlebrow* not as the term of opprobrium Virginia Woolf sometimes used to scorn work that fell short of her aesthetic aspirations, but rather, following Faye Hammill's definition, as an affirmative term for "writers who were not wholly aligned with either high modernism or popular culture" (6). She notes, "It is important to recognize the forms of stylistic experimentation which middlebrow writers engaged in, and which are often overlooked because they do not correspond to the experimental strategies of high modernism" (6).

Chapter 1

1. Early in his career, in an 1890 lecture to the London Spiritualist Alliance, Waite spoke of mysticism as just one branch of the occult sciences, using *occult* in the sense of having to do with hidden or interior knowledge (624–25). However, in a 1904 essay for *Horlick's Magazine*, he had clearly begun to separate mysticism from occultism, articulating the same distinctions that he espoused in *Lamps of Mysticism* (508). In his 1906 *Studies in Mysticism*, he drew sharper distinctions, noting that occultism is often misconstrued to mean either mysticism or those things more properly understood as "psychical research" ("animal magnetism, hypnotism, spiritualism") (5). The "occult," by his definition, is a "science" and, in the words he quotes from Edward Maitland, a "transcendental physics" (6), whereas the mystic is "of the spiritual, belonging to religion" (6). He elaborates, "The practical work of the mystic concerned . . . the soul's union with God . . . It is essentially a religious experiment and is the one ultimate and real experiment designed by true religion" (8). Aren Roukema has found Waite's eventually "stark dichotomy" between occultism and mysticism to be problematic and challenges the "cordon sanitaire" Waite attempted to establish between the one and the other (63). But, regardless of whether, as Roukema argues, the relationship between mysticism and occultism was more complex than Waite's statements allowed, the fact remains that Waite worked to establish boundaries between magic and religion, occultism and Christian mysticism, and such efforts suffuse his writing and that of other fellow Edwardian writers.

2. As recently as 2021, for instance, Mike Zuber's Oxford University Press study of spiritual alchemy identified Waite as "the prolific occultist writer" (175). Waite's biographer, R. A. Gilbert, lamented this kind of identification, suggesting that the modern propensity to categorize Waite as an occultist obscures Waite's emphases and desired self-description (*Magician* 13).

3. Waite, A. E. *The A. E. Waite Reader: A Selection of Occult Essays*. Lamp of Trismegistus, 2021.

4. The term *gramary* emerged in the fourteenth century as a word for occult learning and necromancy; Waite invokes it in "The Bells of Fairyland," among other places, referring to it there as the "forest of gramarye" (*Golden Stairs* 90).

5. In a review of Maitland's biography of Anna Kingsford, Waite extols Maitland before offering his reservations about Kingsford herself: "We all know Mr. Maitland's earnestness; we all know his singleness of purpose; we all know the unswerving devotion with which he has dedicated himself to one object, and that of all things highest—'a perfect system of thought and rule of life'; we all know that he believes himself to have been led to that object through a course of transcendental experience to which no one has ever laid claim; we all know that the sincerity of his claim has been justified by the facts of his life as few transcendental claims have been ever justified palpably before the eyes of the world. We believe also with Mr. Maitland that he has passed through the first mystical experience which he calls the baptism of the spirit, and for myself I should like to add that, so far as one mystic may speak of another's progress, I have always regarded Mr. Maitland as one who has attained a high point in the ascent of Mount Carmel, as St. John of the Cross would say" (*Light* 115).

6. The British literary tradition has been hospitable to a rich history of poets writing about mystical experience: the *Dream of the Rood*-poet, Langland, the *Pearl*-Poet, Spenser, Herbert, Vaughn, Crashaw, Rossetti, and Hopkins, among others. Arguably, though, it was MacDonald who helped to pioneer the use of the novel form for representing Christian mystical experience, for, the novel had long been the genre of ordinary, everyday experience, with novels of the supernatural largely dedicated to mystery and horror, as in the Gothic tradition. Glen Cavaliero has previously explored the "impact of metaphysical themes and subject-matter on [English] naturalistic fiction" (*Supernatural* vi–vii) from Radcliffe to Murdoch and Spark, but his book's thematic approach, while enormously valuable, does not sufficiently illumine this movement's embeddedness in a place and time that brought together an interrelated group of writers dedicated to the same end. The movement shaped by MacDonald and Waite demands more particular analysis of the type of Christian mysticism that came to define a key trend in the Edwardian mystical novel.

7. Notably, Waite's *Golden Stairs* was published in the same year as his *Azoth*, further evidence that MacDonald's writing was on Waite's mind when he penned his own fantasy story. It is also significant that Waite authored this work in the 1890s, a period that the British journalist and writer Holbrook Jackson "identified [in 1913] . . . as the one in which the revival of mysticism began" (Shaw 226).

8. This sentiment correlates with his friend Arthur Machen's provocative claim in *Hieroglyphics* that truly great fiction is characterized neither by mimetic accuracy nor by clever artifice nor by stylistic prowess but rather by its ability to evoke "ecstasy" and connect readers to a realm of "wonder, awe, mystery, sense of the unknown, desire for the unknown" (18).

9. The sapphires in this section may be one of many links to MacDonald's *Golden Key*, for, a "row of small sapphires" borders the golden key's keyhole (72, 77).

10. Metron is also the name of "the Spirit of the North" and guardian spirit of Chevalier Louis de B.—in *Ghost Land*, a popular occult book reputed to be the

autobiography of the Chevalier, as translated and edited by Emma Hardinge Britten in 1876 (204). Waite's comments about *Ghost Land* reflect the characteristic skepticism with which he viewed much of the occult writing and activity he assessed during his prolific career. With no little scorn, he remarked in his own autobiography, "I am content to leave the question whether the Chevalier lived only in the second-rate and typically feminine imagination of Emma Harding because, in the universe of evidential things, there was no room for him anywhere else" (*SLT* 73).

11. Notably, he also imitates MacDonald's penchant for featuring wise women, locating such spiritual wisdom in the figure of an old woman.

12. G. K. Chesterton, for instance, panned Waite's 1902 collection of poetry, *A Book of Mystery and Vision*, for what he saw as its "celestial snobbishness" and Gnostic-like exclusivity (247).

13. With these alchemical allusions, Waite was clearly inspired by his reading of Mary Anne Atwood (1810 to 1910), wife of an Anglican priest, who published a detailed history of the hermetic tradition called *A Suggestive Inquiry into the Hermetic Mysteries* (1850), a study of spiritual alchemy that Mike Zuber has described as "traditionally Christian views, merely dressed up in esoteric garb" (170). This rare book was one Waite read "with joy" in his twenties, "enchanted" by Atwood's "strange, semi-archaic, stilted style" and initially in awe of her as a kind of "High Priestess" (*SLT* 93). Atwood's key ideas about spiritual alchemy were ones he adapted for his 1893 book *Azoth; or, The Star in the East*, published during the same year as Waite's first publication of *The Golden Stairs*. According to Zuber, Waite drew from Atwood a "highly teleological conception" that "saw humanity consciously working towards the 'perfection of the supreme summit of evolution' in the spiritual intellectual, moral, and even physical order" (181). Over the course of his career, however, Waite moved away from his initial zeal for alchemy and toward other forms of esoteric study (Gilbert, *Magician* 96).

14. The interiority of MacDonald's spiritual perspective is characteristic of broader Gnostic and mystical traditions. For instance, in one of the most famous sections of the Gospel of Thomas, verse 70, Jesus exhorts listeners, "If you bring forth what is within you, what you have will save you. If you do not have that within you, what you do not have within you [will] kill you" (*Gospel of Thomas* 51). And one of the landmark works of Western mysticism by St. Theresa of Avila is titled the *Interior Castle*.

15. For Chesterton, that is not a wholly disagreeable point of arrival. With customary flair, he writes, "Everybody knows, of course, and everybody feels (which is more convincing) that there are ultimately things beyond our ken, but there is no hard and fast line to be drawn in the matter . . . I do not think Mr. A. E. Waite mad because he is a mystic; if anything, I think anyone who is not a mystic must be as mad as a hatter" (246).

16. Knight and Mason draw attention to the Incarnational turn that arose in the mid-nineteenth century (161–62) and marked fin-de-siècle fiction and

poetry in the wake of Victorian medievalism and the theological character of poets like Gerard Manley Hopkins (202). Yet, they leave aside Waite and his circle of Edwardian writers of mystical fiction.

17. Indeed, his expanded 1927 revision of *The Golden Stairs*, called *The Quest of the Golden Stairs*, was much worse—a "disastrous failure," in Gilbert's words, "combining [Victorian literary fairy tales'] worst features with a pale mysticism buried deep beneath a dense mass of verbiage" (*Bibliography* 69).

18. A version of this essay has been published as "A. E. Waite, George MacDonald, and the Golden Stair from Victorian Fantasy to Edwardian Mystical Fiction." *Renascence* 77.2 (Spring 2025): 63–87.

Chapter 2

1. See, for instance, Richard Ellman. "Two Faces of Edward." *Edwardians and Late Victorians*, edited by Richard Ellmann, Columbia University Press, 1959, pp. 188–210. See also John Batchelor, "Edwardian Literature." *The Edwardian Novelists*, Gerald Duckworth, 1982, pp. 1–26.

2. As an exception to that, Brian Sudlow argues, "In England, the poems of Gerard Manley Hopkins, the pamphlets of G. K. Chesterton and the novels of Robert Hugh Benson signify the most important revival in Catholic literary production perhaps since Thomas More and Robert Southwell in the sixteen century" (1). By contrast, Nicholas Freeman compares him negatively to the "radical yet traditional Anglo-Catholic" Arthur Machen, referencing Benson as "a Catholic propagandist" (243).

3. Of course, MacDonald himself was equally fond of the realist novel, which was the dominant mode of the nineteenth-century novel, though it is his fairy fiction that has survived as the most popular representation of his oeuvre.

4. Benson affirms as much in his 1907 lecture *Mysticism*, asserting that God is both immanent and transcendent, and either view taken separately "leads to error" (23), in the former case to Materialism (24) and in the latter case to heresies such as Gnosticism and Christian Science (26). It is the Incarnation, he argues, that prevents either error: "Christianity . . . holds both these truths, and finds their reconciling in the Incarnation of the Son of God. In this doctrine we see the reasonable relations of Spirit and matter, of the creature and the Creator . . . This is the doctrine of the Incarnation. 'God is a Spirit': 'The Word was made flesh.' And from this in turn flows out with absolute inevitability, the sacramental system of the Catholic Church" (28).

5. Here Benson's view of the faculty for mystical perception stresses "grace" rather than human will.

6. *Richard Raynal* was a historical novel that Benson published in 1906.

7. "*Seigneur, donnez-moi la foi du charbonnier*!" is the priest's exclamation (174). This episode—and several others—so strikingly mirror aspects of Dostoevsky's 1880 novel *The Brothers Karamazov*, itself an exemplar of a mystical novel in the Russian literary tradition, that one might think Benson had read Dostoevsky's novel, but the Russian novel was apparently not translated into English till several years after Benson's novel was published, and there is no evidence that Benson could read the Russian language.

8. Here is another Dostoevskian parallel, with a scene reminiscent of Grigory's attempts to teach Smerdyakov biblical literacy and being denigrated as Balaam's ass and of Stinking Lizaveta's head being like that of a wooly animal.

9. This instance is one of several in *The Light Invisible*'s narratives that contradict Paschal Baumstein's claim about the centrality of the will in Benson's theology (100). The passivity here bespeaks that quality of mystical experience identified by William James as typical of such experiences (413).

10. Zoë Lehmann Imfeld briefly discusses "The Watcher" in connection to Augustine, but in a slightly different way. She focuses on the terrifying, "disembodied face" he sees in a rhododendron bush after shooting the bird and suggests that the chapter "explores a paradox that is central to the Christian and particularly Augustinian concept of evil. The demonic here is both the opposite of being, and shockingly and effectively present" (*Victorian Ghost Story* 28). Given the way this experience imprints itself in his memory, Imfeld rightly observes that he parallels characters in other ghost stories who are "haunted by the shadow of the worst of themselves" (28).

11. This story is one striking example of how Benson anticipates the idea of substitutionary prayer—prayer through which one literally bears another's burden—that Charles Williams develops in his theology. See, for instance, "The Practice of Substituted Love" in Williams's *He Came Down from Heaven* (82–94). Williams writes, "We are to love each other . . . by acts of substitution. We are to be substituted and to bear substitution. All life is to be vicarious—at least, all life in the kingdom of heaven is to be vicarious" (86).

12. In addition to this scene's Gothic resonances, it also conjures Shakespearean echoes of Lear's storm and his recognition of the suffering subjects he has not justly cared for in his kingdom: "Poor naked wretches, wheresoe'er you are,/ That bide the pelting of this pitiless storm,/ How shall your houseless heads and unfed sides,/ Your loop'd and window'd raggedness, defend you/ From seasons such as these? O, I have ta'en/ Too little care of this!" (3.4.32–27).

13. Ironically, during the priest's dying days, the servant Parker watches, waits, and offers help whenever it is needed, a significant side character who, like Gerasim in Tolstoy's *The Death of Ivan Ilych* (1886), quietly exemplifies the Christlike compassionate action that the priest reproaches himself for having failed to exhibit.

14. My reference to the priest's "dark night of the soul" may strike scholars of mysticism as unduly colloquial. Arguably, though, Benson and others writing

about mysticism in his milieu helped to seed a more generic and popular usage of St. John of the Cross's poetic exploration of the "*noche oscura del alma*." For instance, a few years later, in Evelyn Underhill's seminal 1911 book *Mysticism*, she describes the mystical life as a "Drama of Faith," with multiple acts, of which one is "the desolation of that 'dark night of the soul' in which it seems abandoned by the Divine" (121). She also emphasizes the psychological dimension of this mystical "stage," referring to it as an "intense sense of the Divine Absence" (170). In Benson's narrative, soon after a deep spiritual gloom descends upon the priest, the "Body" of Christ suddenly disappears, though the darkness of this experience eventually yields to a more profound illumination of Christ's presence.

15. Though neither Benson nor his biographers document his familiarity with Dostoevsky's great mystical novel *The Brothers Karamazov*, this episode presents parallels to the moment in book 7 of Dostoevsky's novel when Alyosha recognizes the risen Christ (485–86).

16. Benson's self-criticism, however, looks forward to Emile Mersch, S. J.'s discussion of misconceptions about the mystical body of Christ. A little more than two decades later, he wrote, "It is another, though less serious mistake, to rely more on imagination and sentiment than on reason and faith . . . Some, for example, absolutely insist on picturing the Mystical Body to themselves, by means of an image that they consider to be a perfect representation of the reality. Certainly we need images; we cannot think without phantasms, and Scripture provides many of them in connection with the doctrine of the Mystical Body. The error lies in mistaking the image for a definition and in thinking that just because they are able to conceive some huge ethereal and invisible organism or a kind of living atmosphere in which men's souls are somehow fused one into the other, they therefore possess a perfect knowledge of the mystery of the Head and members. It goes without saying that whoever allows himself to be so misled by his imagination is exposing himself to all kinds of absurdities" (7).

Chapter 3

1. As Lawrence Cunningham notes, *Mysticism* has "never gone out of print" since its initial publication (106).

2. According to Thomas Willard, the Arthurianism in that novel "had considerable influence" on fellow novelist Charles Williams (280). Willard suggests, "Underhill may have inspired the new Grail community in Williams's *War in Heaven*. . . . Even more important, her novel recreated the classic dichotomy between the mystic's *via negativa* and the artist's *via positiva* in a way that appealed to Williams" (280).

3. Todd Johnson echoes this view in observing, "The medieval world provided a link between the realms of matter and spirit defined by her neoplatonic

mind set" ("Anglican Writers" 404). As I go on to argue, however, this link was mediated by Underhill's exposure to the Arts and Crafts movement.

4. There she explains that the awareness of the "spiritual artist" is "possible to all men: without it, they are not wholly conscious, nor wholly alive" (30). Her book is dedicated, therefore, to putting into "plain and untechnical language" the mystic's world view and "to suggest the practical conditions under which ordinary persons may participate in [the mystics'] experience" (16).

5. As James Whitlark observes, this dimension of the story has strong Eastern elements: "the maya, or unreality of life, the frustrated desires of wandering ghosts (as in Buddhist myth), the impersonal divine 'Force,' and his reincarnation" (286).

6. In the opening essay in *Arts and Crafts Essays*, the designer Walter Crane laments how art has become a veritable religion in his day and a source for people to beautify their homes, even as the designer and worker are disregarded: "[I]t is a somewhat singular state of things that at a time when the Arts are perhaps more looked after, and certainly more talked about, than they have ever been before, and the beautifying of houses, to those to whom it is possible, has become in some cases almost a religion, so little is known of the actual designer and maker . . . of those familiar things which contribute so much to the comfort and refinement of life—of our chairs and cabinets, our chintzes and wall-papers, our lamps and pitchers—the Lares and Penates of our households . . ." (2–3).

7. Unlike Morris, some Arts and Crafts leaders did explicitly connect their craftsmanship to a Divine Reality beyond. For instance, the bookbinder T. J. Cobden-Sanderson sounds very much like a mystic in his idealistic "Ecce Mundus" (1902), where he declares, "[M]an . . . tends to become one with the universe, and the universe one with man, in point of WORK, so that ultimately man shall learn to work as the world works, on the grand scale, magnificently, & feel within himself, singing, the world's great tune and rhythm" (par. 35). Shortly thereafter, he concludes with the sublime exclamation, "ECCE MUNDUS ECCE COELUM" (par. 40). Likewise, the eminent Arts and Crafts architect William Lethaby expressed similar transcendent ideals, but about architecture, in his 1891 book *Architecture, Mysticism, and Myth*: "The main purpose and burthen of sacred architecture—and all architecture . . . is thus inextricably bound up with a people's thoughts about God and the universe" (2).

8. Underhill's emphasis on the individual rather than society, particularly in her early writings, has elicited some criticism. For instance, despite respect for Underhill's work, Grace Jantzen has asserted that "part of the legacy of Evelyn Underhill is the pervasive notion that spirituality can grow and flourish without attention to social justice or active efforts to dismantle oppressive structures," a legacy Jantzen regards as "pernicious" (80–81). Although the sixteen-year-old Underhill once described herself as a Socialist (Jantzen 79), Jantzen suggests

that in the course of Underhill's life "she did not get beyond individual charity to working against unjust structures" (96).

9. In a different article on Underhill's pneumatological development, Johnson reiterates this assessment, adding that Underhill does not clearly distinguish early on between symbols and sacraments: "While von Hugel could span a sacramental bridge between the divine and human spheres by anchoring it in the Incarnation of Christ, Underhill was left without such a sacramental principle because of her continued reluctance to accept Christ's pre-existence. The result was an attempt to define God's presence in the world in universal terms without any specific point of reference, resulting in a lack of distinction between symbols which point to God and sacraments through which one encounters God" ("Pneumatology" 114). While Johnson is right to observe a blurring of theological distinctions in Underhill's early work, it is important to note that there are several instances in *The Gray World* when Willie seems actually to *experience* the Divine through art or craft as opposed to seeing it as a mere symbol of the Divine. And, as we have seen, Underhill herself uses the word *sacrament* in relationship to Willie's experiences as a craftsman.

10. See also Delicata (535) and Dixon (655), among others.

11. Many years ago, Clay Kinsner observed that we are just beginning to understand the impact of mystical texts on "other forms of literature" (176), but a study of Underhill's fiction reveals that the reverse is true as well; in other words, we are just beginning to understand the impact of different forms of art on mysticism or, more broadly, spirituality.

12. In different terms, Justine McCarthy claims that Underhill's early work is characterized by "spiritual elitism" and a "disparaging of the ordinary" (85). "Her early mysticism," McCarthy asserts, "was practical in method but not in application" because of her "unconcern with improving anything in the visible universe" (85).

13. A version of this article appeared in *Studies in Medievalism* 28 (Summer 2019): 53–76.

Chapter 4

1. Machen typically uses the word *occult* not in the general sense of alluding to knowledge that is hidden, but rather in reference to astrology, magic, witchcraft, mesmerism, animal magnetism, spiritualism, psychometry, and the like (*Things* 16).

2. For instance, "mystical novel" suits not only Underhill's novel *Column of Dust* (1909), which Milbank analyzes, but also the Underhill novels Milbank leaves aside, *The Gray World* (1904) and *The Lost Word* (1907), neither of which seem Gothic, but both of which explore mysticism. Further, the term *mystical*

novel is inclusive enough to embrace the kind of fiction both MacDonald and Waite wrote.

3. Machen's choice of a hermit for his persona may suggest his separation from literary society and its conventional views; it may also be an instance of Machen's penchant for connecting himself to figures popular in medieval lore.

4. All references in the analysis to follow will be to the final, revised version of the novel, unless otherwise indicated.

5. Machen once described Cervantes's *Don Quixote* as a "picaresque both of mind and body," in contrast to *Gil Blas*, which he considered a "picaresque of the body," and *Tristram Shandy*, which he thought a "picaresque of the mind alone" (*Things* 116).

6. Notably, Machen's own growing up years were characterized by wandering the hills and valleys of the Welsh countryside, an experience he describes as being immersed in an enchanted fairyland (*Far Off Things* 21). He goes on to connect this perception to a precocious mystic sensibility: "[A]s a child, I realised something of the spirit of the mystic injunction. Everywhere, through the darkness and the mists of the childish understanding, and yet by the light of the child's illumination, I saw *latens deitas*; the whole earth, down to the very pebbles, was but the veil of a quickening and adorable mystery" (*Far Off Things* 26).

7. Edward Darnell's response to the mystic *sound* rather than the *sense* of Mary's word's presents parallels to a famous passage describing Lucian Taylor's writing endeavors in *Hill of Dreams*, written between 1895 and 1897: "[H]e tried to find that quality that gives to words something beyond their sound and beyond their meaning, that in the first lines of a book should whisper things unintelligible but all significant. Often he worked for many hours without success, and the grim wet dawn once found him still searching for hieroglyphic sentences, for words mystical, symbolic" (171).

8. John Howard connects the image of the Daystar to Christ by referencing 2 Peter 1:19 (340). This connection is significant, for the Christian resonance of the Daystar image marks Edward's inner movement toward a more explicitly Christian interpretation of his mystical experiences.

Conclusion

1. Auerbach distinguishes Woolf's subjectivism from what he calls the "extremely subjective, individualistic, and often eccentrically aberrant impression of reality" characteristic of earlier novels such as *À rebours* by Huysmans. Woolf's juxtaposition of multiple consciousnesses in *To the Lighthouse* and elsewhere, he thinks, "differentiates it from the unipersonal subjectivism which allows only a single and generally a very unusual person to make himself heard and admits only that one person's way of looking at reality" (536).

2. Higgins, Sørina. "The Oddest Inkling." https://sorinahiggins.wordpress.com/the-oddest-inkling/.

3. Of course, that is not to mention this group's famous American counterpart, the Harvard academic William James, whose *Varieties of Religious Experience*, published in 1902, has become such an important resource for the study of mysticism.

4. Side by side with that article is one by Amy Frykholm about Dame Julian of Norwich's mystical theology.

5. Their findings confirm what Robert Bellah and his colleagues identified decades earlier in *Habits of the Heart*, their 1985 landmark study of religion in the United States. In that study, Bellah et al. dubbed this turn toward hyper-individualistic religion "Sheilaism"—based on the example of a young nurse named Sheila who named her religion after herself because of the extreme individualism of her beliefs (221). They found her radically subjective sense of religion to be "significantly representative" of larger cultural trends (221).

6. For a fascinating account of "spiritual but not religious" patterns in the history of North America, see Robert Fuller's 2001 book, *Spiritual but Not Religious: Understanding Unchurched America.*

7. Ward was connected to Underhill as one of her spiritual directors.

Works Cited

Alexander, Michael. *Medievalism: The Middle Ages in Modern England.* Yale UP, 2007.

Armstrong, Christopher J. R. *Evelyn Underhill (1875–1941): An Introduction to Her Life and Writings.* Eerdmans, 1975.

Auerbach, Erich. "The Brown Stocking." *Mimesis: The Representation of Reality in Western Literature*, translated by Willard B. Trask, Princeton UP, 1953, pp. 525–53.

Batchelor, John. "Edwardian Literature." *Edwardian and Georgian Fiction*, edited by Harold Bloom, Chelsea House Publishers, 2005, pp. 123–48.

Batchelor, John. "Edwardian Literature." *The Edwardian Novelists*, Gerald Duckworth, 1982, pp. 1–26.

Baumstein, Paschal. "Impact of the Will on Mysticism: Compiling Benson's Theory." *Faith and Reason*, vol. 9, no. 2, Summer 1983, pp. 97–106.

Beck, Mordechai. "The Tree of God's Mysteries: The Jewish Kabbalah Offers a Way of Understanding God in the World—One That Has Profoundly Influenced Christianity." *The Christian Century*, vol. 141, no. 1, Jan. 2024, pp. 64–67.

Bellah, Robert, et al. *Habits of the Heart: Individualism and Commitment in American Life.* U of California P, 1985.

Benson, Arthur. *Hugh: Memoirs of a Brother.* Longmans, Green, 1915.

Benson, Robert Hugh. *The Book of the Love of Jesus: A Collection of Ancient English Devotions in Prose and Verse.* Sir Isaac Pitman and Sons, 1904.

Benson, Robert Hugh. *Confessions of a Convert.* Longmans, Green, 1913.

Benson, Robert Hugh. "The Life of Jesus Christ in His Mystical Body." *The Quest*, vol. 2, no. 1, Oct. 1910, pp. 7–30.

Benson, Robert Hugh. *The Light Invisible.* Burns, Oates, and Washbourne, 1903.

Benson, Robert Hugh. *A Mirror of Shalott.* Benziger Brothers, 1907.

Benson, Robert Hugh. *Mysticism.* Edited by Francis Aveling, Sands, 1907. Westminster Lectures, 3rd series.

Benson, Robert Hugh. *The Necromancers.* 1909. Sphere Books, 1974.

Benson, Robert Hugh. *Poems.* Burns and Oates, 1914.

Bishop, Morchard. "Foreword." *Arthur Machen: Artist and Mystic*, edited by Mark Valentine and Roger Dobson, Caermaen Books, 1986, pp. v–vi.

Blakesley, Rosalind P. *The Arts and Crafts Movement*. Phaidon Press, 2006.

Bloom, Clive. *Bestsellers: Popular Fiction Since 1900*. 3rd ed., Palgrave Macmillan, 2021.

Bloom, Harold. "Introduction." *Modern Critical Views: Walter Pater*, Chelsea House Publishers, 1985, pp. 1–22.

Boaden, Ann. "Singing the Heart's Song: George MacDonald." *The Lutheran Journal*, vol. 93, 2023, pp. 6–13.

Britten, Emma Hardinge, translator and editor. *Ghost Land; or Researches into the Mysteries of Occultism*. Alfred Mudge, 1876.

Burton, Tara Isabella. *Strange Rites: New Religions for a Godless World*. PublicAffairs, 2020.

Callahan, Annice. *Evelyn Underhill: Spirituality for Daily Living*. UP of America, 1997.

Carle, Naomi, et al., editors. "Introduction: Venturing Beyond the Garden Party." *Edwardian Culture: Beyond the Garden Party*, Routledge, 2018, pp. 1–14.

Carlyle, Thomas. *Past and Present*. 1843. Oxford UP, 1950.

Cavaliero, Glen. *Charles Williams: Poet of Theology*. Eerdmans, 1983.

Cavaliero, Glen. *The Supernatural and English Fiction*. Oxford UP, 1995.

Chapman, Raymond. *The Practical Mystic: Evelyn Underhill and Her Writings*. Canterbury, 2012.

Chesterton, G. K. "Mysticism: Its Use and Abuse." *The Speaker*, vol. 6, 31 May 1902, pp. 246–47.

Childs, Donald J. "T. S. Eliot and Evelyn Underhill: An Early Mystical Influence." *The Durham University Journal*, vol. 80, no. 1, 1987, pp. 83–98.

Clemens, James. *Mysticism and the Mid-Century Novel*. Palgrave Macmillan, 2012.

Cobden-Sanderson, T. J. *Ecce Mundus and the Arts and Crafts Movement*. Facsimile of the 1902 and 1905 eds., Garland, 1977.

Coloumbe, Charles. "Hermetic Imagination: The Effect of the Golden Dawn on Fantasy Literature." *Mythlore*, vol. 21, no. 2, 1996, pp. 345–55.

Corelli, Marie. *The Life Everlasting: A Reality of Romance*. Methuen, 1911.

Corner, Martin. "Mysticism and Atheism in *To the Lighthouse*." *Studies in the Novel*, vol. 13, no. 4, Winter 1981, pp. 408–23.

Crane, Walter. "Of the Revival of Design and Handicraft: With Notes on the Work of the Arts and Crafts Exhibition Society." *Arts and Crafts Essays*, 1903. Forgotten Books, 2012, pp. 1–21.

Cumming, Elizabeth, and Wendy Kaplan. *The Arts and Crafts Movement*. Thames and Hudson, 1991.

Cunningham, Lawrence. "Evelyn Underhill's *Mysticism*: An Appreciation." *Spiritus*, vol. 12, no. 1, Spring 2012, pp. 106–12.

Danielson, Henry. *Arthur Machen: A Bibliography; with Notes, Biographical and Critical by Arthur Machen*. Introduction by Henry Savage, Henry Danielson, 1923.

Delicata, Nadia. "Evelyn Underhill's Quest for the Holy: A Lifetime Journey of Personal Transformation." *Anglican Theological Review*, vol. 88, no. 4, 2006, pp. 519–36.

Dixon, Joy. "'Dark Ecstasies': Sex, Mysticism and Psychology in Early Twentieth-Century England." *Gender and History*, vol. 25, no. 3, Nov. 2013, pp. 652–67.

Domestic and Foreign Missionary Society of the Protestant Episcopal Church in the United States of America. *Book of Lesser Feasts and Fasts 2018*. Church Publishing, 2019.

Dostoevsky, Fyodor. *The Brothers Karamazov*. Translated by Andrew MacAndrew, Bantam, 2003.

Downes, William Philip. "Mysticism." *The Biblical World*, vol. 54, no. 6, Nov. 1920, pp. 619–24.

Eliot, George. *George Eliot's Life as Related in her Letters and Journals*. Edited by J. W. Cross, 1st ed., vol. 3, Estes and Lauriat, 1895. *HathiTrust*, babel.hathitrust.org/cgi/pt?id=njp.32101075374320&seq=9.

Ellmann, Richard. "Two Faces of Edward." *Edwardians and Late Victorians*, edited by Richard Ellmann, Columbia UP, 1959, pp. 188–210.

Ferguson, Christine. "Reading with the Occultists: Arthur Machen, A. E. Waite, and the Ecstasies of Popular Fiction." *Journal of Victorian Culture*, vol. 21, no. 1, 2016, pp. 40–55, https://doi.org/10.1080/13555502.2015.1123170. Accessed 3 July 2022.

Francis, John R. "Evelyn Underhill's Developing Spiritual Theology: A Discovery of Authentic Spiritual Life and the Place of Contemplation." *Anglican Theological Review*, vol. 93, no. 2, Spring 2011, pp. 283–300.

Freeman, Nicholas. "Arthur Machen: Ecstasy and Epiphany." *Literature and Theology*, vol. 24, no. 3, Sept. 2010, pp. 242–55.

Frykholm, Amy. "Julian the Theologian." *The Christian Century*, May 2023, pp. 58–62.

Fuller, Robert. *Spiritual but Not Religious: Understanding Unchurched America*. Oxford UP, 2001.

Gilbert, R. A. *A. E. Waite: A Bibliography*. Aquarian Press, 1983.

Gilbert, R. A. *A. E. Waite: Magician of Many Parts*. Crucible, 1987.

Gilbert, R. A. "'The One Deep Student': Yeats and A. E. Waite." *Yeats Annual*, vol. 3, 1985, pp. 3–13.

Godwin, Joscelyn. *The Theosophical Enlightenment*. State U of New York P, 1994.

The Gospel of Thomas: The Hidden Sayings of Jesus. Tr. Marvin Meyer. New York: HarperOne, 1992.

Gough, Val. " 'The Razor Edge of Balance': Virginia Woolf and Mysticism." *Woolf Studies Annual*, vol. 5, 1999, pp. 57–77.

Graf, Susan Johnston. *Talking to the Gods: Occultism in the Work of W. B. Yeats, Arthur Machen, Algernon Blackwood, and Dion Fortune*. State U of New York P, 2015.

Grayson, Janet. *Robert Hugh Benson: His Life and Works*. UP of America, 1998.

Greene, Dana. *Evelyn Underhill: Artist of the Infinite Life*. Crossroad, 1990.

Griffiths, Richard. *The Pen and the Cross: Catholicism and English Literature, 1850–2000*. Bloomsbury Publishing, 2010. *ProQuest Ebook Central*, ebook-central.proquest.com/lib/lakeforest/reader.action?docID=5309556&ppg=1.

Hammill, Faye. *Women, Celebrity and Literary Culture Between the Wars*. U of Texas P, 2007.

Heelas, Paul et al. *The Spiritual Revolution: Why Religion Is Giving Way to Spirituality*. Blackwell Press, 2005.

Hein, Rolland. *George MacDonald: Victorian Mythmaker*. Wipf and Stock, 1993.

Higgins, Sørina. "The Oddest Inkling." *WordPress*, https://sorinahiggins.wordpress.com/the-oddest-inkling/.

Hopkins, Gerard Manley. *Gerard Manley Hopkins*. Edited by Catherine Phillips, Oxford UP, 1990.

Howard, John. "The Impossible History: Machen's 'A Fragment of Life.' " *The Secret Ceremonies: Critical Essays on Arthur Machen*, edited by Mark Valentine and Timothy J. Jarvis. Hippocampus Press, 2019, pp. 333–43.

Hunter, Jefferson. *Edwardian Fiction*. Harvard UP, 1982.

Imfeld, Zoë Lehmann. "Decadent Horror Fiction and Fin-de-Siècle Neo-Thomism." *Horror and Religion: New Literary Approaches to Theology, Race and Sexuality*, edited by Eleanor Beal and Jonathan Greenaway. U of Wales P, 2019, pp. 57–74.

Imfeld, Zoë Lehmann. *The Victorian Ghost Story and Theology: From Le Fanu to James*. Palgrave, 2016.

Inge, William Ralph. *Christian Mysticism: Considered in Eight Lectures Delivered Before the University of Oxford*. Methuen, 1899.

Izzo, David Garrett. *The Influence of Mysticism on 20th Century British and American Literature*. McFarland, 2009.

James, William. *The Varieties of Religious Experience: A Study in Human Nature; Being the Gifford Lectures on Natural Religion Delivered at Edinburgh in 1901–1902*. Longmans, Green, 1902.

Jantzen, Grace M. "The Legacy of Evelyn Underhill." *Feminist Theology*, vol. 2, no. 4, Sept. 1993, pp. 79–100.

Johnson, George. *Mourning and Mysticism in First World War Literature and Beyond: Grappling with Ghosts*. Palgrave Macmillan, 2015.

Johnson, Todd E. "Anglican Writers at Century's End: An Evelyn Underhill Primer." *Anglican Theological Review*, vol. 80, no. 3, Summer 1998, pp. 402–13.

Johnson, Todd E. "Evelyn Underhill's Pneumatology: Origins and Implications." *The Downside Review*, vol. 116, no. 403, 1998, pp. 109–36.

Joshi, S. T. *The Weird Tale*. Wildside Press, 1990.

Kane, Julie. "Varieties of Mystical Experience in the Writings of Virginia Woolf." *Twentieth-Century Literature*, vol. 41, no. 4, Winter 1995, pp. 328–49.

Kaplan, Wendy. *Leading "The Simple Life": The Arts and Crafts Movement in Britain, 1880–1910*. The Wolfsonian-Florida International University, 1999.

Kinsner, Clay. "The Female Mystics, Women's Studies, and the Negotiations of Discourse." *Studies in Medievalism*, vol. 10, 1998, pp. 164–83.

Knight, Mark. "The Limits of Orthodoxy in a Secular Age." *Nineteenth-Century Literature*, vol. 73, no. 3, Dec. 2018, pp. 379–98.

Knight, Mark, and Emma Mason. *Nineteenth-Century Religion and Literature: An Introduction*. Oxford UP, 2006.

Kripal, Jeffrey. "Eyeing the Burning Wings: Analyzing the Mystical Experience of Love in Evelyn Underhill's *Mysticism* (1911)." *Roads of Excess, Palaces of Wisdom: Eroticism and Reflexivity in the Study of Mysticism*, U of Chicago P, 2001, pp. 33–84.

Larsen, Timothy. *Incarnation, Doubt, and Reenchantment: George MacDonald in the Age of Miracles*. IVP Academic, 2018.

Lethaby, W. R. *Architecture, Mysticism, and Myth*. 1891. Architectural Press, 1974.

Lindop, Grevel. *Charles Williams: The Third Inkling*. Oxford UP, 2015.

Lovecraft, H. P. *Supernatural Horror in Literature*. Dover, 1973.

Lover of Books [A. E. Waite]. "Dealings in Bibliomania." *Horlick's Magazine*, vol. 1, 1904, pp. 405–16.

MacDonald, George. *The Golden Key*. 2nd Revised ed., Farrar, Strauss, and Giroux, 1984.

Machen, Arthur. "Aristotle and Art." *Literature*, vol. 2, no. 24, 2 Apr. 1898, pp. 367–68. *HathiTrust*, babel.hathitrust.org/cgi/pt?id=uc1.31210019742897&seq=379.

Machen, Arthur. "Arthur Machen BBC Interview." 1937. *YouTube*, uploaded by Carla Arnell, 26 June 2024, www.youtube.com/watch?v=WxJ_CCWUXMo.

Machen, Arthur. *Arthur Machen Selected Letters: The Private Writings of the Master of the Macabre*. Edited by Roger Dobson, Godfrey Brangham, and R. A. Gilbert, Aquarian Press, 1988.

Machen, Arthur. *Dr. Stiggins: His Views and Principles*. Alfred A. Knopf, 1925.

Machen, Arthur. *Eleusinia and Beneath the Barley*. 1931. Necronomicon Press, 1988.

Machen, Arthur. *Far Off Things*. London, Martin Secker, 1922.

Machen, Arthur. "A Fragment of Life." *The White People and Other Weird Stories*, edited by S. T. Joshi, Penguin, 2011, pp. 149–222.

Machen, Arthur. *The Glorious Mystery*. Covici-McGee, 1924.

Machen, Arthur. "A Great Experiment: Miss Evelyn Underhill's New Novel." *T. P.'s Weekly*, vol. 14, no. 366, 12 Nov. 1909, p. 627. *HathiTrust*, babel.hathitrust.org/cgi/pt?id=coo.31924069714370&seq=631.

Machen, Arthur. *The Great God Pan and The Hill of Dreams*. Dover Publications, 2006.

Machen, Arthur. "The Great Quest." *The Academy*, vol. 80, no. 2029, 25 March 1911, pp. 352–53. *HathiTrust*, babel.hathitrust.org/cgi/pt?id=pst.000020223762&seq=362.

Machen, Arthur. *Hieroglyphics: A Note upon Ecstasy in Literature*. 1902. Alfred A. Knopf, 1923.

Machen, Arthur. "The Middle Ages." Review of *The Mediaeval Mind* by Henry Osborn Taylor. *The Academy*, vol. 80, no. 2040, 10 June 1911, pp. 708–09. *HathiTrust*, babel.hathitrust.org/cgi/pt?id=rul.39030024876239&seq=730.

Machen, Arthur. *Mist and Mystery*. Darkly Bright Press, 2022.

Machen, Arthur. "The Novel of the White Powder." *The White People and Other Weird Stories*, edited by S. T. Joshi, Penguin, 2011, pp. 67–82.

Machen, Arthur. "Realism and Symbol." *The Academy*, vol. 75, no. 1891, 1 Aug. 1908, pp. 109–10. *HathiTrust*, babel.hathitrust.org/cgi/pt?id=njp.32101065266668&seq=107.

Machen, Arthur. *The Secret Glory*. 1922. Tartarus Press, 1998.

Machen, Arthur. *Things Near and Far*. Martin Secker, 1923.

Machen, Arthur. "Trying the Spirits: Father Benson's New Novel." *T. P's Weekly*, vol. 14, no. 369, 3 Dec. 1909, p. 726. *HathiTrust*, babel.hathitrust.org/cgi/pt?id=coo.31924069714370&seq=730.

"Magistery, *N.*, Sense I.4." Oxford English Dictionary, Oxford UP, Sept. 2024, https://doi.org/10.1093/OED/1044040744.

Martin, Stoddard. *Orthodox Heresy: The Rise of "Magic" as Religion and Its Relation to Literature*. St. Martin's Press, 1989.

Martindale, Cyril Charlie. *The Life of Monsignor Robert Hugh Benson*. Longmans, Green, 1916. 2 vols.

McCarthy, Justine Scott. *Edges of the Mind: Psychic Margins and the Modernist Aesthetic in Vernon Lee, Evelyn Underhill, May Sinclair, Dion Fortune and Jane Harrison*. Sept. 2000. Queen Mary, PhD dissertation.

McGinn, Bernard. "'The Violent Are Taking It by Storm' (Mt. 11:12): Reflections on a Century of Women's Contributions to the Study of Mystical Spirituality." *Spiritus*, vol. 13, no. 1, Spring 2013, pp. 17–35.

Mersch, Emile, S. J. *The Whole Christ: The Historical Development of the Doctrine of the Mystical Body in Scripture and Tradition*. Translated by John R. Kelly, S. J., Ex Fontibus, 2018.

Mesman, Jessica. "The Woman Behind Tarot's Strange Beauty." *The Christian Century*, vol. 140, no. 5, May 2023, pp. 42–47.

Milbank, Alison. *God and the Gothic: Religion, Romance, and Reality in the English Literary Tradition*. Oxford UP, 2018.

Milbank, John. "Fictioning Things: Gift and Narrative." *Religion and Literature*, vol. 37, no. 3, Autumn 2005, pp. 1–35.

Molnár, Géza von. "Mysticism and a Romantic Concept of Art: Some Observations on Evelyn Underhill's Practical Mysticism and Novalis' Heinrich von Ofterdingen." *Studia Mystica*, vol. 6, no. 2, 1983, pp. 66–75.

Morris, William. *News from Nowhere and Other Writings*. Edited by Clive Wilmer, Penguin, 1993.

Morson, Gary Saul. "Prosaics: An Approach to the Humanities." *The American Scholar*, vol. 57, no. 4, Autumn 1988, pp. 515–28.

Murdoch, Iris. *Existentialists and Mystics: Writings on Philosophy and Literature*. London, Penguin, 1997.

Murdoch, Iris. *Metaphysics as a Guide to Morals*. Penguin, 1992.

Neff, Rebeccah Kinnamon. "'New Mysticism' in the Writings of May Sinclair and T. S. Eliot." *Twentieth-Century Literature*, vol. 26, no. 1, Spring 1980, pp. 82–108.

Otto, Rudolf. *The Idea of the Holy*. 1923. Translated by Tr. John W. Harvey, Oxford UP, 1958.

Owen, Alex. *The Place of Enchantment: British Occultism and the Culture of the Modern*. U of Chicago P, 2004.

Paulsell, Stephanie. *Religion Around Virginia Woolf*. U of Pennsylvania State P, 2019.

Pazdziora, J. Patrick. "Cynical Mysticism: The Role of Fairies in Late-Victorian Esotericism." *Literature and Theology*, vol. 31, no. 3, 2017, pp. 285–304. Oxford Academic, https://doi.org/10.1093/litthe/frw021. Accessed 11 July 2022.

Pope Pius XII. "*Mystici Corporis Christi.*" The Holy See, 29 June 1943, www.vatican.va/content/pius-xii/en/encyclicals/documents/hf_p-xii_enc_29061943_mystici-corporis-christi.html.

Poston, Carol. "Evelyn Underhill and the Virgin Mary." *Anglican Theological Review*, vol. 97, no. 1, Winter 2015, pp. 75–89.

Ramsey, Michael. "Evelyn Underhill." *Religious Studies*, vol. 12, no. 3, 1976, pp. 273–79.

Reiter, Geoffrey. *"Man Is Made a Mystery": The Evolution of Arthur Machen's Religious Thought*. 2010. Baylor University, PhD dissertation. Print.

Reiter, Geoffrey. "Through the Ancient Wood: Envisioning Apophatic Mysticism in *A Fragment of Life*." *Arthur Machen: Critical Essays*, edited by Antonio Sanna, Lexington Books, 2021, pp. 225–39.

Review of *Initiation* by Robert Hugh Benson. *The Spectator*, vol. 112, no. 4475, 4 April 1914, pp. 573–74.

Reynolds, Aidan, and William Charlton. *Arthur Machen: A Biography*. John Baker (The Richards Press), 1963.

Reynolds, Philip L. "On the Origins of 'Mystics' and 'Mysticism': From Pseudo-Dionysius to the Anglo-American Mystical Revival in Five Steps." *Boston Colloquy in Historical Theology*, 6 Aug. 2022. www.academia.edu/105274618.

Roberts, R. Ellis. "Arthur Machen." *The Sewanee Review*, vol. 32, no. 3, July 1924, pp. 353–56.

Roeschlein, Michael. "E. M. Forster and 'The Part of the Mind That Seldom Speaks': Mysticism, Mythopoeia, and Irony in 'A Passage to India.'" *Religion and Literature*, vol. 36, no. 1, 2004, pp. 67–99.

Roukema, Aren. *Esotericism and Narrative: The Occult Fiction of Charles Williams*. Brill, 2018.

Ruskin, John. *The Stones of Venice*. Edited by J. G. Links, Da Capo, 2003.

Sauer, Michelle M. "Evelyn Underhill (1875–1941): The Practical Mystic." *Women Medievalists and the Academy*, edited by Jane Chance, U of Wisconsin P, 2005, pp. 183–99.

Shakespeare, William. *The Riverside Literature Series: King Lear*. 1906. Riverside Press, 1909.

Shaw, Jane. *Pioneers of Modern Spirituality: The Neglected Anglican Innovators of A 'Spiritual but Not Religious' Age*. Church Publishing, 2018.

Shaw, Jane. "Varieties of Mystical Experience in William James and Other Moderns." *History of European Ideas*, vol. 43, no. 3, 2017, pp. 226–40.

Shirley, Ralph. "Notes of the Month." *The Occult Review*, edited by Shirley Ralph, vol. 19, no. 1, Jan. 1914, pp. 1–13.

Shuster, George N. "Robert Hugh Benson and the Aging Novel." *The Catholic Spirit in Modern English Literature*, Macmillan, 1922, pp. 208–28.

Starrett, Vincent. "Foreword." *The Glorious Mystery*, Covici-McGee, 1924.

Staudt, Kathleen Henderson. "Rereading Evelyn Underhill's *Mysticism*." *Spiritus*, vol. 12, no. 1, Spring 2012, pp. 113–28.

@StephenKing. "The greatest horror tales I ever read is a tie between "The Great God Pan," by Arthur Machen (novella) and THE CEREMONIES, by T. E. D. Klein." *X*, 9 Feb. 2024, 10:55 a.m., x.com/StephenKing/status/1755998901289578809.

Stoeber, Michael. "Evelyn Underhill on Magic, Sacrament, and Spiritual Transformation." *Worship*, vol. 77, no. 2, Mar. 2003, pp. 132–51.

Stutz, Chad. *Robert Hugh Benson and the Catholic Literary Revival in Edwardian England*. 2002. University of Nevada, MA thesis.

Sudlow, Brian. *Catholic Literature and Secularisation in France and England, 1880–1914*. Manchester UP, 2011.

Sweetser, Wesley D. *Arthur Machen*. Twayne, 1964.

Trilling, Lionel. *E. M. Forster*. 2nd ed., New Directions, 1965.

Underhill, Evelyn. *The Column of Dust*. Methuen, 1909.

Underhill, Evelyn. "The Death of a Saint." *Horlick's Magazine*, vol. 2, 1904, pp. 173–77.

Underhill, Evelyn. *The Gray World*. Century, 1904.

Underhill, Evelyn. *The House of the Soul and Concerning the Inner Life*. Seabury, 1947.

Underhill, Evelyn. *The Letters of Evelyn Underhill*. 1943. Edited by Charles Williams. Darton, Longman, and Todd, 1991.

Underhill, Evelyn. *The Lost Word*. William Heinemann, 1907.

Underhill, Evelyn. *The Making of a Mystic: New and Selected Letters of Evelyn Underhill*. Edited by Carol Poston, U of Illinois P, 2010.

Underhill, Evelyn. "The Mountain Image." *Horlick's Magazine*, vol. 2, 1904, pp. 375–80.

Underhill, Evelyn. *Mysticism: A Study in the Nature and Development of Man's Spiritual Consciousness*. E. P. Dutton, 1961.

Underhill, Evelyn. *Practical Mysticism*. 1914. Ariel Press, 1986.

Valentine, Mark. *Arthur Machen*. Seren (Poetry Wales Press), 1995.

Valentine, Mark, and Roger Dobson. "Introduction." *Arthur Machen: Artist and Mystic*, Caermaen Books, 1986, pp. vii–ix.

Van Vechten, Carl. "Arthur Machen, Dreamer and Mystic." *Literary Digest International Book Review*, vol. 1, no. 3, Feb. 1923, pp. 36–37. *HathiTrust*, babel.hathitrust.org/cgi/pt?id=mdp.39015078843219&seq=222&q1=machen.

Vermeule, Blakey. "God Novels." *The Work of Fiction: Cognition, Culture, and Complexity*, edited by Alan Richardson and Ellen Spolsky, Ashgate, 2004, pp. 147–65.

Waite, A. E. *The A. E. Waite Reader: A Selection of Occult Essays*. Lamp of Trismegistus, 2021.

Waite, A. E. "Anna Kingsford." *Light: A Journal of Physical, Occult, and Mystical Research*, vol. 16, no. 791, 7 March 1896, pp. 115–17. *Internet Archive*, archive.org/details/IAPSOP-light_v16_n791_mar_7_1896.

Waite, A. E. "Assembly of the London Spiritualist Alliance." *Light: A Journal of Physical, Occult, and Mystical Research*, vol. 10, no. 521, 27 Dec. 1890, pp. 624–26. *HathiTrust*, babel.hathitrust.org/cgi/pt?id=umn.31951p01018787v&seq=636.

Waite, A. E. *A Book of Mystery and Vision*. 1902. Read Books, 2011.

Waite, A. E. "By-Ways of Periodical Literature, Part 1." *Walford's Antiquarian Magazine*, vol. 11, 1887, pp. 179–87.

Waite, A. E. "By-Ways of Periodical Literature, Part 2." *Walford's Antiquarian Magazine*, vol. 12, 1887, pp. 65–74.

Waite, A. E. *The Golden Stairs: Tales from the Wonder-World*. Theosophical Publishing Society, 1893.

Waite, A. E. *Lamps of Western Mysticism*. 1923. Rudolph Steiner Publications, 1973.

Waite, A. E. "The Latin Church and Freemasonry." *The Occult Review*, vol. 8, no. 3, Sept. 1908, pp. 146–50. *HathiTrust*, babel.hathitrust.org/cgi/pt?id=umn.31951000842868t&seq=154.

Waite, A. E. *The Occult Sciences: A Compendium of Transcendental Doctrine and Experiment*. Kegan, Paul, Trench, Trübner, 1891.

Waite, A. E. "The Policy of Union." *Horlick's Magazine*, vol. 1, 1904, pp. 507–11. *HathiTrust*, babel.hathitrust.org/cgi/pt?id=coo.31924007283868&seq=519.

Waite, A. E. "Preface." *Memorabilia: Reminiscences of a Woman Artist and Writer*, by Isabelle de Steiger, Rider, 1927, pp. v–xi.

Waite, A. E. *Shadows of Life and Thought: A Retrospective Review in the Form of Memoirs*. Selwyn and Blount, 1938.

Waite, A. E. *Studies in Mysticism and Certain Aspects of the Secret Tradition*. Hodder and Stoughton, 1906.

Waller, Philip. "Roman Candles: Catholic Converts Among Authors in Late-Victorian and Edwardian England." *Politics and Culture in Victorian Britain: Essays in Memory of Colin Matthew*, edited by Peter Ghosh and Lawrence Goldman, Oxford UP, 2006.

Watt, Ian. *The Rise of the English Novel.* U of California P, 1957.

Wheeler, Michael. "The Light of the Word: Incarnation." *St. John and the Victorians*, Cambridge UP, 2012, pp. 52–82.

Whitlark, James. *Evelyn Underhill, Late Nineteenth- and Early Twentieth-Century British Women Poets*. Edited by William B. Thesing, Thomson Gale, 2001.

Willard, Thomas. "Acts of the Companions: A. E. Waite's Fellowship and the Novels of Charles Williams." *Secret Texts: The Literature of Secret Societies*, edited by Marie Mulvey Roberts and Hugh Ormsby-Lennon, AMS Press, 1995, pp. 269–302.

Williams, Charles. *He Came Down from Heaven and the Forgiveness of Sins*. Apocryphile Press, 2005.

Wilmer, Clive, editor. "Introduction." *News from Nowhere and Other Writings*, by William Morris, Penguin, 1993, pp. ix–xli.

Woelfel, Craig Bradshaw. "Stopping at the Stone: Rethinking Belief (and Non-Belief) in Modernism Via *A Passage to India*." *Twentieth-Century Literature*, vol. 58, no. 1, Spring 2012, pp. 26–59.

Wood, Juliette. "The Grail in Welsh Tradition." *Eternal Chalice: The Enduring Legend of the Holy Grail*, I. B. Tauris, 2008, pp. 53–83.

Woolf, Virginia. "Modern Fiction." *The Essays of Virginia Woolf*, vol. 4, edited by Andrew McNeille, Hogarth Press, 1984, pp. 157–65.

Zuber, Mike A. *Spiritual Alchemy: From Jacob Boehme to Mary Anne Atwood*. Oxford UP, 2021.

Index